The Return of the Neighborhood
as an Urban Strategy

THE URBAN AGENDA

Series Editor, Michael A. Pagano

A list of books in the series appears at the end of this book.

The Return
of the Neighborhood
as an Urban Strategy

EDITED BY MICHAEL A. PAGANO

University of Illinois at Chicago

PUBLISHED FOR THE
COLLEGE OF URBAN PLANNING
AND PUBLIC AFFAIRS (CUPPA),
UNIVERSITY OF ILLINOIS AT CHICAGO,
BY THE UNIVERSITY OF ILLINOIS PRESS
Urbana, Chicago, and Springfield

The College of Urban Planning and Public Affairs of the University of Illinois at Chicago and the University of Illinois Press gratefully acknowledge that publication of this book was assisted by a grant from the John D. and Catherine T. MacArthur Foundation.

Library of Congress Control Number: 2015946184
ISBN 978-0-252-03989-8 (hardcover)
ISBN 978-0-252-08141-5 (paperback)
ISBN 978-0-252-09802-4 (e-book)

Contents

Preface and Acknowledgments

The University of Illinois at Chicago (UIC) has hosted a forum on urban issues since 1995, when the first forum was convened under the auspices of the Great Cities Institute at UIC. The Winter Forum met annually until 2005, convening scholars, public intellectuals, policy makers, and elected officials from the Chicago region as well as from other parts of the country. Starting in 2005, UIC in partnership with the City of Chicago hosted the Richard J. Daley Urban Forum annually for six years. This forum was designed as a convening of key public, private, and nonprofit leaders in an academic arena to discuss, analyze, and propose pragmatic and innovative solutions to enhance the lives of city dwellers around the globe.

In 2012, UIC chancellor Paula Allen-Meares revitalized the UIC annual conference on urban issues, retitling it the UIC Urban Forum, and charging it with the responsibility of bringing together policy makers, academics, public intellectuals, students, community activists, and citizens to discuss, debate, and recommend policy action to the pressing and intractable challenges of cities and metropolitan regions. The activities of the UIC Urban Forum are directed toward two major goals: staging a major annual event to advance a national and global dialogue about the urban future; and disseminating policy options, recommendations, and best practices.

PARTNERSHIP AND COLLABORATION

The UIC Urban Forum works in collaboration with a multiplicity of partners, including foundations, the nonprofit community, governments, the corporate sector, and the media. The partners of the 2014 UIC Urban Forum included the Chicago Community Trust, the John D. and Catherine T. MacArthur Foundation, Abbott, Walgreen's, UIC's College of Urban Planning and Public Affairs, and UIC's Institute for Policy and Civic Engagement, whose financial support was instrumental in the success of the forum. The MacArthur grant was provided as a subvention in support of underwriting the costs of publishing and disseminating the book.

The UIC Urban Forum also partnered with the local National Public Radio affiliate, WBEZ, which supplied moderators for the morning panels. The support of WBEZ CEO Goli Sheikholeslami in strengthening the reach of the forum's impact is deeply appreciated.

The UIC Urban Forum also has a contractual partnership with the University of Illinois Press. The edited white papers from the UIC Urban Forum are prepared for a series called the Urban Agenda. Each annual volume publishes the conference's proceedings as well as a synopsis of the panel "conversations with local officials" from the conference; also included are short "reflection" pieces on individual white papers and the conversation that ensued at a panel around which the white paper was organized. This volume is the third installment of the partnership between the UIC Urban Forum and the press. The encouragement and insight of Bill Regier, the director of the University of Illinois Press, are gratefully acknowledged. The importance of the press's editorial assistance in improving the presentation of the papers cannot be overestimated. The monograph, as a result, is better and more accessible to a large audience.

Finally, the UIC Urban Forum's primary internal partner is the UIC College of Urban Planning and Public Affairs (CUPPA). The project director of the UIC Urban Forum is the dean of the college, and the executive committee consists of CUPPA's director of the Great Cities Institute and a delegate from the chancellor's office.

THE 2014 UIC URBAN FORUM

The theme of the 2014 UIC Urban Forum, from which the book takes its title, was "The Return of the Neighborhood as an Urban Strategy," and the invitation to attend the event included this statement: "Metropolitan regions are a complex web of activities, systems and networks, of people, businesses, and capital, and of commercial, industrial and residential areas. The strength, value, welfare and resilience of cities and metropolitan regions reflect their core building blocks, namely, their neighborhoods. Sustainable capital and societal investments in people and firms at the neighborhood level—from micro-enterprises to factories, from social spaces for collective and social action to private facilities, from affordable housing and safety to gated communities, from accessible jobs and transportation to opportunities for growth and development, from public education in the neighborhood to cooperative, charter and private education—reflect contested and diffuse paths to enhancing the quality of life for individuals, households and neighborhoods. The 2014 UIC Urban Forum will engage policymakers, researchers, public intellectuals and citizens in a dynamic discussion and debate about the broad issues surrounding the role neighborhoods can and do play in building strong, livable urban regions."

The 2014 event was cochaired by Cook County Board president Toni Preckwinkle, LISC Chicago executive director Susana Vasquez, and UIC chancellor Paula Allen-Meares. The daylong event was held on September 18, 2014, beginning with two morning panels moderated by WBEZ news reporters. The four afternoon panels were organized around the themes of the four white papers. The first of two keynote speakers, Cook County Commissioner Bridget Gainer, spoke eloquently about the importance of viable neighborhoods to strengthening a metropolitan region and the need to ensure the productive conversion of vacant land in pursuit of that ideal.

The second keynote presentation was made by three middle-school students from Bradwell School of Excellence and their teacher, Linsey Rose. The students spoke passionately of their dreams, aspirations, and goals as well as the role their neighborhood plays in their lives. Just two months prior to the UIC Urban Forum, these three students and twenty-four of their classmates sent the following letter to the editor to the *Chicago Tribune* (July 28, 2014):

> This is us.
>
> We saw your news trucks and cameras here recently and we read the articles, "Six shot in South Shore laundromat" and "Another mass shooting in Terror Town." We saw the reporters with fancy suits in front of our laundromat. You spent less than 24 hours here, but you don't really know us.
>
> Those who don't know us think this is a poor neighborhood, with abandoned buildings everywhere, with wood covering the windows and broken doors. Those who don't know us see the police on the corner and think that we're all about violence and drugs. They see the candy wrappers and empty juice bottles and think that we don't care. Uneducated, jobless and thieves. You will be scared of these heartless people. When you see us coming, you

might hurry and get in your car and lock the doors. Then speed through these streets at 60 mph like you're on the highway, trying to get out of this ghetto.

We want you to know us. We aren't afraid. We know that man on the corner. He works at the store and gives us free Lemonheads. Those girls jumping rope are Precious, Aniya and Nivia. The people in the suits are people not going to funerals, but to church. That little, creepy dog is Saianis, Lamaur's dog. We are the kids who find crates so we can shoot hoops. When the sun shines here, it's not God saying he wants to burn us; he sees us all with bright futures. Those who know us look at the ones who want to go to college, not the ones who dropped out of school. If you listen, you'll hear the laughter and the chattering from the group of girls on the corner who are best friends and really care about each other. Do you see the smile on the cashier's face when the kids walk in? Why? Because this neighborhood is filled with love. This isn't Chiraq.

This is home. This is us.

By Demarion, Makyla, Lamaur, Dai'sean, JahLisa, Rondayle, DaShun, Clifford, Angel, Ashford, Keziah, Jakobe, Richard, Ariana, Jahmia, Kiara, Raquel, Adora, Nathaniel, Deamia, Maleek, Tania, Damiontaye, Samaira, Carlos, Deajiah, Ramijee and Jamariah

The 2014 UIC Urban Forum was organized by an executive committee that chose the theme of the conference, a committee of UIC scholars that identified the white papers and the authors, an external advisory board that recommended participants for the morning panels, and an operations committee responsible for organizing and planning the conference. The executive committee, which I chaired, included the UIC Great Cities Institute director Teresa Córdova, and the associate chancellor for government and public affairs Michael Redding. The UIC Committee of Academic Advisors included Rachel Weber, Elizabeth Todd-Breland, Nilda Flores-González, Steve Schlickman, Michelle Boyd, and Janet Smith.

The external board of advisors includes the following:

- Clarence Anthony, executive director, National League of Cities
- MarySue Barrett, president, Metropolitan Planning Council
- Randy Blankenhorn, executive director, Chicago Metropolitan Agency for Planning
- Henry Cisneros, former secretary, HUD; former mayor, San Antonio; founder and chairman, CityView
- Michael Coleman, mayor, Columbus
- Rahm Emanuel, mayor, Chicago

- Lee Fisher, president and CEO, CEOs for Cities
- Karen Freeman-Wilson, mayor, Gary
- Bruce Katz, director of the Metropolitan Policy Program, Brookings Institution
- Jeff Malehorn, president and CEO, World Business Chicago
- Terry Mazany, president and CEO, Chicago Community Trust
- Toni Preckwinkle, president, Cook County Board

Participants on the panels included the following:

- Robin Steans, executive director of Advance Illinois, Steans Family Foundation
- Philip Blackwell, retired senior minister, First United Methodist Church at Chicago Temple
- Brian Bannon, commissioner, Chicago Public Library
- Robert Winn, VPHA, associate vice president for community-based practice, University of Illinois at Chicago
- Niala Boodhoo, host, *Afternoon Shift*, WBEZ
- Isiah Thomas, CEO and founder, Isiah International, LLC
- Terry Mazany, president and CEO, Chicago Community Trust
- Herman Brewer, bureau chief, Economic Development, Cook County
- Bernita Johnson Gabriel, executive director, Quad Communities Development
- Richard Steele, host, WBEZ
- Mary Pattillo, Harold Washington Professor, professor of sociology and African American studies, Northwestern University
- Teresa Córdova, director and professor, Great Cities Institute, University of Illinois at Chicago
- Michael Goldberg, vice president and executive director, Heartland Alliance
- MarySue Barrett, president, Metropolitan Planning Council
- Craig Howard, director of community and economic development, MacArthur Foundation
- Alice O'Connor, professor of public policy, University of California at Santa Barbara
- Rachel Weber, associate professor, Department of Urban Planning and Policy, University of Illinois at Chicago
- Tom Tresser, public defender, CityLab Chicago
- Jason Ervin, alderman, City of Chicago

- Laura Washington, columnist, *Chicago Sun-Times*, and political analyst, ABC 7
- Pedro Noguera, Peter L. Agnew Professor of Education, New York University
- Elizabeth Todd-Breland, assistant professor, Department of History, University of Illinois at Chicago
- Cynthia Nambo, principal, Instituto Justice Leadership Academy
- Victoria Chou, interim dean of education, Dominican University
- Lorraine Forte, editor in chief, Catalyst Chicago
- Nik Theodore, professor of urban planning and policy, University of Illinois at Chicago
- Nilda Flores-González, associate professor, Department of Latin American and Latino Studies, University of Illinois at Chicago
- Grace Hou, president, Woods Fund
- Michael D. Rodriguez, executive director, Enlace Chicago
- Mary Schmich, columnist, *Chicago Tribune*

The success of the 2014 UIC Urban Forum can be credited to those who tirelessly planned, staged, and programmed the event. These tasks for an event the size of the Urban Forum create challenges that only an experienced, dedicated, and professional staff can handle effectively. Cybele Abrams and Jenny Sweeney mastered the complexities of the event with aplomb and goodwill. We are grateful for their capacity to make the event appear seamless. Many others were involved in the planning of the event. Jennifer Woodard, director of strategic engagement at the University of Illinois, was extraordinarily successful in securing the participation of many panelists; Darcy Evon and Rona Heifetz undertook the advancement work of the project; Norma Ramos, the communications officer of the Institute for Policy and Civic Engagement (a major financial supporter of the event) and Bill Burton from the UIC Office of External Affairs managed the communications and marketing of the conference; the graduate assistants assigned to the project, Stephanie Truchan, Bree Medvedev, and Megan Houston, performed superbly; and Jasculca-Terman Associates, especially Kristi Sebestyen, managed the event flawlessly.

The editorial assistance and manuscript supervision by Stephanie Truchan, who was responsible for both the book production process and for writing the summary of the panelists' conversations ("Not Your Parents' Neighborhood" in part 3, excels at synthesizing the key "takeaways" of the conference). Stephanie worked with all the contributors to this volume.

The seven hundred registrants of the one-day conference were challenged to examine the manifold ways that neighborhoods undergird and sometimes challenge the creation and growth of healthy cities and metropolitan regions. Change and growth for the improvement of the human condition can occur only when opportunities for deliberation and dialogue present themselves. The 2014 UIC Urban Forum was designed to facilitate conversation and change.

The annual UIC Urban Forum offers thought-provoking, engaged, and insightful conferences on critical urban issues in a venue to which all of the world's citizens are invited.

Michael A. Pagano
Project Director, 2014 UIC Urban Forum
Dean, UIC College of Urban Planning and Public Affairs
Chicago, December 2014

PART ONE

OVERVIEW

Neighborhoods Matter . . .
Neighborhood Matters

JANET L. SMITH

UNIVERSITY OF ILLINOIS AT CHICAGO

Neighborhoods are real places where people live, work, and play. They also function as sites for investigating urban dynamics and launching policy interventions, providing a space to implement and study change—and hopefully improve things—over time. These are not mutually exclusive activities. Our frameworks for experiencing neighborhoods and interpreting what happens in them are shaped by many of the same social norms, historical moments, and cultural preferences, which in turn determine their significance to policy makers and academics at different points in time. In this chapter, I examine what is driving the current interest in neighborhoods, focusing on both the historical role they have played in urban policy and research, and contemporary forces that make neighborhoods a compelling space for investigation and intervention. Understanding the lineage of neighborhood based theory and practice is critical since it continues to shape our expectations for policy outcomes and, as I argue in this chapter, has also misled some of our current policy prescriptions.[1]

Neighborhoods today are ground zero for several thorny policy problems, including foreclosures, housing affordability, education reform, economic mobility, and immigration.

- Foreclosure: The foreclosure crisis that hit in 2008 triggered awareness of whole neighborhoods in trouble as homes were abandoned when families moved out because they could not make their mortgage payments and lending institutions let them sit empty. Cook County is in the top ten for foreclosure filings in the United States, and in Chicago several communities, primarily African American and lower income, now have a disproportionate rate of "zombie properties"—foreclosed properties that have been sitting unresolved for three or more years.[2]

- Housing affordability: Before the recession, housing affordability was a problem for a growing number of families of all income levels, but especially for lower-income renters squeezed by rising housing costs. Even now, as economic recovery continues, the United States is at the highest ever reported level of "worst-case housing needs": 8.48 million very low-income renter households, which is a 43.5 percent increase since 2007.[3] This is due in part to the slow economic recovery from the recession, but more critically, the circumstances that produced the housing bubble in the first place including housing price inflation and wage stagnation.[4]

- Public education: Many say our public education system is in turmoil, with traditional neighborhood schools closing while a shift toward privatization has generated new charter and contract schools.[5] Over the last decade, the number of annual school closures has ranged from around 1,200 to 2,200 annually, mostly of "regular" public schools. In 2012, the closing of nearly two thousand schools affected 321,000 students.[6] A year later, Chicago closed fifty schools affecting 12,000 students, one of the largest closures in the United States. The overwhelming majority of schools were in lower-income African American communities that had lost population the previous decade.[7]

- Mobility: The abilities to move within space and up the income ladder are both tied to neighborhoods, the conditions of which can either hold residents back or move them forward.[8] The ongoing debate this last decade has been over how best to help improve neighborhoods that are largely poor and have been so for some time; do you help people move out and disperse them into better neighborhoods, or do you focus on improving the neighborhood they live in?[9] Both approaches generally aim to reduce concentrated poverty on the presumption that it will reduce a culture of poverty.[10]

- Immigration: A different type of mobility problem, immigration can present a challenge to communities. Immigrants seek employment and need social services. At the same time, they trigger a rising immigrant civil society to help respond to these needs and also to weave newcomers into the local and national political fabrics.[11] A major driver of growth in cities through the 1990s, many new immigrants are now bypassing them for the suburbs, where they can find employment and where second-generation families are buying homes.

Neighborhoods have always been home to urban-policy solutions. The current focus in broad terms is on the role they play in reducing poverty through various strategies to bring different income groups together. At the national level, we can trace this policy trajectory back to the Clinton administration and its embrace of the HOPE VI program, which aimed to transform "severely distressed" public housing developments into New Urbanist communities with low- and higher-income families living side by side. The Obama administration's Choice Neighborhoods extends HOPE VI, promoting the rebuilding of whole neighborhoods struggling with the effects of distressed public and subsidized housing. Both cede control of the process and responsibility back to local government, relying heavily on public-private partnerships and more importantly private capital investment to redress and make whole deteriorating subsidized housing. Choice Neighborhoods considers schools, services, and infrastructure. To date, the results have been wide-ranging, and generally successful at improving housing quality but not necessarily at increasing income.[12] However, this program is still a work in progress.

Mobility has been prescribed as the ticket to opportunity, to help poor people move out of concentrated poverty and into better (ideally middle-income) neighborhoods that offer better schools, positive social capital, and access to employment networks.[13] While embraced by many liberals and conservatives, both mobility and the transformation of public housing also harken back to the urban renewal efforts of the 1960s, which is blamed for once again causing damage by uprooting people, often only to be resegregated in other racially concentrated low-income neighborhoods.[14] In contrast, while there is broad recognition that investment in neighborhoods can potentially solve many problems, providing benefits to both the people and place, many are leery of this strategy as private investment has led to gentrification and displacement rather than incumbent upgrading.[15] This includes a long history of public investment in "urban renewal" and a host of neighborhood regeneration schemes that historically have not been at a scale sufficient to make a positive impact, yet have been successful in pushing poor people out.[16]

To begin my discussion of neighborhood research, policy, and practice, I offer a brief overview of how neighborhoods are conceived, delving into their significance in theory and practice, and in relation to community. I then review three periods in the United States, beginning with late modernity.[17] I focus on the roles that urban sociology and urban planning have played in shaping our expectations for neighborhoods and in shaping debates about what makes them healthy and what makes them change over time. I close with a discussion of the limits to current approaches and propose reframing neighborhood research and policy to recognize neighborhoods as critical urban commodities.[18] As spaces that have always in some way mediated social reproduction and capitalism, this current period presents specific challenges for neighborhoods and their occupants, who are now both consumers and the consumed.

WHAT IS A NEIGHBORHOOD?

This is not an easy question to answer. As Ludwig Wittgenstein said, "Something that we know when no one asks us, but no longer when we are supposed to give an account of it, is something that we need to remind ourselves of."[19] That is somewhat true here, too; to a certain degree, *neighborhood* is a term we use freely but rarely call for a precise definition. At a minimum, most would agree that a neighborhood is a place in which people live, or at a more personal level, it is the area surrounding one's home.[20] Neighborhoods are also assumed to have some sort of boundary to differentiate one from another. However, these are not easily pinned down when asking people who presumably know, such as residents or researchers.[21] Cognitive mapping exercises, for example, have shown that perceptions of neighborhood boundaries vary with each individual.[22] A recent study suggests that even when the boundaries are fixed, perceptions of the size of a neighborhood will vary depending on the characteristics of the occupants and the neighborhood.[23]

Researchers also have different views on what constitutes a neighborhood and how we identify them in studies. As a physical place, it is a unit of analysis—"the neighborhood"—made up of people and other smaller units of analysis that aggregate to constitute neighborhood characteristics. Social scientists have been producing neighborhood studies since the early 1900s using data the U.S. Census delineates by "tracts" as a proxy for a neighborhood.[24] Then and now, the average size of a tract is about four thousand people, which can be a small or large geography, depending on the density. Planners around the same time assumed this size was sufficient to support a local school and other amenities expected in a neighborhood.[25] More recently, employing walkability standards, it is assumed that these features should be within a certain walking distance (usually a half-mile radius), which then dictates a certain density and land use mix.

Census tracts were also "designed to be relatively homogeneous units with respect to population characteristics, economic status, and living conditions."[26] For the most part, this continues to be the case; even as the United States becomes more racially and ethnically diverse, its census tracts do not.[27] A hundred years ago, homogeneity was assumed to be a precondition for neighborhood stability and health. While this has changed over time and has more recently been challenged by policies and planning practice that promote "mixed" neighborhoods, homogeneity—and its presumed relationship to health and poverty—continues to be a highly problematic measure that is discussed throughout this chapter.

Accepting the notion that a neighborhood is of a certain size and scale, a mix of residential and other uses, and bounded in some way, social scientists and planners have debated how to interpret homogeneity and the degree to which it is intentional in the United States. For many, neighborhoods are places where proximity matters; whether by choice or not, living as neighbors is a form of communing. At a minimum, there is a common experience of being in a place—whatever the conditions—that is shared and affects all living there in some way. However, more commonly, it is assumed that there is some synergy between the place and the people, and that what is in common is neither arbitrary nor a coincidence. In other words, the reason we are likely to find people with the same characteristics, economic status and living conditions sharing space is because people seek out other people like them to live among and, in some manner, will act collectively as a community to maintain the status quo of that space over time.

While highly debated, planning practice and urban theory have reinforced this image with years of research, which subsequently has shaped how we think about the relationship between neighborhood and community.[28] It began with the rise of human ecology and the neighborhood unit in the 1920s and has been sustained to a certain extent by political economists and geographers in their efforts to reframe urban dynamics beginning in the 1960s. And both periods continue to influence our thinking about neighborhoods today and our expectations for them in solving urban problems.

NEIGHBORHOODS IN THE MODERN CITY

A hundred years ago, human ecologists assumed neighborhoods were natural areas where people of similar social, ethnic, or demographic background lived together. They were microcosms of our larger society that provided windows into the social relations that were needed for modern cities to function. This image prevailed for several decades, until political economists and geographers (among others) challenged the underlying logic for the organization of urban space and its commodification as the United States began shifting from an industrial to a postindustrial economy. As this section outlines, even as our understanding of neighborhoods and how they function as urban spaces has evolved, the human ecologists' conceptualization has endured, in part because planning and urban policy have continued to reproduce its logic and assumptions about why people live where they do, why neighborhoods change, and what makes them healthy.

The Neighborhood as a Microcosm (1900s–1950s)

In the early 1900s, social theorists believed that differentiation or spatial sorting into smaller groups—whether by race, ethnicity, or class—was a "natural" process. As opposed to social stratification, which sorts hierarchically, differentiation was considered by many to be essential to the functioning of the modern city; without it, there would be disorder and social dysfunction. For human ecologists at the University of Chicago (the Chicago School), the modern industrial city had a particular order to it, with neighborhoods organized in concentric rings radiating out from the central business district (CBD), which was the economic engine and heart that sustained the organism's metabolism.[29] Immediately surrounding the CBD was the zone of transition, which was the port of entry for new immigrants to the city. These neighborhoods, often a mix of industry and poor-quality housing that allowed workers to live nearby, were considered transitional because people generally would leave them once they had sufficient resources to move to a better neighborhood. The "derelict" behavior found in these neighborhoods was assumed to be the result of the poor people living together, usually new immigrants with limited resources and social capital not yet assimilated to U.S. culture. In contrast, residents at the Hull House, which was in Chicago's zone of transition, viewed these poor living conditions as social problems that were not solely the fault of the people living in them.

The Chicago School's depiction of neighborhoods prevailed even as new explanations of urban spatial formation and change were developed. The zone of transition was a functional way station, necessary for economic growth but dysfunctional for communities, as evidenced by the high rates of poverty, crime, and mortality, and directly attributed to the mix and type of people living there but also the transient nature of the space.[30] In contrast, neighborhoods in the surrounding zones were viewed as functional communities in which people with similar backgrounds—usually race or ethnicity, but also class—lived together not only because they chose to but because others chose *not* to live there. Likening this sorting and self-selection to the natural process by which a plant species would invade and take over the space of another plant species, human ecologists described the dynamics shaping city space as a process of invasion and succession. They believed it was natural that people from one group moving into a neighborhood occupied by another group would eventually push the original occupants out, who subsequently were expected to do the same wherever they moved. Not only did this sorting process validate differentiation, the collective behavior—the act of moving together—was evidence of community cohesion because whole groups of people moved together from one neighborhood to the next.

Filtering was also offered to explain these patterns of migration, particularly post-depression and post–World War II.[31] Focusing on the housing market and life cycle of families, neighborhood change was a logical if not a natural progression that occurred in response to social reproduction; as households formed and became families with children they sought larger homes, and for the most part, many Americans could afford to "move up and out." While still implicit in filtering theory, this explanation of neighborhood change shifted attention away from race and ethnicity as drivers of change and also from viewing the process as an invasion; instead, it was presented as people moving into new homes on the periphery who were then freeing up their older homes for others with lower incomes to move in. Helping to generate these new homes were urban planners.

Planners at the time mirrored to a certain extent human ecologists' perspective of urban neighborhoods. Lewis Mumford, for example, believed that "neighborhoods, in some primitive, inchoate fashion exist wherever human beings congregate, in permanent family dwellings; and many of the functions of the city tend to be distributed naturally—that is, without any theoretical preoccupation or political direction—into neighborhoods."[32] In other words, they are a product of the people residing in a common space but they also serve a purpose and play a role in keeping the city functioning. While neighborhood planning "has been practiced since the early days of America's settlement," it began to mature in the 1920s as more people searched for social cohesion in the bustling industrial city.[33] Perhaps most influential and most influenced by the Chicago School was Clarence Perry, best known for his "neighborhood unit" approach to planning. Perry proposed a set of principles for building new neighborhoods that could adapt to the automobile age (fig. 1).[34] However, he also sought to "insulate affluent city residents from the disruptive influence of forced interaction with supposedly incompatible groups."[35] The neighborhood unit was designed to guard against invasion and succession of lower income people into middle class communities. Replicated in some form in many cities but also more importantly their suburbs, many middle-class neighborhoods were developed across the United States following the neighborhood unit approach.[36]

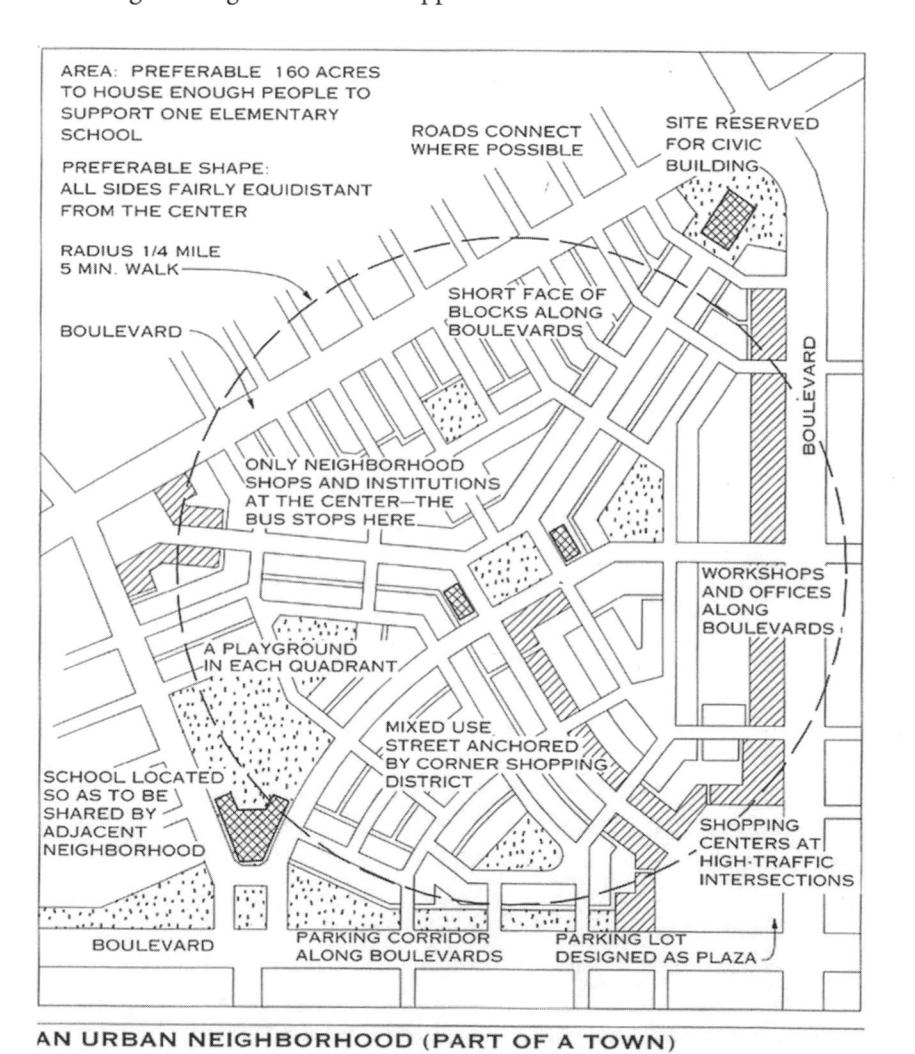

AN URBAN NEIGHBORHOOD (PART OF A TOWN)

Figure 1. Neighborhood Unit Principles. Reproduced from C. Perry, *A Plan for New York and Its Environs* (New York: New York Regional Planning Association, 1929), 34–35.

Neighborhoods as Sites for Consumption (1960s–1980s)

By the 1960s, criticism had grown not just of the neighborhood unit but also of the urban planning profession as it pushed for modernizing neighborhoods through urban renewal.[37] A blunt critic, Jane Jacobs, wrote: "Neighborhood is a word that has come to sound like a Valentine. As a sentimental concept, 'neighborhood' is harmful to city planning. It leads to attempts at warping city life into imitations of town or suburban life. Sentimentality plays with sweet intentions in place of good sense." For Jacobs, diversity is what made a community in the city as did "the eyes on the street" provided by watchful neighbors.[38] The death of cities was assured, she claimed, as long as planners continued their efforts to "renew" old neighborhoods and replace them with monolithic and out-of-scale residential development like the large public housing projects growing up in cities, or worse the exclusive neighborhood unit in our suburbs. From her perspective, it was the unplanned and diverse spaces (both the use and the people) found in mercantile cities like New York and Boston, and industrial cities like Chicago, that were real neighborhoods and made the city function.

Along these lines, Herbert Gans maligned the neighborhood unit's physical determinism and the Chicago School's conceptualization of "slums" that justified urban renewal.[39] Based on his empirical research in Boston's West End, he found a vibrant ethnic lower-income enclave that, while homogeneous and somewhat insular, functioned well because it developed organically and over time. In this period and in direct response to top-down urban renewal, a number of advocates reframed neighborhoods as organs of local government and democratic decision making; what was in common was the need to control and participate meaningfully in planning for renewal of their neighborhoods.[40]

Around the same time, some cities began organizing their planning practice into neighborhood units, in part to accommodate new requirements to engage citizenry in decisions around urban renewal and redevelopment.[41] Unlike Perry's planned neighborhood unit, these were to be more bottom-up and focused on process rather than top-down and physical design oriented. Many like Gans argued for more social orientation: "Neighborhood planning is necessary, of course, but a social and political type which supports community, state, and federal programs for elimination of poverty" is what he thought was needed.[42] Paul Davidoff coined the phrase "advocacy planning" to describe an alternative approach to neighborhood work.[43] In response to urban renewal in particular, he and others pushed to change the way public participation worked so that residents were consulted before the plan was made rather than after it was completed. Davidoff also argued for pluralism, allowing for many plans to be produced by and with different constituency groups on the premise that there is no single public interest. Similarly, Sherry Arnstein laid out her ladder of participation to distinguish powerless consulting from engagement that empowered and gave residents real control in the process but also the allocation of resources.[44]

The community development movement also began in the 1960s with the creation of our first nonprofit community development corporations (CDCs). Formed to get private and public resources back into disinvested communities, CDCs were born in places like Newark, New Jersey, and New Haven, Connecticut—neighborhoods left behind by middle-class families who had moved to the suburbs. These were comprehensive efforts, often filling many voids and working to rebuild infrastructure and housing while providing services, food, and job training.[45] Many were successful in developing the physical space. However, despite the declared war on it, reducing poverty was a larger challenge for these CDCs as was the issue of racial segregation, which as Alice O'Connor reminds us, was never the intention of community development policy.[46]

The 1960s also marked a shift in neighborhood scholarship, which took two directions, both fitting of the changes occurring across many cities, interpreting conditions differently and in important ways. The in-migration of African Americans primarily from the South to northern industrial cities triggered a new explanation for change: racial tipping. Researchers concluded that there was a point at which a predominantly white neighborhood would tip and rapidly resegregate to become a black neighborhood once a threshold was met.[47] While this varied, the consensus based on empirical evidence was that it was between 5 and 30 percent black.[48] In a way, tipping was a specific form of invasion succession (blacks succeed whites) and filtering (whites freed up space for blacks).

Racial tipping was the primary explanation in urban sociology for neighborhood change through the early 1980s, providing the basis for several policy prescriptions to prevent the out-movement of whites and resegregation but also to "open up" communities to African Americans. This included equity assurance programs to assuage fears of property depreciation, placing a cap on African Americans moving into a neighborhood (set at a percent below the tipping point; considered illegal since it restricted choice) and housing centers to help people make affirmative moves (which is not the same as steering).[49] These local strategies all came in direct reaction to the behavior of various actors in the real-estate transaction, including the Federal Housing Administration (FHA), which underwrote mortgage lending and stated in its manual that "if a neighborhood is to retain stability, it is necessary that properties shall continue to be occupied by the same racial classes." This practice was reinforced by the real-estate industry, which until passage in 1968 of the Fair Housing Act was able to outright discriminate and steer families to purchase and rent housing in neighborhoods with people of their same race or ethnicity.[50] While the Fair Housing Act aimed to prevent discrimination, it was not designed to promote integration—an issue that scholars and advocates still debate.[51]

Although the Chicago School was still highly influential, a growing critical voice was coming from political economists and geographers, many grounded in Marxism, questioning the very foundation of human ecology. Specifically, they found the invasion succession argument flawed and based on social theory contrived to find order in a city that was becoming more diverse.[52] By framing the city as naturally segregated by race, ethnicity, and class, the Chicago School overlooked many key factors shaping urban spatial patterns a hundred years ago. This included the social, political, and legal conditions that prevented people from integrating and the deliberate actions of institutions opposed to racial or ethnic integration.[53] Also, excluded was the use of restrictive covenants that prevented people from accessing whole neighborhoods because of their race, ethnicity, and/or religion, which were finally deemed unenforceable by the U.S. Supreme Court in 1948.[54] However, before that ruling, about 80 percent of property in Chicago and Los Angeles had covenants barring purchase by black families.[55]

Prior to this period, Marxists and political economists had not really paid attention to neighborhoods, in part because their analysis was at a systems level. Still, they recognized that these enclaves provided a separate space outside the workplace for social interaction, the production of culture, and social reproduction.[56] However, neighborhoods were now also recognized as sites for investment and disinvestment driven by both private capital and the state (e.g., urban renewal). David Harvey's study of the relationship between city disinvestment and suburban investment spatialized the flow of capital and put it squarely in (or out of) neighborhoods.[57] Studies of urban revitalization began to distinguish neighborhood improvement and "incumbent upgrading" from gentrification.[58] Neil Smith reframed invasion and succession, claiming the process was driven by revanchist motivations of middle-class (and usually white) people to reclaim the city from the poor (usually not white).[59] Neighborhoods became the commodity market for profit-seeking capital—first by young professionals and then later by a whole collection of investors, developers, and real-estate professionals. As John Logan and Harvey Molotch explained, the exchange value trumped use value.[60] The idea that neighborhoods were a community of like-minded people was a sentimentality to buy and sell, but so was the idea of living the bohemian lifestyle in an edgy neighborhood, which in real-estate terms was code for lower-income and often ethnic neighborhoods in transition.[61] As Pattillo describes, once settled in, newcomers generally rid the neighborhood of its diversity and charm.

With this back-to-the-city movement also came a whole new way to classify neighborhoods in relation to how gentrified they were (e.g., über, hyper, turbo) but also awareness that not all city neighborhoods were experiencing reinvestment.[62] Furthermore, gentrification became urban policy—whether written or not—as cities embraced the positive cash flow of investment and influx of households with resources and income rather than need and poverty.[63] Chris Silver described this period as "decades of revisions" and as a "movement to resurrect a pattern of urban social, political, and spatial relationships centered on self-contained and self-sustaining residential clusters."[64] While some people were truly moving back to the city, many were also finding ways to preserve what they had and fight against the pressures of investment or disinvestment. In either case, the neighborhood was a key part in launching U.S. urban revitalization—as something to package and sell—and that continues today.

Neighborhoods as Sites for Investment (1990s–present)

Low interest rates and a recovering economy in the early 1990s encouraged investment. Gentrification expanded and the renaissance of U.S. cities was in full swing. However, as the national economy was improving, not all boats were rising with the tide. While the federal government had been investing in community development policy for several decades and nonprofits had built thousands of housing units, few felt that planners had made measurable progress on the social front envisioned during the 1960s. A growing concern was that perhaps we were just "gilding the ghetto"—making it look good but not changing the conditions that made people poor and deterred private investment.[65]

Growing attention to poverty, and particularly generational poverty, by social scientists suggested that the neighborhoods in which poor people lived were contributing to this problem.[66] Policy researchers began investigating the idea that there might be a "culture of poverty" that kept people from getting out of low-income neighborhoods, including those high-rise public housing developments that Jane Jacobs had condemned in the 1960s. These homogeneous neighborhoods, presumed to be lacking in positive role models for youth, generated negative social capital in the form of gangs and drug dealers; in some cities, such neighborhoods were barriers to much needed private investment.[67]

During the early years of the Clinton administration, debates about whether we should invest in people or place stirred up concerns among community developers and others who believed in doing both.[68] National policy followed a two-pronged path: place-based strategies like public housing transformation and empowerment zones, and people-based dispersal strategies such as housing choice vouchers. Both were premised on the belief that poverty must be deconcentrated if people are going to get out of it.[69] Liberal think tanks like the Urban Institute and researchers such as William Julius Wilson pushed policy makers to look seriously at ways to address the problems in high-poverty neighborhoods. Fresh research from implementation of the *Hills v. Gautreaux* settlement in Chicago showed promising though tempered outcomes from moving seven thousand families from predominantly black public housing developments into predominantly white or mixed-race middle-income and usually suburban neighborhoods. The results were favorable for children's education and employment for the adult parents who moved.[70] This prompted the U.S. Department of Housing and Urban Development (HUD) to launch the Moving to Opportunity (MTO) program to "test housing mobility strategies more systematically," however, unlike Gautreaux it focused on controlling the poverty rate of neighborhoods rather than controlling their racial composition.

Early research on high-poverty neighborhoods suggested that redistribution was a partial answer but not a full solution.[71] When the MTO program started, HUD had outlined a larger agenda to respond to the concentrated poverty problem. In addition to moving people to low-poverty neighborhoods, the federal government would help families link to jobs in economic opportunity areas, and "promote the revitalization of distressed inner-city neighborhoods."[72] To this end, the Clinton administration implemented several programs, including HOPE VI, which had originated under George H. Bush to redevelop "severely distressed" public housing (about 7–8 percent of its stock), and the Empowerment Zone program in selected cities to help create jobs and shore up local businesses.[73] The latter had limited reach and results.[74] HOPE VI, on the other hand made an impact—though the outcomes have varied. HOPE VI provided grants up to $50 million to public-housing authorities to demolish high-rise public housing and replace them with low-rise, mixed-income developments. Besides a means to deconcentrate poverty, the redeveloped sites were expected to help produce positive social capital and to be an asset to the surrounding neighborhoods. To produce these results, HUD turned to the Congress for New Urbanism (CNU) for guidance. CNU's mission is to "change the practices and standards of urban design and development to support healthy regions and diverse, complete neighborhoods."[75] CNU developed a guide based on its design principles to help housing authorities transform the dense monolithic space of high-rise public housing.[76]

Critical of public housing and suburban sprawl, New Urbanists found both to be problematic because they were homogeneous spaces. There also was a scale problem: one was too dense and the other not dense enough. Their solution was a hybrid space that had enough density to support a diversified economy and a mix of income groups. Like the original neighborhood unit, attention was given to the mix and location of different land uses; however, the intent was to produce a space that supported diversity, at least in income and housing tenure. The New Urbanist neighborhood was a packaged idea of what an urban neighborhood should look like in terms of scale that partly mirrored actually existing places but also represented a new type of space, one that was aesthetically compelling but also that resonated with a growing interest in environmental conservation. Countering sprawl, other movements such as "smart growth" and "transit oriented development" and "walkability" design principles complemented New Urbanism.[77]

All these ideas fit under a broad rubric of place making—the process of creating spaces that were convivial and supportive, interactive and connected. In some way, all were nostalgic and at the time fit well with what might best be described as a public longing for community, representing an imagined place from our collective past.[78] These representations, while different in appearance from the neighborhood unit, functioned much the same way: they provided a template for developing complete urban spaces that could also by design produce community in the form of positive social capital among a diverse group of people. This image of the neighborhood was compelling. Unlike gentrification, which was "unplanned," requiring individual developers and consumers to align their interests, New Urbanism was a complete vision of the space that could be implemented in toto as a mixed-use planned unit development. In this sense, in addition to selling the "inner city," we were being offered a version of the inner-city neighborhood without the individual risk or edginess.

The New Urbanist images of redeveloped public housing helped sell a vision of a future in which public housing fit into the existing fabric of our cities. It was appealing to many who wanted to target investment to help both people and place.[79] To date, however, the impact on the physical space is more evident in the new housing stock and, in some cases, spillover private investment when compared to the outcomes for the people, which have been limited and certainly have not significantly reduced poverty or necessarily produced the social relationships envisioned. In some cases, an unintended result of redevelopment may have been new racial tension compounded by class differences in the mixed-income and race developments.[80]

Public-housing transformation also reminded us that there were many low-income people in need. In addition to HOPE VI, the Clinton administration also pushed asset building strategies to benefit both people and place.[81] This included the individual development account (IDA), which was a matched savings program to help lower-income families invest in their education, small-business development, or buying a home. The vast majority of families applied their IDA savings toward housing taking advantage of low-interest rates on mortgages. From the perspective of asset building, most policy makers thought these individual purchases would spill over to the neighborhood; however, research suggests this rarely happened and was limited.[82]

At the neighborhood scale was asset-based community development (ABCD), which "considers local assets as the primary building blocks of sustainable community development"—residents' skills, local associations, and local institutions.[83] ABCD spawned a small movement to turn around how we viewed community development, focusing on strengths rather than deficits, and helping residents put their assets to work to generate income and improve their community. Many foundations also embraced ABCD, responding to the founders' claim that this was unlike traditional community development, which made people dependent rather than empower them.[84]

A similar message came from Michael Porter in his "Competitive Advantage of the Inner City," however, framed slightly differently.[85] From his perspective, the "inner city" had many advantages but CDCs were not helping the communities they served through their job creation efforts. Instead, he recommended that these organizations focus on helping people by developing their job skills and changing their attitudes about working and leave the job creation to the private sector since this was their expertise. Of course, Porter and ABCD proponents had their critics, who did not agree that CDCs should diminish their role in poor communities. Interestingly, even as Porter and asset building both prevailed, so have CDCs—though some would argue that the CDCs heeded Porter's advice and focused on their unique competitive advantage: producing affordable housing.

Opening the door to private-sector investment in lower-income neighborhoods is what many believed was needed, especially after decades of disinvestment. And the private sector to some extent responded. The result was an array of new public-private partnerships aimed at bringing private capital into urban neighborhoods in order to right the disinvestment patterns. This included lending institutions seeking to invest in previously redlined communities. While not all were predatory, many were not necessarily well-intended when entering these "emerging" new markets.[86] To help fuel homeownership, the federal government had developed new programs that could help lower-income families enter the market, in part on the premise that this was an asset building strategy and in particular because it would help "minority" families increase wealth.[87] Lending institutions also offered various loan products to entice families to purchase homes, and for some these were beyond their means. This helped expand ownership among African Americans and Latinos as well as immigrants.[88] It also, however, helped to set the stage for the most recent recession and the high rates of foreclosure in many lower income and non-white neighborhoods as well as immigrants.[89]

Neighborhoods as Sites for Investigation (1990s–present)

Efforts to improve poor neighborhoods have also generated new research. Interest once again in the ecology of neighborhoods triggered a wide array of hypotheses linking health, educational achievement, employment, and wealth to name a few "effects" that neighborhoods were assumed to have on people.[90] However, while it made sense that people are affected by where they live, it was harder to really determine which attribute or set of attributes contributed more or less—or even if there was a causal link—to poverty. A new generation of research on "neighborhood effects" was launched to investigate the relationship between neighborhoods and individual outcomes with growing attention to quasi-experimental and randomized designed studies to assure robust results.

This included the MTO research, which randomly assigned families—all volunteers—living in public housing and other assisted developments to one of three groups: experimental, comparison, and control. Families in the experimental group received housing vouchers to use only in low-poverty neighborhoods, while the comparison families could move to any neighborhood with their vouchers. The control group did not move, remaining in their original developments. All were tracked over a ten-to-fourteen-year period to observe economic, educational, and health outcomes. After twenty-plus years of research, including the extensive MTO study, the empirical evidence is still relatively inconclusive as to how neighborhoods actually affect people—in essence, how they matter.[91]

George Galster comes to a similar conclusion based on an exhaustive review of research on neighborhood effects.[92] He does, however, offer several observations, including this one:

> First, in both the U.S. and Western Europe high concentrations of poverty or socially disadvantaged households (which typically are heavily Hispanic- and especially black-occupied neighborhoods in the U.S. and immigrant-occupied neighborhoods in Western Europe) have been consistently empirically linked to weaker cohesion and structures of informal social controls in their neighborhoods. This situation produces, in turn, negative consequences like increased youth delinquency, criminality, and mental distress, although this mechanism has not yet been linked to other important outcomes like labor market performance. However, in both U.S. and Western European research the aforementioned concentrations of poverty or disadvantage retain their relationship with a variety of child and adult outcomes even after intra-neighborhood levels of social control and cohesion are taken into account. Clearly, more than this mechanism is at work.[93]

Clearly, there is a lot more to unpack here. While there appear to be relationships between poverty and race and between ethnicity and immigrant status, we really cannot say how or why neighborhoods matter other than that they are locations in which people are experiencing these effects together. A link suggests only that a relationship exists. As Galster thoughtfully reminds us, "Put bluntly, it is risky for policy-makers to naively observe a correlation between neighborhood indicators and individual outcomes of interest and design programmatic strategies as if neighborhoods were a 'black box.' At best, inefficiencies and, at worse, negative unforeseen consequences, are all-too-likely to follow in these circumstances."[94]

The big unknown in neighborhood effects research is causality. At this time we cannot easily conclude what particular set of conditions, if changed, will have a greater likelihood of improving a person's economic situation. Still, most agree that neighborhoods do matter. Further, we do have more evidence now about neighborhood effects and linkages (fig. 2). Like clinical research on new drugs, Galster suggests we think of these different linkages as having some "dosage" amount that will either cure or exacerbate the problem.

Figure 2. Potential Linkages of Neighborhood Effects (Galster, "Mechanism(s) of Neighborhood Effects Theory, Evidence, and Policy Implications")

Social-Interactive Mechanisms

- Social contagion
- Collective socialization
- Social networks
- Social cohesion and control
- Competition
- Relative deprivation
- Parental mediation

Environmental Mechanisms

- Exposure to violence
- Physical surroundings
- Toxic exposure

Geographic Mechanisms

- Spatial mismatch
- Public services

Institutional Mechanisms

- Stigmatization
- Local institutional resources
- Local market actors

I would like to suggest another set of linkages to consider: what I call "systemic institutional mechanisms." This includes economic and income equality and environmental racism. Racism is the use of power—intentional or unintentional—to isolate, separate, and exploit others based on racial or ethnic identity. Environmental racism is the result of decisions that impact our built and natural environments and that directly or indirectly affect people with less power, which in the United States has been and continues to be, though not exclusively, nonwhites. Income inequality, which measures how income is distributed, is not the same as economic inequality. Economic inequality describes the conditions affecting an individual's ability to create wealth, which varies over time and space, and different economic structures and systems.[95] Both are systemic because they operate at a level that affects all neighborhoods, though not the same way, and they are institutional because they are sustained and reproduced through various institutions at all levels of society and government. Without inclusion of these linkages, we will continue to sustain prescriptions that are not only ineffective but also pin responsibility on the people who have the problem to also solve it, whether it is poverty, educational attainment, housing affordability, or unemployment. The following section discusses this in greater depth.

NEIGHBORHOOD AS CONTESTED SPACE

Neighborhoods are dynamic places, constantly changing with the ebb and flow of people, capital, and policy. Over time, the various theories developed to explain these dynamics have identified physical, social, and institutional factors that cause neighborhoods to change. They offer at best only partial explanations of the complex relationships and factors shaping the day-to-day events in our urban areas. What these explanations do reveal are the social concerns at the time they were developed and what social scientists, planners, and policy makers perceived the problem to be. I conclude with a discussion of the common threads that continue to weave together a specific view of neighborhoods today in terms of what makes them healthy to live in. This includes assumptions about social differentiation and collective efficacy that originated with the Chicago School. I argue that what is missing, at least in the mainstream research and contemporary policy, is full analysis of the institutions at work that as Greg Squires clearly argues produce uneven development including lending institutions and housing policy.[96] I propose that we consider adding to the list the systemic institutional mechanisms of environmental racism and economic and income inequality. Currently, while the effects of both do appear in the linkages as "symptoms" (to continue Galster's medical metaphor) that are studied or are the target of policy intervention, they are not outright identified as causal variables. The limits to the current approach are evident in the current underlying logic of neighborhood-based strategies to reduce poverty, which assumes now that a healthy neighborhood will have a mix of income groups.

The Healthy Neighborhood

Policy makers and researchers have long turned to the various theories already described in this chapter to guide the development of programs and practical applications that can produce "positive" neighborhood change. This includes different forms of intervention, either to offset negative results of change (e.g., loss in property values, decreasing quality of life) or to encourage change so as to induce positive results (e.g., increasing property values, improving quality of life). The key policy questions that neighborhood research continues to ask are what makes a neighborhood healthy, and what assures it will stay that way? And while we cannot always make direct linkages between theory and policy, as the previous analysis illustrates, social science hegemony at particular points in time has clearly shaped how the policy problems associated with neighborhoods are framed and the subsequent solutions to them.[97] For example, in 1974, HUD provided an extensive list of criteria for a "healthy" neighborhood in its model of neighborhood change (fig. 3).[98] Visibly, these indicators of neighborhood health represent a particular form of neighborhood that assumes racial or ethnic homogeneity and class are important as well as high rates of ownership. These indicators continue to be germane to contemporary discussions of revitalization and preservation goals and strategies.[99]

As planning and policy has moved toward framing mixed-income neighborhoods as healthy communities, the question we need to ask is whether or not the entire "package" of variables should be reassessed. Research on "mixed" race neighborhoods in the 1990s, for example, proved that tipping and resegregation are not inevitable.[100] However, while these findings challenge the assumption about ethnic homogeneity, the results are still framed as contrary to conventional wisdom. In other words, the research itself assumes that ethnically diverse neighborhoods are the exception and not the

Figure 3. Indicators of a "Healthy" Stable Neighborhood (adapted from Mitchell, *Dynamics of Neighborhood Change*)

Social

- Middle to high social status
- Moderate to upper income levels
- Ethnic homogeneity
- High school graduates and above
- Family-oriented or childless adults
- White-collar and/or skilled blue-collar workers
- Pride in neighborhood and house
- Good neighborhood reputation
- Neighborhood perceived as safe
- Socially cohesive

Public Services

- Services efficient and appropriate
- Some reliance on private services

Physical

- Good property upkeep
- Sound structural condition
- Good location
- Neighborhood well-maintained

Economic

- High owner investment
- Good property values
- Property insurance available
- High confidence in future value

rule.[101] While disconcerting for diversity proponents, the cautionary tone seems warranted given the longstanding and culturally reinforced perceptions consumers have about racial segregation in the United States.[102]

A similar caution has been taken with mixed-income neighborhoods. While there was a groundswell of support for the New Urbanist transformation of public housing into so-called mixed-income neighborhoods, developers proceeded with caution and restricted the number of poor public-housing renters. Understandably, much was unresolved on this front prior to building the first developments.[103] It was unknown if people were actually willing to mix along lines of class and housing tenure and, if they were, what actually constituted a ratio of low- to higher-income households, renters to owners, or whites to nonwhites sufficient to make a healthy mix. A key point of debate was the effect that renters and, more pointedly, poor people would have on neighborhood stability.[104] Historically, both have been treated as destabilizing factors in a neighborhood on the assumption that poor people lack both economic and social capital when compared to higher-income people, and renters are transient and therefore less connected to the community than property owners.[105] While it is hard to disentangle income and social capital, research has found evidence that they are not always positively correlated.[106] Furthermore, despite research showing few critical distinctions between renters and owners, the perception that poor renters destabilize a neighborhood is evident in new developments that favor homeowners over renters and limit the number of lower-income tenants.[107]

While framed as promoting a healthy mix, restricting the number of rental units for people who need them the most raises questions about the logic and intention of public-housing transformation. Generally speaking, the operating assumption behind current efforts to develop mixed-income neighborhoods is that they are expected to be better communities with a higher quality of public and private services, lower crime rates, and better access to jobs than homogeneous low-income neighborhoods. They are also assumed to benefit poor people through interaction with higher-income people with social capital, which further assumes that higher-income people are willing to play this role and that if they do, it will produce certain results that will help reduce poverty. However, not taken into consideration are the systematic barriers that affect these outcomes, including individual prejudices but also the institutional racism and classism operating outside of these developments.[108] Putting that aside, if the goal is to produce material benefits to lower-income families, then the question to ask is this: do people have to live in a mixed-income neighborhood to get them, especially when higher-income people living in homogeneous "economic enclaves" usually have these benefits? As I have argued elsewhere, I think the answer is no; more importantly, we need to question why this approach is even acceptable.[109]

Reframing the Problem

As discussed earlier, some political economists and geographers frame neighborhood dynamics differently. Change occurs because of shifts in production and reproduction. According to Logan and Molotch, "within the Marxian framework, neighborhood is essentially a residual phenomenon" within this process.[110] A limitation to this framework is the lack of agency and the overdetermination of what produced change and the outcomes of it. For example, gentrification once started will continue to completion, and higher-income people will replace lower-income residents. At least the role of institutions, including the state, is recognized. Still, as with human ecologists, the world divides into homogeneous groups each in its own space; however, the social differentiation observed is hierarchical and based in power.

For some, interpreting neighborhood dynamics changed with the introduction of Henri Lefebvre's *The Production of Space*, which framed space as a process and its production fluid over time.[111] David Harvey and other geographers have shown how neighborhood change was a flow of capital in relation to spatial production and the process of social reproduction. From this perspective, the ebb and flow of capital through space is evident in neighborhoods, and the resulting spatial patterns provide evidence that can help us understand the current state of production and reproduction. For example, Harvey found changes in the "inner city" that were directly related to changes in suburban space and in other parts of the world.[112] Squires further demonstrated how these changes were also tied to institutional racism as well as individual discrimination.[113]

Critical analyses grounded in various traditions—for example, neo-Marxism, feminism, postmodernism—have taken this interpretation of space further with investigations that relate gentrification and public-housing transformation to neoliberalism situating neighborhood change in the global financial system.[114] This became evident when the mortgage crisis revealed how tightly neighborhoods around the country were connected to global capital through secondary markets and mortgage-backed securities.[115] From this perspective, neighborhoods generally are contingent products.[116] The dynamics shaping the space are explained by the social relations of reproduction, which are shaped by and at the same time shaping class dynamics and capital accumulation. And from this critical perspective, gentrification and the transformation of public housing into mixed-income neighborhoods are public strategies to clear some but not all poor people out to make room for higher-income people to move in, and both are possible because we have put in place systems and institutions to make it possible. Furthermore, while income mixing reduces concentrated poverty—which by default it has to—it will do nothing significant to reduce poverty overall because it does not deal with the systems and institutions that produce poverty including environmental racism and economic and income inequality. It is these mechanisms that need to be investigated and for which intervention is needed.

CONCLUSION: A PROPOSITION

Neighborhoods matter today because they are clear physical targets for investment and disinvestment.[117] These two produce the conditions that then produce neighborhood effects including poverty. The forces behind disinvestment are what we need to focus on since, when compared with investment, they are more elusive in shaping urban patterns. We can see investment and can trace it to investors, but disinvestment isn't necessarily traced back to a "disinvestor" since many actors and institutions are responsible, some intentional in their actions (e.g., FHA lending practices before fair housing) while others not.

A form of disinvestment shaping our uneven neighborhood U.S. landscape is known as environmental racism, which Bullard coined to describe the strong correlation between environmental and subsequent health disparities found across the United States between white and non-white neighborhoods, and now more commonly between rich and poor regardless of race.[118] But, as stated earlier, correlation is not the same as causation. Over time, the accrued evidence has shown through empirical research and validated with millions of dollars in legal settlements that in fact institutions have contributed directly to disparities because they determine where toxic waste and pollutants are located and maintained through regulation (e.g., zoning, permits), and for the most part overwhelmingly in poor and nonwhite communities.

While some may argue that a landfill or a petroleum coke storage facility can be an investment in a community because it creates jobs and pays taxes, it is also a form of disinvestment because it reduces the value of the land and homes in the neighborhood. But more importantly, it creates conditions that have lasting effects on the lives of the people living there. A growing body of research correlates environmental threats and health disparities with poverty and race and spatial segregation.[119] This research raises serious questions about the linkages between environmental conditions to education outcomes, economic opportunities and violence as well as poor health, and more broadly to long-term deprivation in our communities and the country. Researchers have also documented resistance and strong social cohesion among residents in many of these affected neighborhoods to "stop the dumping" on communities of color.[120] In fact, the U.S. Environmental Protection Agency has an Environmental Justice division to help these communities. Still, all this research and activism is noticeably absent from the discussion of neighborhood effects, as is the possible linkage to poverty, education outcomes, violence or poor health.

Also noticeably absent from the discussion has been inequality—until recently. While related, poverty is not the same as inequality. Research generally indicates that in the United States metropolitan area household income segregation grew from 1970 to 2010.[121] Many assume that spatial income sorting—the decision on where to live based on your income—is natural given the relative homogeneity of housing within and across neighborhoods.[122] However, a small but growing body of research suggests that increasing economic inequality is compounding socio-spatial exclusion (polarization). For example, Chicago's income inequality doubled from 1970 to 2010, as did its income polarization.[123] Over that same period, the number of middle-class neighborhoods shrank in Chicago while increasing in the suburbs.[124] We also know there are confounding effects of race and ethnicity in the robust relationship between income inequality and income segregation.[125]

Reframing income and economic inequality as a product of the uneven development witnessed over the past forty years as result of institutional racial discrimination, revanchism, and creative destruction shifts our attention from the victim—both the people and the place—to a significant though not necessarily sole source of the problem.[126] Since 2014, Ferguson, Missouri, has brought national attention, not just to the differences in income levels of whites and blacks but also to how divided we are still on the causes of these differences.[127] Ta-Nehisi Coates's "A Case for Reparations" reminds us that our neighborhood spatial patterns are not simply a result of income sorting, as does the decision by the Koch brothers to store petroleum coke piles in Detroit and in the predominantly African American but also Latino South Side of Chicago.[128] Yet decisions made and sustained by government institutions and lending institutions over the years remind us that simply raising awareness does not undo or even reverse these decisions.

While these recent events remind us that economic and income inequality and environmental racism make all our neighborhoods contested space, the question now is what we will do to change this. I suggest we begin by reframing the problem to focus on the systemic institutional mechanisms that cause poverty, to learn from people affected so we can better understand how these mechanisms produce and allow these neighborhoods to be targets of disinvestment, and to work to develop policy and interventions that can change these mechanisms. I think this charge is supported by the other chapters in this book.

Notes

1. Smith, J., "Interpreting Neighborhood Change," unpublished diss., Cleveland State University, 1998.

2. "Unresolved Foreclosures: Patterns of Zombie Properties in Cook County," Woodstock Institute, accessed November 30, 2014, www.woodstockinst.org/.

3. U.S. Department of Housing and Urban Development, *Worst Case Housing Needs 2011, Report to Congress—Summary* (Washington, D.C.: U.S. Department of Housing and Urban Development, 2013).

4. National Low Income Housing Coalition, "Out of Reach," 2014, http://nlihc.org/oor.

5. Noguera, P., "Cities, Schools and Social Progress: The Impact of School Reform Policies on Low-Income Communities of Color," paper presented at the UIC Urban Forum, Chicago, Illinois, September 18, 2014, see also his chapter in this book; P. Lipman, *The New Political Economy of Urban Education: Neoliberalism, Race, and the Right to the City* (New York: Routledge, 2011).

6. "Fast Facts: Closed Schools," National Center for Education Statistics Institute of Education Sciences, 2013, accessed November 30, 2014, http://ies.ed.gov/.

7. Kunichoff, Y., "One Year after Closings, How Are Chicago's Public Schools Now?," *In These Times*, June 5, 2014, accessed November 30, 2014, http://InTheseTimes.com/.

8. Pattillo, M., "Mobility and Neighborhoods," paper presented at the UIC Urban Forum, Chicago, Illinois, September 18, 2014; see also her chapter in this book.

9. Imbrosio, D., *Urban America Reconsidered: Alternatives for Governance and Policy* (Ithaca, N.Y.: Cornell University Press, 2010).

10. Joseph, M., "Is Mixed-Income Development an Antidote to Urban Poverty?," *Housing Policy Debate* 17, no. 2 (2006): 209–34.

11. Theodore, N., "Migrant Civil Society and the Metropolitics of Belonging," paper presented at the UIC Urban Forum, Chicago, Illinois, September 18, 2014, see also his chapter in this book; Martin, N., "'There Is Abuse Everywhere': Migrant Nonprofit Organizations and the Problem of Precarious Work," *Urban Affairs Review* 48 no. 3 (2012): 389–416.

12. Levy, D., Z. McDade, and K. Dumlao, *Effects of Living in Mixed-Income Communities for Low-Income Families: A Review of the Literature* (Washington, D.C.: Urban Institute, November 2010).

13. Briggs, X., J. Popkin, and J. Goering, *Moving to Opportunity: The Story of an American Experiment to Fight Ghetto Poverty* (New York: Oxford University Press, 2013).

14. Fullilove, M., *Root Shock: How Tearing Up City Neighborhoods Hurts America, and What We Can Do About It* (New York: One World/Ballantine, 2005); Pattillo, "Mobility and Neighborhoods"; Goetz, E., *New Deal Ruins: Race, Economic Justice, and Public Housing Policy* (Ithaca, N.Y.: Cornell University Press, 2013); Bennett, L., J. Smith, and P. Wright, eds., *Where Are Poor People to Live? Transforming Public Housing Communities* (Armonk, N.Y.: M. E. Sharpe, 2006); Voorhees Center, "The Plan to Voucher Out Public Housing: An Analysis of the Chicago Experience and a Case Study of the Proposal to Redevelop the Cabrini-Green Public Housing Area," Nathalie P. Voorhees Center for Neighborhood and Community Improvement, University of Illinois at Chicago, 2006, accessed November 30, 2014, http://media.wix.com.

15. O'Connor, A., "People and Places: Neighborhood as a Strategy of Urban Development from the Progressive Era to Today," paper presented at the UIC Urban Forum, Chicago, Illinois, September 18, 2014; see also her chapter in this book.

16. Fullilove, *Root Shock*.

17. While not exactly aligned, I credit Chris Silver's review of neighborhood planning for helping me to organize this history of neighborhood theory: Silver, C., "Neighborhood Planning in Historical Perspective," *Journal of the American Planning Association* 51, no. 2 (1985): 161–74.

18. This is the central argument of Betancur, J., and J. Smith, *Claiming Neighborhoods: New Ways of Interpreting Urban Change* (Urbana: University of Illinois Press, forthcoming).

19. Wittgenstein, L., *Philosophical Investigations* (Oxford, U.K.: Basil Blackwell, 1958).

20. Pebley, A. R., and N. Sastry, "Neighborhood, Poverty, and Children's Well-Being: A Review," in *Social Inequality*, ed. K. Neckerman, 119–46 (New York: Russell Sage Foundation, 2004).

21. Taylor, R. B., "Defining Neighborhoods in Space and Time," *Cityscape: A Journal of Policy Development and Research* 14, no. 2 (2012): 225–30.

22. Coulton, C., M. Zane Jennings, and T. Chan, "How Big Is My Neighborhood? Individual and Contextual Effects on Perceptions of Neighborhood Scale," *American Journal of Community Psychology* 51, no. 1–2 (2013): 140–50.

23. Pebley, A., and N. Sastry, "Our Place: Perceived Neighborhood Size and Names in Los Angeles," On-Line Working Paper Series, California Center for Population Research, University of California, Los Angeles, 2009.

24. The U.S. Census began this process in New York City in 1900 and consulted with a community panel on tract boundaries.

25. Perry, C., "Planning a City Neighborhood from the Social Point of View," in *Proceedings of the National Conference of Social Work*, 415–21 (Chicago: University of Chicago Press, 1924).

26. American Community Survey, "Geographic Areas: Definitions," U.S. Census Bureau, accessed November 20, 2014, www.census.gov/acs/.

27. Holloway, S., and R. Ellis, "The Racially Fragmented City? Neighborhood Racial Segregation and Diversity Jointly Considered," *Professional Geographer* 64, no. 1 (2012): 63–82.

28. J. Smith, "Interpreting Neighborhood Change"; Betancur and J. Smith, *Claiming Neighborhoods*.

29. Park, R., E. Burgess, and R. McKenzie, *The City* (Chicago: University of Chicago Press, 1925).

30. Diner, S., *A City and Its Universities: Public Policy in Chicago, 1892–1919* (Chapel Hill: University of North Carolina Press, 1980); J. Smith, "Interpreting Neighborhood Change."

31. Baer, W. C., and C. B. Williamson, "The Filtering of Households and Housing Units," *Journal of Planning Literature* 3 (1988): 127–52.

32. Mumford, L., "The Neighborhood and the Neighborhood Unit," *Town Planning Review* 24 (1954): 256–70, 258.

33. Silver, "Neighborhood Planning in Historical Perspective," 161.

34. Perry, C., *Neighborhood and Community Planning*, vol. 3 (New York: Regional Survey of New York and Its Environs, 1929).

35. Silver, "Neighborhood Planning in Historical Perspective," 166.

36. Ibid.

37. Isaacs, R., "The Neighborhood Unit as an Instrument for Segregation," *Journal of Housing* 5, no. 8 (1948): 215–19.

38. Jacobs, J., *The Death and Life of Great American Cities* (New York: Random House, 1961).

39. Gans, H., *The Urban Villagers* (New York: Free Press, 1962); Silver, "Neighborhood Planning in Historical Perspective."

40. Jacobs, *Death and Life of Great American Cities*; Arnstein, S., "A Ladder of Citizen Participation," *Journal of the American Institute of Planners* 35, no. 4 (1969): 216–24; Davidoff, P., "Advocacy and Pluralism in Planning," *Journal of the American Institute of Planners* 31, no. 4 (1965): 331–38.

41. Silver, "Neighborhood Planning in Historical Perspective"; O'Connor, "People and Places."

42. Gans, Urban Villagers.

43. Davidoff, "Advocacy and Pluralism."

44. Arnstein, "Ladder of Citizen Participation."

45. Keating, D., N. Krumholz, and P. Star, *Revitalizing Urban Neighborhoods* (Lawrence: University Press of Kansas, 1996).

46. O'Conner, A., "Swimming against the Tide: A Brief History of Federal Policy in Poor Communities," in *The Community Development Reader*, eds. J. DeFilippis and S. Saegert, 11–29 (New York: Routledge, 2008).

47. Grodzins, M., *The Metropolitan Area as a Racial Problem* (Pittsburgh, Pa.: University of Pittsburgh Press, 1958); Schelling, T., "Dynamic Models of Segregation," *Journal of Mathematical Sociology* 1 (1971): 143–86.

48. Card, D., A. Mas, and J. Rothstein, "Tipping and the Dynamics of Segregation," *Quarterly Journal of Economics* 123, no. 1 (2008): 177–218.

49. All three were introduced in Oak Park, Illinois, in the early 1970s. The limit on the percent of African Americans on a block was never implemented (Goodwin 1973).

50. U.S. Commission on Civil Rights, "Understanding Fair Housing," Clearinghouse Publication 42, February 1973.

51. Squires, G., and C. Hartman, *The Integration Debate: Competing Futures for American Cities* (New York: Routledge, 2009).

52. Tilley, C., *Big Structures, Large Processes, Huge Comparisons* (New York: Russell Sage Foundation, 1984).

53. Massey, D., and N. Denton, *American Apartheid: Segregation and the Making of the Underclass* (Cambridge, Mass.: Harvard University Press, 1993); Abrams, C., *Forbidden Neighbors* (New York: Harper & Brothers, 1955); Aldrich, H., "Ecological Succession in Racially Changing Neighborhoods: A Review of the Literature," *Urban Affairs Quarterly* 10, no. 3 (1975): 327–48; Squires, G., *Capital and Communities in Black and White* (Albany, N.Y.: SUNY Press, 1994).

54. *Shelley v. Kraemer*, 334 U.S. 1 (1948).

55. U.S. Commission on Civil Rights, 1973.

56. Katznelson, I., "The Centrality of the City in Social Theory," in *The Divided Heritage: Themes and Problems of German Modernism*, ed. I. Rogoff, 253–64 (Cambridge: Cambridge University Press, 1991).

57. Harvey, D., *The Urban Experience* (Baltimore, Md.: Johns Hopkins University Press, 1989).

58. Clay, P., *Neighborhood Renewal* (Cambridge, Mass.: MIT, 1979).

59. Smith, N., *The New Urban Frontier: Gentrification and the Revanchist City* (London: Routledge, 1996).

60. Logan, J., and H. L. Molotch, *Urban Fortunes: The Political Economy of Place* (Berkeley: University of California Press, 1987).

61. Higgins, M., "Life after Brooklyn," *New York Times* magazine, August 22, 2014, describes how people are leaving Brooklyn to find new affordable places to live such as "ethnic" Harlem.

62. Palen, J., and B. London, eds., *Gentrification, Displacement and Neighborhood Revitalization* (Albany, N.Y.: SUNY Press, 1984).

63. Carmon, N., "Neighborhood Regeneration: The State of the Art," *Journal of Planning Education and Research* 17 (1997): 131–44.

64. Silver, "Neighborhood Planning in Historical Perspective."

65. Persky, J., and J. Kain, "Alternatives to Gilding the Ghetto," *National Review* 14 (1969).

66. Wilson, W., *The Truly Disadvantaged: The Inner City, the Underclass, and Public Policy* (Chicago: University of Chicago Press, 1987); Sampson, R., S. Raudenbush, and F. Earls, "Neighborhoods and Violent Crime: A Multilevel Study of Collective Efficacy," *Science* 15 vol. 277, no. 5328 (1997): 918–24.

67. Venkatesh, S., *American Project: The Rise and Fall of a Modern Ghetto* (Cambridge, Mass.: Harvard University Press, 2000).

68. Ellen Gould, I., and M. Turner, "Does Neighborhood Matter? Assessing Recent Evidence," *Housing Policy Debate* 8, no. 4 (1997): 833–66.

69. In addition, welfare reform also sought to encourage people to enter the labor force by limiting the time for receiving assistance to five years but also offering job training.

70. U.S. Department of Housing and Urban Development, "Expanding Housing Choices for HUD-Assisted Families," Washington, D.C. 1996.

71. Jargowsky, P., *Poverty and Place: Ghettos, Barrios, and the American City* (New York: Russell Sage Foundation, 1997).

72. Schroder, M., "Moving to Opportunity: An Experiment in Social and Geographic Mobility," *Cityscape* 5, no. 2 (2001): 57–67, 57.

73. HOPE stands for Homeownership and Opportunity for People Everywhere; HOPE IV was inaugurated in 1993 to provide grants to local public housing authorities to redevelop severely distressed or obsolete public housing projects. HOPE VI began as a demonstration program and in 1998 it was made a permanent program operated by the U.S. Department of Housing and Urban Development and its focus expanded to support transforming public housing into mixed income developments. See http://www.hud.gov/offices/pih/programs/ph/hope6/about/hope6appropriations.pdf.

74. U.S. Government Accountability Office, "Empowerment Zone And Enterprise Community Program: Improvements Occurred in Communities, but the Effect of the Program Is Unclear," Washington, D.C., 2006.

75. Congress for New Urbanism, "CNU Strategic Plan 2012–2017" (2012). See www.cnu.org/strategicplan2012.

76. U.S. Department of Housing and Urban Development, "Expanding Housing Choices for HUD-Assisted Families."

77. See www.SmartGrowthAmerica.org, www.TransitOrientedDevelopment.org/, and www.WalkLive.org/ for more information on these movements.

78. Smith, J., "Cleaning Up Public Housing by Sweeping Out the Poor," *Habitat International* 23, no. 1 (1999): 49–62.

79. Bennett, J. Smith, and Wright, *Where Are Poor People to Live?*

80. Joseph, "Is Mixed-Income Development an Antidote to Urban Poverty?"; Chaskin, R., and M. Joseph, "Social Interaction in Mixed-Income Developments: Relational Expectations and Emerging Reality," *Journal of Urban Affairs* 33, no. 2 (2011): 209–37; Khare, A., M. Joseph, and R. Chaskin, "The Enduring Significance of Race in Mixed-Income Developments," *Urban Affairs Review* 33, no.2 (2014): 209–37.

81. Sherraden, M., *Assets and the Poor: A New American Welfare Policy* (Armonk, N.Y.: M. E. Sharpe, 1991).

82. Weber, R., and J. Smith, "Assets and Neighborhoods: The Role of Individual Assets in Neighborhood Revitalization," *Housing Policy Debate* 14 (2003): 169–202.

83. The Asset-Based Community Development Institute, Northwestern University, accessed November 30, 2014, www.abcdinstitute.org/.

84. Kretzmann, J., "Building Communities from the Inside Out," *National Housing Institute*, 1995, accessed November 30, 2014, www.nhi.org/online.

85. Porter, M., "The Competitive Advantage of the Inner City," *Harvard Business Review*, May–June (1995): 55–71.

86. The term "emerging" was used by Fannie Mae and Freddie Mac to describe these communities.

87. Shapiro, T., "Race, Homeownership and Wealth," *Washington University Journal of Law and Policy* 20, no. 1 (2006): 53–74.

88. Myers, D., and G. Painter, "Homeownership and Younger Households: Progress Among African Americans and Latinos," in *Redefining Urban and Suburban America*, eds. A. Arube, B. Katz, and R. E. Lang, 245–66 (Washington, D.C.: Brookings Institution Press, 2005).

89. Kochhar, R., and A. Gonzalez-Barrera, *Through Boom and Bust: Minorities, Immigrants and Homeownership* (Washington, D.C.: Pew Charitable Trust, 2009).

90. Popkin, S. J., T. Leventhal, and G. Weismann, "Girls in the 'Hood: Reframing Safety and Its Impact on Health and Behavior," *Urban Affairs Review* 45, no. 6 (2010); Turner, M., and M. Rawlings, *Promoting Neighborhood Diversity: Benefits, Barriers, and Strategies (Discussion Papers)* (Washington, D.C.: Urban Institute, 2009).

91. Ludwig, J., G. Duncan, L. Gennetian, L. Katz, R. Kessler, J. Kling, and L. Sanbonmatsu, "Long-Term Neighborhood Effects on Low-Income Families: Evidence from Moving to Opportunity," *American Economic Review Papers and Proceedings* 103, no. 3 (2013): 226–31.

92. Galster, G., "The Mechanism(s) of Neighborhood Effects Theory, Evidence, and Policy Implications," paper presented at the ESRC Seminar: Neighbourhood Effects: Theory and Evidence, St. Andrews University, Scotland, February 4–5, 2010.

93. Ibid., 15.

94. Ibid., 18.

95. Sen, A., "From Income Inequality to Economic Inequality," *Southern Economic Journal* 64, no. 2 (1997): 383–401.

96. Squires, Capital and Communities in Black and White.

97. Metzger, J. "Planned Abandonment: The Neighborhood Life-Cycle Theory and National Urban Policy," *Housing Policy Debate* 11, no. 1 (2000): 7–40.

98. Mitchell, J., *The Dynamics of Neighborhood Change* (Washington, D.C.: U.S. Department of Housing and Urban Development, Office of Policy Development and Research, 1974).

99. J. Smith, "Interpreting Neighborhood Change"; Betancur and J. Smith, *Claiming Neighborhoods*.

100. Lee, B., and P. Wood, "Is Neighborhood Racial Succession Place-Specific?" *Demography* 28, no. 1 (1991): 21–40; Ottensmann, J., "Requiem for the Tipping-Point Hypothesis," *Journal of Planning Literature* 11, no. 2 (1995): 132–41; Nyden, P., M. Maly,

and J. Lukehart, "The Emergence of Stable Racially and Ethnically Diverse Urban Communities: A Case Study of Neighborhoods in Nine U.S. Cities," *Housing Policy Debate* 8 (1997); J. Smith, "Interpreting Neighborhood Change."

101. Holloway and Ellis, "Racially Fragmented City?"

102. Krysan, M., and M. Bader, "Racial Blind Spots: Black-White-Latino Differences in Community Knowledge," *Social Problems* 56, no. 4 (2009): 677–701; Wilson, W., and C. Taub, *There Goes the Neighborhood* (New York: Knopf, 2006).

103. Schwartz, A., and K. Tajbakhsh, "Mixed-Income Housing: Unanswered Questions," *Cityscape* 3, no. 2 (1997): 71–92.

104. J. Smith, "Cleaning Up Public Housing by Sweeping Out the Poor."

105. Putnam, R., *Bowling Alone: The Collapse and Revival of American Community* (New York: Simon and Schuster, 2000).

106. Saegert, S., J. Thompson, and M. Warren, eds. *Social Capital and Poor Communities* (New York: Russell Sage Foundation, 2001).

107. Rohe, W., S. Van Zandt, and G. McCarthy, "The Social Benefits and Costs of Homeownership: A Critical Assessment of the Research," in *Low Income Homeownership: Examining the Unexamined* (Washington, D.C.: Brookings Institution, 2002).

108. Smith, N., "New Globalism, New Urbanism: Gentrification as Global Urban Strategy," *Antipode* 34, no. 3 (2002): 434–57; Smith, J., and D. Stovall, "'Coming Home' to New Homes and New Schools: Critical Race Theory and the New Politics of Containment," *Journal of Education Policy* 23, no. 2 (2008): 135–52.

109. J. Smith, "Interpreting Neighborhood Change."

110. Logan, J., and H. Molotch, *Urban Fortunes: The Political Economy of Place* (Berkeley: University of California Press, 2007), 100.

111. Lefebvre, *Production of Space*; J. Smith, "Interpreting Neighborhood Change"; Betancur and J. Smith, *Claiming Neighborhoods*.

112. Harvey, *Urban Experience.*

113. Squires, *Capital and Communities in Black and White.*

114. N. Smith, "New Globalism, New Urbanism"; Hackworth, J., *The Neoliberal City: Governance, Ideology and Development in American Urbanism* (Ithaca, N.Y.: Cornell University Press, 2007).

115. Ashton, P., "'Troubled Assets': The Financial Emergency and Racialized Risk," *International Journal of Urban & Regional Research,* 36, no. 4 (2012): 773–90.

116. Betancur and J. Smith, *Claiming Neighborhoods.*

117. Ibid.

118. Bullard, R., *Confronting Environmental Racism: Voices from the Grassroots* (Boston: South End Press, 1983); Bullard, R., *Unequal Protection: Environmental Justice and Communities of Color* (San Francisco: Sierra Club Books, 1994); Schweizer, E., "Environmental Justice: An Interview with Robert Bullard," *Earth First! Journal,* 1999, accessed August 12, 2013, www.ejnet.org/ej/bullard.html.

119. Clark, L., D. Millet, and J. Marshall, "National Patterns in Environmental Injustice and Inequality: Outdoor NO_2 Air Pollution in the United States," *PLOS One,*

April 15, 2014, accessed November 30, 2014, www.plosone.org/; Orum, P., R. Moore, M. Roberts, J. Sánchez, *Who's in Danger? Race, Poverty, and Chemical Disasters: A Demographic Analysis of Chemical Disaster Vulnerability Zones* (Brattleboro, Vt.: Environmental Justice and Health Alliance for Chemical Policy Reform, 2014).

120. Bullard, Confronting Environmental Racism.

121. Jargowsky, *Poverty and Place*; Jargowsky, P., "Stunning Progress, Hidden Problems: The Dramatic Decline of Concentrated Poverty in the 1990's," in *Center of Urban and Metropolitan Study, Living Cities Census Series* (Washington, D.C.: Brookings Institution, 2003); Wheeler, C. H., and E. A. La Jeunesse, "Trends in Neighborhood Income Inequality in the U.S.," *Regional Science* 48, no. 5 (2008): 879–91; Watson, T., "Inequality and the Measurement of Residential Segregation by Income in American Neighborhoods," NBER Working Paper 14908, Cambridge, Mass., 2009; Voorhees Center, "The Deepening Divide in Chicagoland," Nathalie P. Voorhees Center for Neighborhood and Community Improvement, University of Illinois at Chicago, 2014, accessed November 30, 2014, www.voorheescenter.com.

122. Thurow, L., "The Income Distribution as a Pure Public Good," *Quarterly Journal of Economics* 85, no. 2 (1971): 327–36; Weinberg, D., "U.S. Neighborhood Income Inequality in the 2005–2009 Period," *U.S. Census Bureau, American Community Survey Reports* (Washington, D.C.: U.S. Government Publishing, 2011).

123. The Gini Coefficient was 0.163 in 1970 and 0.328 in 2010 and the Coefficient of Polarization 0.231 in 1970 and 0.454 in 2010 in Chicago. Voorhees Center, "Joint Report with the University of Toronto on Neighborhood Change in Chicago & Toronto, 1970–2010," forthcoming.

124. Voorhees Center, "Deepening Divide in Chicagoland."

125. Reardon, S. F., and K. Bischoff, *Growth in the Residential Segregation of Families by Income, 1970–2009* (Providence, R.I.: Russell Sage Foundation American Communities Project of Brown University, 2011).

126. Squires, *Capital and Communities in Black and White*; N. Smith, *New Urban Frontier*; Betancur and J. Smith, *Claiming Neighborhoods*.

127. Gandel, S., "The Economic Imbalance Fueling Ferguson's Unrest," *Fortune*, August 15, 2014.

128. Coates, T., "The Case for Reparations," *Atlantic*, May 21, 2014; Hawthorn, M., "Petcoke Firm Threatens Lawsuit over City Rules," *Chicago Tribune*, July 25, 2014, accessed November 30, 2014, www.chicagotribune.com.

PART TWO

WHITE PAPERS

Opportunity without Moving

Building Strong Neighborhoods Where People Can Stay If They Want To

MARY PATTILLO

NORTHWESTERN UNIVERSITY

Andrea Wilson, an African American woman in her twenties, lived with her mother in the same apartment building in Chicago where she, her mother, and her grandmother had all been raised.[1] But now the neighborhood was changing. "The management, now, I don't particularly care for," she began. "They don't want the kids running around. They can't play in front. They don't want you standing in front of the building. You can't do this, you can't do that. It's like you a prisoner in your own home. Basically, they don't want you to do anything." Andrea commented on nearby buildings being converted to condos, new homes going up, and old homes being remodeled. She appreciated that the vacant lots were being filled, that new businesses were opening, and that the schools had new administration, but as a result, she said, "it's getting more expensive to live around here." And along with the new housing and neighbors came the new rules. When the landlord began hassling her family about standing in front of their building, Andrea tried to stand her ground. "We would just sit there and not pay any attention to him. And then finally he just drive off." She felt emboldened by her seniority in the neighborhood to defy the new, more rigid rules. Still, Andrea's stoop-sitting protest was short-lived. The landlord got the last word through the prerogatives of ownership. "He wanted to raise our security [deposit] from $75 to $900 dollars," she recalled. "He wanted to raise our rent to $1,100. We were already paying $875. So by the first of November we had to have . . . [$1,100] rent and a $900 security, which is no way. Got to move. So within a month we were packed up and moved in here."

Andrea was lucky to find an apartment in a federally subsidized building a few blocks away. Her move probably did not alter her own place-based social ties or the demographic character of the neighborhood in major ways. Still, Andrea's case represents the incremental process by which disadvantaged people lose access to (or are excluded from) good neighborhoods. It shows how a neighborhood characterized by improving opportunities slipped out of Andrea's reach, just at the time that policy makers were promoting slogans like "Moving to Opportunity"[2] for low-income and working-class households like Andrea's. This chapter shows how patterns of voluntary and involuntary mobility (and permanence) often undermine the equitable distribution of opportunities across neighborhoods, and how unequal neighborhoods then lead to differential residential mobility. It proposes steps to promote universal opportunity in neighborhoods so that people don't have to move unless they want to.

People move for all kinds of reasons, and neighborhoods are always changing. Because neighborhoods are created, transformed, nourished, depleted, rediscovered, and forgotten by people (and institutions, businesses, and jobs) that move into and out of them, this chapter focuses on how moving behavior is integrally connected to the ability of neighborhoods to thrive as nurturing places for their residents. Moving behavior consists of decisions to move into or out of neighborhoods, as well as to stay put in a certain place. But this residential mobility (or permanence) is deeply structured by inequalities by race, class, disability, citizenship status, and other characteristics that make some people's hold on their homes more tenuous than others', and gives some people much greater choice than others. The incidence of voluntary and involuntary moves (or voluntary and involuntary permanence) is not equally distributed across groups. As a result, advantaged groups—for example, whites, middle- and upper-income households, professionals, U.S. citizens—have greater ability to leave neighborhoods when they perceive them to be declining, and move to new neighborhoods that they perceive as better. Their moves decrease the resources, political clout, and livability of the neighborhoods they leave behind. Disadvantaged groups have fewer options—whether it's because they cannot pay as much in rent or perhaps they don't have a car. They are no less motivated to live in good neighborhoods, but they are less able to realize that goal. The moving and staying of unequal groups creates an unequal "geography of opportunity" in which neighborhoods vary widely as good or bad places to live, work, go to school, recreate, and be healthy.[3]

Below, I discuss how mobility affects neighborhoods and neighborhood change. I then review the literature on various kinds of mobility and degrees of voluntariness. The aim of the literature review is to show how inequalities in the ability to move and the practice of moving (and staying put) create inequalities across neighborhoods because neighborhood advantages and disadvantages accrue depending on who lives there. These inequalities across neighborhoods, in turn, affect the (educational, labor market, health, safety) outcomes of families living in them. Moreover, because neighborhood characteristics and neighborhood change can motivate more moving, residential mobility can be both the cause and the effect of who lives in a neighborhood and its overall quality. I conclude by arguing that breaking this cycle of moving, neighborhood change, and more moving—and thus building more uniformly strong and enriching neighborhoods—does not result from tinkering with mobility, but instead requires the de-commodification of housing and the decoupling of place and opportunity.

MOBILITY AND NEIGHBORHOODS

The U.S. Census Bureau reports that nearly 36 million people, or 11.7 percent of the population, moved between 2012 and 2013.[4] Over five years, roughly one in three Americans moved. While this is a lot of moving—particularly when compared to other advanced nations—residential mobility in the United States has been on the decline since the mid-1960s, when the one-year mover rate was roughly 20 percent, almost twice today's rate.[5] Some moving is inevitable since it is tied to common changes in family status, job location, and individual whim. As table 1 shows, 22 percent of households moved for job-related reasons; 12 percent moved because they had a change in their family situation; and 40 percent moved for housing-related reasons, which includes things like starting an independent household, wanting a bigger or better home, or wanting lower housing costs. While only 3 percent of households in the American Housing Survey reported their main reason for moving as being displaced involuntarily—which includes foreclosures, evictions, natural disasters, or government displacement—6 percent listed it as one of the reasons for their move (data not given in table 1). Hence, there is never just one reason for moving, and it is often difficult to disentangle push and pull factors.

Instead of creating single-reason categories, it makes more sense to posit a continuum of residential mobility from voluntary to involuntary. At the

Table 1. Main Reason for Moving by Selected Household Characteristics, American Housing Survey, 2011

	All Households	Owner	Renter	Black	Hispanic	Poor	In City	In Suburb
Displaced	3%	2%	4%	4%	4%	4%	3%	4%
Job Related	22%	14%	25%	16%	19%	20%	24%	21%
Family Related	12%	13%	12%	10%	12%	12%	11%	12%
Housing Related	40%	52%	37%	44%	44%	40%	40%	41%
Other/No Report	18%	15%	18%	21%	15%	19%	18%	18%
All Factors Equal	5%	5%	5%	4%	7%	4%	5%	5%

Source: U.S. Department of Housing and Urban Development and U.S. Census Bureau, *American Housing Survey for the United States: 2011*, table C-06-AO, 2011, accessed June 12, 2014, http://www.census.gov/.

most voluntary end of the spectrum would be a person who is financially, logistically, and socially comfortable in their current housing unit, but decides he would be happier with an attached garage or a home office, or if she were closer to public transportation or a park. Completely voluntary moves are prompted more by taste than necessity, by personal considerations rather than the demands of others, and by aspirational desires rather than hardships. Extreme involuntary moves, on the other hand, are compulsory, forced by an external party, and unwanted. Eviction, demolition, and physical violence are actions that force involuntary moves. Most moves fall somewhere between these two extremes.

No matter what the impetus for or the autonomy in moving, the neighborhood is both the starting point and the destination of residential mobility. Alongside individual circumstances, tastes, and the social context, the built environment also makes possible or constrains certain kinds of moves. If there is no public transportation in a neighborhood, it is not attractive for people without cars. If there are no homes built at grade level, no buildings with elevators, or no curb ramps, a neighborhood will be difficult to navigate for those with physical disabilities. If there are no jobs within a reasonable commute, only families who can afford extensive child care or a stay-at-home parent will want to move there. If a neighborhood has only six-bedroom McMansions, it will not attract single, older, or working-class people. And a neighborhood that replaces all of its play lots with dog parks may push out families with children. Moreover, neighborhoods are more than the people who live there. Schools, churches, businesses, factories, organizations, and public spaces equally contribute to the feel and functioning of neighborhoods. To a greater or lesser extent, the users of these institutions are mobile and the physical structures or open spaces can be demolished, repurposed, or replaced. While the mobility of institutions and jobs is of crucial importance to the health and sustainability of neighborhoods, I focus this chapter instead on how the mobility of residents impacts neighborhoods, and how neighborhood qualities, in turn, prompt residential mobility.

Finally, why and where people move and the neighborhoods they move to are structured by markets. Housing is a commodity.[6] The expansion of the market ever further into the spheres of land and housing is an emergent feature of modern capitalism and is neither natural nor given. Urban space is configured by the demands of capitalist production and accumulation, the commodification of space, and the resulting social conflicts between people and groups with unequal political, economic, and symbolic resources.[7] As a result of these processes, some groups have privileged and unbridled access to urban resources—effective sanitation, convenient shopping, clean air, reliable electricity, good schools—and others are completely left out, through price, law, violence, and other forms of exclusion. Moreover, the capitalist class needs people to move. "The drive to relocate to more advantageous places" incites a cycle of neighborhood improvement and decline that benefits developers, land speculators, real estate agents, construction firms, raw-materials producers, and the politicians who align with them.[8]

When people buy, sell, or rent houses or apartments, the neighborhood necessarily comes along with it. John Logan and Harvey Molotch argue that the desire to improve the profitability of land use stands central to the ways in which coalitions of economic and political elites (or "growth machines") govern cities, which in turn shapes the neighborhood contexts within which families and households move.[9] Within land and housing prices are capitalized the quality of schools, access to transportation, neighborhood amenities, the race and income of neighbors, and crime rates. Housing prices and rents are also the result of political and legal decisions about taxation, zoning, desegregation, policing, labor, and infrastructure, among many other things. Seeking to achieve the highest possible return on land investments, elites aim for increasing rents, which creates involuntary mobility for people with less money. Hence, people are not moving freely across places, nor are places the natural results of the people who move in and out of them. A discussion of residential mobility and neighborhoods that does not recognize the dominant role of capitalist market makers and state actors misidentifies the causes of urban inequalities as individual choices and preferences, rather than the structural context within which such choices and preferences are exercised.

The following sections discuss various kinds of mobility under the broad categories of "moving in," "moving out," and "forced moves," with the variable of voluntariness or involuntariness discussed throughout. Each section also discusses how various kinds of mobility are related to the establishment of neighborhoods as places of greater and lesser opportunity.

MOVING IN

What kinds of forces draw people into neighborhoods and what affects if their entry is met with delight, indifference, or disdain? There are myriad in-moving scenarios that could be explored, such as: population growth prompted by transit-oriented development; poor people moving to the suburbs;[10] chain migration into immigrant enclaves;[11] families moving to take advantage of high-performing schools; oil and other energy boomtowns that attract new workers; the construction of new retirement communities for baby boomers; or the substantial population movement to the South and West.[12] In this section, I focus on two types of neighborhood in-migration that have received considerable popular and scholarly attention: low-income families using Housing Choice Vouchers to move into nonpoor neighborhoods, and high-income families moving into lower-income neighborhoods, commonly called gentrification.

A 2008 article in the *Atlantic* fingered displaced public housing residents and relocating Housing Choice Voucher users as the causes of rising crime in the suburbs of Memphis.[13] The unfriendly reception that poor families faced having moved into these suburbs should not have been surprising given the considerable evidence of antipathy for rental, affordable, subsidized, and public housing, and their residents, especially in better-off neighborhoods.[14] Nonetheless, tenant-based rental assistance, which gives families vouchers to rent apartments in the private market, is currently by far the largest federal housing program. In many cities, families—many of whom are black and Hispanic—are encouraged to use their vouchers to make "opportunity moves"—that is, to move into areas with low poverty rates and higher proportions of white families, often in the suburbs.[15] Many big cities like Chicago, Baltimore, Dallas, and Minneapolis offer "mobility counseling" to encourage families with vouchers to make these opportunity moves.[16] While low-income families often express autonomous desires to move into safer and better neighborhoods, the incentive of counseling plus the disincentive of losing out on a voucher make opportunity moves not fully voluntary.

Rigorous research followed the *Atlantic* article indictment that crime goes up when subsidized families move in. Michael Lens used data on two hundred metro areas, finding a small but not robust *negative* correlation—the opposite as posited by the *Atlantic* article—between the number of voucher holders in a neighborhood and crime rates in cities, while crime in suburban neighborhoods was unaffected by voucher holders.[17] Using data on ten cities, Ingrid Ellen and colleagues initially found a positive correlation between an increase in voucher households and crime in a neighborhood, but more detailed, time-sequenced analyses pointed to the fact that voucher households were moving to areas where crime was already increasing, rather than being the cause of it.[18] The authors argued that their findings "should provide some comfort to communities concerned about the entry of voucher holders" but also "should be troubling to policymakers," since vouchers are supposed to improve families' residential options, not limit them to neighborhoods that may be in decline. Finally, Susan Popkin and colleagues asked the same question in Chicago and Atlanta: are neighborhoods that were the destinations for families relocated from demolished projects in Chicago and Atlanta experiencing increased crime? They found that crime declined in most of the destination neighborhoods of displaced public-housing residents, but crime would have gone down *even more* if those relocated public-housing families had not moved in. In other words, relocation stunted the crime decline in neighborhoods that received large numbers of public-housing residents. However, in both Chicago and Atlanta, only a few neighborhoods reached sufficient density of relocated families to really make an impact on crime rates. Overall, the authors came to a conclusion not too unlike that reached by Ellen and colleagues: "our story is not the popular version of previously stable communities spiraling into decline because public housing residents moved in, but rather a story of poor families moving into areas that were already struggling."[19]

Even prior to the *Atlantic* debate, many scholars had studied what happened to neighborhoods when low-income families moved in, either with vouchers or to live in newly built subsidized housing.[20] George Galster and colleagues found that housing prices went up when a few families with housing vouchers moved into higher-cost, stable white communities in Baltimore, likely because the houses they moved into had to pass a quality inspection to be eligible for the program.[21] But they also found that the concentration of many voucher families in areas that already had low or declining property values had a further negative effect on neighborhood property values.[22]

Chang-Moo Lee and colleagues found that public-housing units, Low Income Housing Tax Credit (LIHTC) units, and Housing Choice Voucher units had small to modest negative effects on nearby housing prices in Philadelphia, but public-housing homeownership programs and new construction Section 8 housing had modest positive effects.[23] Amy Schwartz and colleagues and Ellen and colleagues found large and sustained positive effects of federally and city-subsidized low-income housing, respectively, on property values in New York.[24] Overall, then, the in-migration of low-income households does not have uniformly negative impacts on neighborhoods, and the evidence actually suggests that the most negative impacts are not in advantaged communities—which likely have substantial resources to absorb new low-income families—but rather in places that are economically fragile or that already have high concentrations of subsidized housing and low-income families.[25] These empirical facts, however, have not seemed to stop advantaged residents from fleeing neighborhoods when poor people and minorities move in.

As nonpoor neighborhoods absorb new poor in-migrants, some poor neighborhoods are the new destinations of the wealthy. *Gentrification* is a woefully imprecise and loaded word, but it seems to be the most recognizable description of the process whereby affluent or upwardly mobile people (and the businesses that cater to them) move into poor and working-class neighborhoods.[26] Such movement into disadvantaged neighborhoods does not simply reflect the new gritty fancies of gentrifiers. Smith shows how gentrification is "lubricated by state donations" through the use of eminent domain, tax incentives and tax breaks, land giveaways, and direct subsidies to investors.[27] At the same time that policy makers aim to "de-concentrate poverty" by pressuring poor people to make opportunity moves away from the urban core, they are hoping to replace those departing residents with middle- and upper-income newcomers.

The scope of gentrification in U.S. cities should not be overstated, however. For example, Ingrid Ellen, Katherine O'Regan, and Keren Horn show that only about 29 percent of higher-income movers in the American Housing Survey moved to relatively low-income neighborhoods, with nonwhite households, renters, and those without a college degree—not the usual gentrifier profile—*more* likely to do so.[28] Owens shows that in the decades from 1970 to 2010, no more than about 20 percent of census tracts in metropolitan areas across the country experienced "ascending" socioeconomic profiles.[29] Moreover, census tracts in white suburbs—not the stereotypical targets of gentrification—made up the largest category of ascending neighborhoods, although minority neighborhoods were more likely to ascend in the more recent decades. In other words, gentrification is not a predominant pattern of in-migration across the country. Nonetheless, the dramatic and generally voluntary influx of upper-income white (and nonwhite) households into working-class minority communities in New York, Denver, Boston, Washington, D.C., Seattle, and other cities is a visibly stark phenomenon that has consequences for neighborhoods.

Whether they are artists, gays and lesbians, bankers, new college graduates, or black and Hispanic professionals on an uplift mission, when these new people move into a neighborhood to capitalize on cheap rents, a favorable location, a storied past, or architectural charm they mean business. Brett Williams studied the "upscaling" of a neighborhood in Washington, D.C., in the 1980s where the commercial change lagged behind the influx of new residents. She describes how newcomers reacted to the existing neighborhood and what they envisioned instead: "Most new homeowners find the stores uninteresting, inadequate, unpleasant, and sometimes frightening. They feel threatened by the groups of men who stand talking. . . . One man, a realtor, vows that his agency is there 'to clean the neighborhood up' and complains, 'We need a florist. We need a bank. We need a *good* restaurant.' When I asked him about the Greek, Malian, Salvadoran, and Guatemalan restaurants there already, he replied, 'We deserve better.' Michael laughingly pleads, 'All I want is a place where I can buy twelve kinds of mustard.'"[30] As this quotation indicates, the interactions between newcomers and established residents in gentrifying neighborhoods include contestations over neighborhood resources, the use of public space, and appropriate public behaviors.[31] When well-off people move into poor neighborhoods, they attract stores, banks, and amenities that longtime residents often appreciate.[32] Yet, at the same time, the newcomers have little tolerance for loud music, corner loitering, informal vending, and even legal ethnic businesses that had been the way of life before they got there. As a result, established residents express feeling policed, excluded, and increasingly unable to find their way in what used to be familiar territory. As Andrea Wilson said in the opening vignette, "It's like you a prisoner in your own home."

Quantitative studies have focused more on the impact of gentrification on crime, schools, and displacement. The findings are not totally consistent on the question of crime, with results varying across city and by the type of crime.[33] Derek Kreager and colleagues' study of Seattle argues that such inconsistent results across studies might be due to changes over time in the effects of gentrification. They posit "a tipping-point in gentrification, where the positive association between early gentrification and crime reverses once neighborhoods fully turn over and the gentrification process completes."[34] On schools, gentrifiers are often active in efforts to improve specific local public schools that their own children attend,[35] and they may contribute to the growth of charter schools,[36] but a study in Chicago suggests that there are no generalized benefits to the school system from their presence,[37] and research in Boston suggests that they may contribute to overall racial segregation.[38]

Finally, the question of if the in-migration of upper-income households displaces lower-income households has garnered considerable attention. Although Rowland Atkinson found empirical support for displacement in London,[39] recent quantitative analyses find that poor households are no more likely to move out of gentrifying neighborhoods than out of neighborhoods not experiencing such change.[40] Some studies find that poor households are actually more likely to stay put in such neighborhoods likely due to satisfaction with observed changes.[41] There is also evidence, however, that when poor families do move, they are *replaced* by higher-income households,[42] thus decreasing the overall availability of affordable housing for new low-income families[43] and contributing to the upward socioeconomic profile of such neighborhoods.[44] These findings underscore the relationship between moving in and moving out. The more space that advantaged residents claim by moving into a neighborhood, the less space that is available for low-income residents. The next section discusses moving out and adds some historical examples.

MOVING OUT

The old adage has it that people "move up and out." The idea is that as people move up the socioeconomic ladder, they move out of their current neighborhoods to "better" ones. For many decades, "out" has had literal geographic connotations as people moved farther out of the city core, and then into suburbs, and eventually into exurbs, although this centrifugal tendency has begun to weaken.[45] There are many manifestations and forms of "up-and-out" mobility. Here, I focus on three areas on which there is considerable research: white flight, black middle-class out-migration, and spatial assimilation. I consider how each type of mobility mixes elements of voluntary and involuntary moves and how they combine to create inequalities in neighborhood characteristics and quality.

White flight refers to the departure of whites from inner-city neighborhoods beginning around World War II. White flight had many causes.
There were certainly pulls to peripheral areas of cities and to new suburban
areas, which were being heavily subsidized by the federal government and
being made accessible by federally built highways.[46] Through its mortgage
insurance guidelines the federal government basically restricted these new
neighborhoods to whites.[47] Alongside pull factors were many (perceived)
push factors. The word *flight* refers to the threat that whites perceived from
growing black populations, especially in northern cities, as the Great Migration of blacks from the South to the North was well underway. Boustan
estimates that 2.7 whites left northern and western cities for every black
person who arrived.[48] This means that fifty-two thousand whites left the
average northern and western city between 1940 and 1970 in response to
black in-migration. In the 1950s and 1960s, whites fled southern cities as
desegregation legislation opened up schools, public spaces, and neighborhoods to blacks.[49]

It is too simple, however, to conceive of white flight as either a voluntary
(and racist) reaction to the specter of black neighbors or as a voluntary preference for single-family detached homes in the urban periphery and suburbs.
Even for whites who cherished their neighborhoods and wanted to stay in
the central city (albeit usually not in racially integrated neighborhoods), the
withholding of public and private financing to city neighborhoods made it
impossible for them to maintain their aging homes or buy other ones nearby.[50]
As their neighborhoods deteriorated, downtown politicians declared them
slums, which further stymied investments.[51] Many of these white families
experienced their moves as being precipitated by external decisions, not their
own, although their total rejection of remaining in black neighborhoods il-
lustrated considerable voluntariness. In the end, the racist practices of the
federal government fed upon, amplified, and facilitated the racism of families
who were fleeing changing neighborhoods. Together these factors established
durable patterns of racial segregation, uneven development across sectors
of the metropolis, and metropolitan fragmentation that acts as a powerful
mechanism of exclusion and resource hoarding.[52]

Another example of "moving out" is black middle-class out-migration,
which refers to the departure of middle-class blacks from the neighborhoods
in which blacks had settled in the era of white flight.[53] The Fair Housing Act
of 1968, among other legal victories, created new possibilities for upwardly
mobile African Americans to move up and out. But the same patterns of
gross inequalities in metropolitan investments that made white flight not

completely voluntary pertain to the residential mobility decisions of middle-class blacks, as well. If property owners in white neighborhoods were denied bank loans and federal mortgage insurance because their homes were too old or because their neighborhoods were changing racially, black neighborhoods were completely excluded from conventional financing altogether. As a result, blacks were easy targets for predatory hucksters peddling loans that carried all of the responsibilities and risks of ownership with none of the financial benefits or securities.[54] Moreover, the downward cycle of housing deterioration, deindustrialization, unemployment, crime, and drugs—all of which have been borne disproportionately by black neighborhoods—made the decision to move out as much a necessity as a desire.

Empirically, there has been vigorous debate about the extent of black middle-class out-migration, especially if out-migration is meant to refer to moving to predominately white or suburban neighborhoods. Evidence of increasing class segregation among African Americans and the increasing concentration of black poverty supports the out-migration thesis.[55] On the other hand, high levels of black-white segregation, even for middle-class blacks, challenges the idea that middle-class blacks have left black neighborhoods for white ones.[56] Also, blacks and Hispanics of all classes are much *less* likely than similar whites to leave high-poverty neighborhoods and much *more* likely than similar whites to move into them.[57] Reconciling these poles, Lincoln Quillian shows that black middle-class households largely settled in white neighborhoods that were getting less white, and more poor over time.[58] Other scholars have shown that middle-class blacks often establish and move to black nonpoor neighborhoods that are adjacent to areas of high poverty.[59]

A final example of moving out is spatial assimilation. This theory picks up where black middle-class out-migration leaves off by exploring the destinations, or "locational attainment," of those who move up and out. The theory posits that upwardly mobile households "attempt to leave behind less successful members of their groups and to convert occupational mobility and economic assimilation into residential gain, by 'purchasing' residence in places with greater advantages and amenities."[60] The empirical operationalization of "greater advantages and amenities" often includes the proportion of the population that is white, the neighborhood income level, and suburban location. These assumptions are not without critique since construing "whiteness" as a proxy for advantage reinforces the privileges of whiteness, and suburban location is an ever more unjustifiable signifier of advantage.[61]

The empirical evidence generally supports spatial assimilation theory for white ethnics and for Asian immigrants and their children.[62] The story for Hispanics is more complicated, with Mexicans more able to translate their socioeconomic success into neighborhoods with a greater proportion of whites, whereas Cubans and Puerto Ricans especially those with darker skin—are less able to do so.[63] Moreover, stagnant trends in white-Hispanic segregation levels and the rise of hyper-segregation for Hispanics also suggest decreasing spatial assimilation.[64] Black households are the least likely to be able to translate improving socioeconomic circumstances into neighborhoods with higher incomes and more whites.[65] Indeed, there is considerable evidence that high-income blacks live in neighborhoods that have lower median incomes and fewer amenities than low-income whites.[66]

Hence, when blacks and Hispanics move up, they do not usually move out to neighborhoods that are equal to the neighborhoods where whites and Asians live. These facts raise the importance of thinking not only of moves as voluntary or involuntary, but also of *destinations* as voluntary or involuntary. To be sure, no one uses brute force to determine where black, Hispanic, Asian, or white households move, but these outcomes are also far from random. Exclusionary zoning, informational asymmetries, local historical knowledge and experience, racial steering, discriminatory and affirmative preferences, prohibitive pricing, jurisdictional fragmentation, and plain old racism all shape the context within which people move, curtailing the voluntariness of any residential choices.[67]

Moving up and out is both caused by and contributes to neighborhood inequalities. Upwardly mobile families move out of their old neighborhoods because the schools are under-resourced, the trash is not picked up, the potholes go unfilled, and the police cannot keep them safe. Where they go, they join up with people who make about the same amount of money as they do, went to college as they did, and work in similar kinds of jobs, so that together they—and only they—can benefit from the revenues generated from higher housing prices, business taxes, commercial receipts, and private investments. As Kendra Bischoff and Sean Reardon show, affluent households are more segregated from everyone else than are poor households. These inclinations are supported by the ultra-local control of a wide range of important social goods. In essence, inequalities in being able to move up and out drive neighborhood outcomes; simultaneously, unequal opportunities across neighborhoods drive the process of moving up and moving out.[68] Thus, more equal neighborhoods would make moving up and out less of an imperative, a point to which I return later.

FORCED MOVES

While it is clear that the types of moves discussed above are not all completely voluntary, foreclosures, evictions, and displacement by demolition constitute moves that are more clearly involuntary. Forced moves are disproportionately experienced by the most vulnerable populations.

The target selling of disadvantageous mortgages to black and Hispanic communities has been uncovered through federal and state lawsuits against banks.[69] Black and Hispanic homeowners and communities, and low-income communities, have been especially devastated by the foreclosure crisis.[70] Obviously, families must involuntarily leave their homes when banks repossess them. Scholars have just begun to study the impact of foreclosures on families and neighborhoods.[71] For example, Janet Currie and Erdal Tekin find that an increase in foreclosures at the zip-code level is correlated with increases in emergency room visits and hospitalizations.[72] In other words, concentrated foreclosures are unhealthy for neighborhood residents. These studies do not determine causation, however. Thus, it is not clear whether poor health causes foreclosure—which would support the idea that the most vulnerable populations are at risk for forced moves—or foreclosure causes poor health.[73] More certain is the fact that foreclosures have a negative impact on nearby property values.[74] The impact of foreclosures on crime seems mixed. Some research finds that higher foreclosure rates lead to more crime in a neighborhood,[75] others find no direct correlation,[76] and still others find mixed or time- or context-dependent results.[77] This early research suggests that forced moves through foreclosures may have negative effects on a range of neighborhood outcomes.

The equivalent of foreclosures for homeowners is eviction for renters. The study of eviction represents a nearly unexplored area of research.[78] Chester Hartman and David Robinson state: "Each year, an untold number of Americans are evicted or otherwise forced to leave their homes involuntarily. The number is likely in the many millions, but we have no way of gauging even a modestly precise figure for renters, because such data are simply not collected on a national basis or in any systematic way in most localities where evictions take place."[79] Matthew Desmond advances this research by showing how eviction is structurally patterned in the city of Milwaukee, Wisconsin, where it disproportionately impacts African Americans and, to a lesser extent, Hispanics.[80] Black women experienced the highest incidence of eviction, whereas white women compared to white men show similar or perhaps lower rates of eviction. Desmond and colleagues add that families with children are more likely to be evicted and neighborhoods with higher proportions of children are particularly vulnerable for concentrated evictions.[81] Other studies document the particular exposure to eviction of public-housing residents, women leaving welfare, and formerly incarcerated men.[82] Of course, incarceration itself is a form of forced mobility that is unequally perpetrated across populations and has severe and concentrated negative consequences for neighborhoods.[83] Drawing the connection between eviction and neighborhood health, Desmond concludes: "This study has identified eviction as a key mechanism driving high levels of residential mobility in poor neighborhoods. With roughly one in 14 renter-occupied households evicted annually, eviction is frankly commonplace in Milwaukee's black inner-city neighborhoods."[84]

Finally, the most extreme and violent form of mobility happens through demolition, clearance, and violence. Mid-twentieth-century urban renewal in the United States uprooted perhaps a million people across the country, leveling whole neighborhoods to make way for highways, luxury housing, public housing, civic centers, or office buildings.[85] Sometimes the plans fell through, and the land just sat vacant, with nothing to show for the dispossession of former residents. In the twenty-first century, attention has turned to tearing down the public housing built in the previous century as a primary mode of forced displacement.[86]

There are also countless international examples of the same story and of resistance to it. Keisha-Khan Perry documents the activism of Afro-Brazilian women in the city of Salvador against the slow destruction of their neighborhood over the course of more than forty years.[87] Liza Weinstein and Xuefei Ren study activism against urban renewal in Shanghai and Mumbai.[88] In one case in Mumbai, a coalition of movement organizations successfully halted state urban renewal activities, which had already demolished ninety thousand homes, leaving four hundred thousand people homeless. Finally, forced migrations due to civil and international war, drug trafficking, agricultural and extractive industries, and ecological destruction create humanitarian crises on a global scale.[89] While these examples dwarf the concerns of mobility and neighborhood vitality in the United States, they highlight the common thread that someone more powerful and with more resources decided they wanted the land of a more vulnerable group, and that their demands were determinative of the overall "geography of opportunity."[90] Whether the outcome looks like voluntary residential moving up and out, gentrification, displacement, or a forced move is mostly a matter of degree.

PATHS FORWARD

The voluntariness of mobility increases with household resources. Having more money obviously gives people more options, makes their choices more determinative of neighborhood trajectories, and protects them from displacement. Intangible resources such as information, voice, social clout, and racial privilege are also important. The fact that housing and neighborhoods are decisions that entwine a plethora of crucial concerns—financial investments, education, safety, health, social status—is the biggest hurdle to convincing advantaged households to stay if and when less advantaged households move in, or, alternatively, to move into disadvantaged areas without speculative intentions. Hence, only policies that move toward the de-commodification of housing and the decoupling of place and opportunity will move in the direction of greater neighborhood vitality and equity. Such interventions will also mitigate the unhealthy cycle of severe neighborhood deterioration and rapid neighborhood enrichment and will increase the ability of low-income households to make voluntary moves or to voluntarily stay in place. In essence, moving rich, middle-class, and poor people around is not an effective route by which to arrive at universally strong neighborhoods, since residents' unequal resources get translated to the neighborhood level. The neighborhoods of rich people attract investments and political attention and jobs and parks and grocery stores, while the neighborhoods of poor people too often do not. Hence, we must commit to making extra investments in struggling neighborhoods, while places that have significant private wherewithal should be given basic public support but no more. Right now we do the exact opposite. As targeted neighborhood investments begin to bear fruit, neighborhood quality will even out, and people's moves will be less impacted by fear, aversion, and force, and will be more motivated by life stage, preference, and fancy. What do such strategies of de-commodification and decoupling look like?

Public housing has been the largest effort to create housing outside of the capitalist market. It flourished at a time when the 1949 Housing Act stated, "The Congress hereby declares that the general welfare and security of the Nation and the health and living standards of its people require . . . the realization as soon as feasible of the goal of a decent home and a suitable living environment for every American family."[91] Yet, public policy is moving in the opposite direction. Federal funds for the renovation and maintenance of existing public housing have declined from \$4 billion in

1999, to under $2 billion in 2014. Over 250,000 units of public and subsidized housing have been demolished.[92] The woes of public housing are well-rehearsed, but New York City has a stock of nearly 350 developments housing over four hundred thousand people. It has not initiated efforts to demolish public housing as in other cities, and in the city's hot real-estate market, public housing stands as the most durable and protected safeguard against the complete removal of poor families from new neighborhoods of opportunity. Public housing is an important housing type for all kinds of communities since it can offer housing stability and quality to families who cannot pay market rents.

Other kinds of "social ownership"—or housing that is not owned or operated for profit and thus renders no speculative gain for owners while offering protection against eviction for residents—include housing built, owned, and managed by nonprofit organizations, limited-equity cooperatives, and community land trusts.[93] Under social ownership, the elimination of profit and speculation moderates prices and puts housing and the neighborhoods where it is located within reach of more people. Community land trusts (CLTs)—which combine land ownership by a nonprofit entity, long-term land leases for users (or even buyers), restrictions on the profitability of resales in order to preserve affordability, and collective governance—are a particularly powerful and promising tool.[94] Writing in 2012, Tom Moore and Kim McKee reported: "The last decade has been marked by a period of rapid growth with over half of the USA's 230 CLTs formed since 2000. Although there is no dedicated fund for CLTs to access, their activities have been facilitated by a national lobbying body since 2006 and funded by combinations of public, private and charitable finance."[95] Efforts should be undertaken to expand this form of social ownership, especially in areas rich in resources and amenities or forecasted to move in that direction.

In addition to growing the stock of de-commodified housing, which will create more accessible and stable neighborhoods, policies that decouple where someone lives from important goods like schools, air quality, transportation, and access to doctors, open space, and good food would also minimize the ways in which cycles of moving in and moving out maintain a geography of opportunity—and inopportunity. Some current federal interventions—namely Choice Neighborhoods, Promise Neighborhoods, and Promise Zones—aim to do this through targeted investments in poor neighborhoods.[96] These are important models that will require wildly more resources than are currently allocated. Our goal should be to make neighborhoods inconsequential for people's happiness and well-being. Put another way, all neighborhoods should facilitate and contribute to good outcomes for their residents; all neighborhoods should be places rich in opportunity.

Inequalities across places rest firmly on the fragmentation of metropolitan areas that allow some jurisdictions to hoard resources while others are left to languish. The jurisdiction of local government over matters pertaining to land use and resource management is part of a culturally entrenched idea in the United States that "local government, the government closest to the people, is the best government," such that "local citizens oppose nearly anything that would threaten the existence, powers, services or autonomy of their local governments."[97] The U.S. model is quite different from the European model, where appropriations for life-sustaining things like education, child care, and health care are managed at the national level and thus create fewer inequalities across local places.[98] A large body of research indicates that the fragmented and diffuse U.S. metropolitan landscape frustrates efforts at building vibrant, safe communities across the metropolis.[99] And as the research on such regional approaches illustrates, simple coordination is insufficient for radically altering the distribution of valued goods and resources.[100] The efforts needed to truly decouple place from opportunity must come either from states, whose constitutions and legislations authorize the powers of local jurisdictions, or from the federal government, which obviously has its own revenue-generating and redistributive capacities, as well as levers with which to influence the actions of states and localities.

To conclude, let's return to the opening vignette. With larger stocks of public and long-term affordable housing or stronger controls on housing prices through things like CLTs, Andrea Wilson's landlord would not have been able to get her out of the apartment by jacking up the rent. Moreover, if neighborhoods were more equally endowed with good schools and access to transportation and protection from crime, then there would not be drastic swings in housing prices that create "the new hot places to move to" and "the places that people can't exit fast enough." If we decouple place and opportunity, Andrea Wilson may voluntarily move to be closer to work or farther from a rude neighbor; in any case, we can feel confident that she will end up in a place that has a lot to offer her and her family.

Martin Luther King and other civil rights leaders called for a "Marshall Plan" to eradicate poverty.[101] Contemporary activists and scholars have called for a Marshall Plan focused specifically on black urban communities.[102] Putting together the issues of poverty and racial disadvantage in a Marshall Plan for poor and predominately minority neighborhoods would target substantial resources to these areas and include mechanisms to de-commodify some housing in order to disrupt the relationship between resources and the ability to stay in place. When the kinds of opportunities that people need to survive and thrive are more equally apportioned across all places, residential mobility will be less consequential. The question always is if we have the political will to do this work.

Notes

1. See Mary Pattillo, *Black on the Block: The Politics of Race and Class in the City* (Chicago: University of Chicago Press, 2007).

2. Xavier de Souza Briggs, Susan J. Popkin, and John Goering, *Moving to Opportunity: The Story of an American Experiment to Fight Ghetto Poverty* (New York: Oxford University Press, 2010); U.S. Department of Housing and Urban Development, *Moving to Opportunity for Fair Housing Demonstration Program: Final Impacts Evaluation*, 2011, accessed October 3, 2014, www.huduser.org/.

3. Xavier de Souza Briggs, ed., *The Geography of Opportunity: Race and Housing Choice in Metropolitan America* (Washington, D.C.: Brookings Institution, 2005).

4. U.S. Census, "Reasons for Moving: 2012 to 2013," 2014, accessed October 3, 2014, www.census.gov.

5. Aida Caldera Sánchez and Dan Andrews, "Residential Mobility and Public Policy in OECD Countries," *OECD Journal: Economic Studies* 1 (2011), accessed June 12, 2014, http://dx.doi.org.

6. Mary Pattillo, "Housing: Commodity versus Right," *Annual Review of Sociology* 39 (2013): 509–31.

7. Manuel Castells, *The Urban Question: A Marxist Approach* (Cambridge, Mass.: MIT Press, 1977); David Harvey, *Social Justice and the City* (Baltimore, Md.: Johns Hopkins University Press, 1973).

8. David Harvey, *The Condition of Postmodernity* (Malden, Mass.: Blackwell, 1990), 106.

9. John R. Logan and Harvey Luskin Molotch, *Urban Fortunes: The Political Economy of Place* (Berkeley: University of California Press, 1987).

10. Elizabeth Kneebone and Alan Berube, *Confronting Suburban Poverty in America* (Washington, D.C.: Brookings Institution, 2013).

11. Monica Boyd, "Family and Personal Networks in International Migration: Recent Developments and New Agendas," *International Migration Review* (1989): 638–70.

12. John D. Kasarda, "Jobs, Migration, and Emerging Urban Mismatches," in *Urban Change and Poverty*, eds. Michael G. H. McGeary and Laurence E. Lynn, 148–98

(Washington, D.C.: National Academy Press, 1988); Rakesh Kochhar, Roberto Suro, and Sonya M. Tafoya, "The New Latino South: The Context and Consequences of Rapid Population Growth," Pew Hispanic Center, 2005, accessed May 25, 2015, www .pewtrusts.org; U.S. Census, "Geographical Mobility/Migration," 2014, accessed June 12, 2014, www.census.gov.

13. Hanna Rosin, "American Murder Mystery," *Atlantic*, July 2008, accessed June 12, 2014, www.theatlantic.com.

14. Victoria Basolo and Dorian Hastings, "Obstacles to Regional Housing Solutions: A Comparison of Four Metropolitan Areas," *Journal of Urban Affairs* 25, no. 4 (2003): 449–72; Edward Goetz, "Words Matter: The Importance of Issue Framing and the Case of Affordable Housing," *Journal of the American Planning Association* 74 (2008): 222–29; David L. Kirp, John P. Dwyer, and Larry A. Rosenthal, *Our Town: Race, Housing, and the Soul of Suburbia* (New Brunswick, N.J.: Rutgers University Press, 1995); Pattillo, *Black on the Block*; Rolf Pendall, "Opposition to Housing: NIMBY and Beyond," *Urban Affairs Review* 35, no. 1 (1999): 112–36.

15. Briggs, Popkin, and Goering, *Moving to Opportunity*.

16. Mary Cunningham et al., Improving Neighborhood Location Outcomes in the Housing Choice Voucher Program: A Scan of Mobility Assistance Programs, Urban Institute, 2010, accessed June 12, 2014, www.urban.org/.

17. Michael C. Lens, "The Impact of Housing Vouchers on Crime in US Cities and Suburbs," *Urban Studies* 51 (2014): 1274–89.

18. Ingrid Ellen, Katherine O'Regan, and Michael C. Lens, "American Murder Revisited: Do Housing Vouchers Cause Crime?," *Housing Policy Debate* 22, no. 4 (2012): 1–22.

19. Susan J. Popkin et al., "Public Housing Transformation and Crime: Making the Case for Responsible Relocation," *Cityscape* 14, no. 3 (2012): 137–60, 153.

20. For a detailed discussion, see Lance Freeman and Hilary Botein, "Subsidized Housing and Neighborhood Impacts: A Theoretical Discussion and Review of the Evidence," *Journal of Planning Literature* 16 (2002): 359–78.

21. George C. Galster, Peter Tatian, and Robin Smith, "The Impact of Neighbors Who Use Section 8 Certificates on Property Values," *Housing Policy Debate* 10, no. 4 (1999): 879–917.

22. Also see Anna M. Santiago, George C. Galster, and Peter Tatian, "Assessing the Property Value Impacts of the Dispersed Housing Subsidy Program in Denver," *Journal of Policy Analysis and Management* 20, no. 1 (2001): 65–88.

23. Chang-Moo Lee, Dennis P. Culhane, and Susan M. Wachter, "The Differential Impacts of Federally Assisted Housing Programs on Nearby Property Values: A Philadelphia Case Study," *Housing Policy Debate* 10, no. 1 (1999): 75–93.

24. Amy Ellen Schwartz et al., "The External Effects of Place-Based Subsidized Housing," *Regional Science and Urban Economics* 36, no. 6 (2006): 679–707; Ingrid

Gould Ellen et al., "Does Federally Subsidized Rental Housing Depress Neighborhood Property Values?," *Journal of Policy Analysis and Management* 26, no. 2 (2007): 257–80.

25. Douglas S. Massey et al., *Climbing Mount Laurel: The Struggle for Affordable Housing and Social Mobility in an American Suburb* (Princeton, N.J.: Princeton University Press, 2013).

26. Japonica Brown-Saracino, *The Gentrification Debates: A Reader* (New York: Routledge, 2010).

27. Neil Smith, "New Globalism, New Urbanism: Gentrification as Global Urban Strategy," *Antipode* 34, no. 3 (2002): 427–50, 446.

28. Ingrid Gould Ellen, Katherine O'Regan, and Keren Horn, "Why Do Higher Income Households Move into Low Income Neighborhoods: Pioneering or Thrift?," *Urban Studies* 50, no. 12 (2013): 2478–95.

29. Ann Owens, "Neighborhoods on the Rise: A Typology of Neighborhoods Experiencing Socioeconomic Ascent," *City & Community* 11, no. 4 (2012): 345–69.

30. Brett Williams, *Upscaling Downtown: Stalled Gentrification in Washington, D.C.* (Ithaca, N.Y.: Cornell University Press, 1989), 99.

31. Derek S. Hyra, *The New Urban Renewal: The Economic Transformation of Harlem and Bronzeville* (Chicago: University of Chicago Press, 2008); Christopher Mele, *Selling the Lower East Side: Culture, Real Estate and Resistance in New York City* (Minneapolis: University of Minnesota Press, 2000); Pattillo, *Black on the Block*; Monique M. Taylor, *Harlem between Heaven and Hell* (Minneapolis: University of Minnesota Press, 2002).

32. Lance Freeman, *There Goes the 'Hood: Views of Gentrification from the Ground Up* (Philadelphia, Pa.: Temple University Press, 2006).

33. Jeannette Covington and Ralph Taylor, "Gentrification and Crime: Robbery and Larceny Changes in Appreciating Baltimore Neighborhoods during the 1970s," *Urban Affairs Quarterly* 25 (1989): 142–72; Yan Y. Lee, "Gentrification and Crime: Identification Using the 1994 Northridge Earthquake in Los Angeles," *Journal of Urban Affairs* 32, no. 5 (2010): 549–77; Andrew V. Papachristos et al., "More Coffee, Less Crime? The Relationship between Gentrification and Neighborhood Crime Rates in Chicago, 1991 to 2005," *City & Community* 10, no. 3 (2011): 215–40; Ralph Taylor and Jeannette Covington, "Neighborhood Changes in Ecology and Violence," *Criminology* 26 (1988): 553–91.

34. Derek A. Kreager, Christopher J. Lyons, and Zachary R. Hays, "Urban Revitalization and Seattle Crime, 1982–2000," *Social Problems* 58, no. 4 (2011): 634.

35. Maia Bloomfield Cucchiara, *Marketing Schools, Marketing Cities: Who Wins and Who Loses When Schools Become Urban Amenities* (Chicago: University of Chicago Press, 2013); Pattillo, *Black on the Block*; Linn Posey-Maddox, *When Middle-Class Parents Choose Urban Schools: Class, Race, and the Challenge of Equity in Public Education* (Chicago: University of Chicago Press, 2014).

36. Tomeka Davis and Deirdre Oakley, "Linking Charter School Emergence to Urban Revitalization and Gentrification: A Socio-Spatial Analysis of Three Cities," *Journal of Urban Affairs* 35, no. 1 (2013): 81–102; Pauline Lipman, *The New Political Economy of Urban Education: Neoliberalism, Race, and the Right to the City* (New York: Routledge, 2011).

37. Micere Keels, Julia Burdick-Will, and Sara Keene, "The Effects of Gentrification on Neighborhood Public Schools," *City & Community* 12, no. 3 (2013): 238–59.

38. Shelley McDonough Kimelberg and Chase M. Billingham, "Attitudes Toward Diversity and the School Choice Process: Middle-Class Parents in a Segregated Urban Public School District," *Urban Education* 48, no. 2 (2013): 198–231.

39. Rowland Atkinson, "Measuring Gentrification and Displacement in Greater London," *Urban Studies* 37 (2000): 149–65.

40. Terra McKinnish, Randall Walsh, and T. Kirk White, "Who Gentrifies Low-Income Neighborhoods?," *Journal of Urban Economics* 67, no. 2 (2010): 180–93; Jacob Vigdor, "Does Gentrification Harm the Poor?," in *Brookings-Wharton Papers on Urban Affairs*, eds. William Gale and Janet Rothenberg Pack, 133–82 (Washington, D.C.: Brookings Institution, 2002). But see Ingrid Gould Ellen and Katherine O'Regan, "How Neighborhoods Change: Entry, Exit, and Enhancement," *Regional Science and Urban Economics* 41, no. 2 (2011): 89–97, which finds some evidence that poor homeowners (not renters) *are* more likely to leave.

41. Lance Freeman and Frank Braconi, "Gentrification and Displacement: New York City in the 1990s," *Journal of the American Planning Association* 70 (2004): 39–53.

42. Lance Freeman, "Displacement or Succession? Residential Mobility in Gentrifying Neighborhoods," *Urban Affairs Review* 40, no. 4 (2005): 463–91.

43. Peter Marcuse, "Gentrification, Abandonment, and Displacement: Connections, Causes, and Policy Responses in New York City," *Washington University Journal of Urban and Contemporary Law* 28 (1985): 195–240.

44. Ingrid Gould Ellen and Katherine O'Regan, "Reversal of Fortunes? Lower-Income Urban Neighbourhoods in the US in the 1990s," *Urban Studies* 45 (2008): 845–69.

45. William H. Frey, "Population Growth in Metro America since 1980," Brookings Institution, 2012, www.brookings.edu, accessed June 12, 2014.

46. Kenneth T. Jackson, *Crabgrass Frontier: The Suburbanization of the United States* (New York: Oxford University Press, 1985).

47. David M. P. Freund, *Colored Property: State Policy and White Racial Politics in Suburban America* (Chicago: University of Chicago Press, 2010); Kevin Fox Gotham, *Race, Real Estate, and Uneven Development: The Kansas City Experience, 1900–2000* (Albany, N.Y.: SUNY Press, 2002).

48. Leah Platt Boustan, "Was Postwar Suburbanization 'White Flight'? Evidence from the Black Migration," *Quarterly Journal of Economics* 125, no. 1 (2010): 417–43.

49. Kevin M. Kruse, *White Flight: Atlanta and the Making of Modern Conservatism* (Princeton, N.J.: Princeton University Press, 2007).

50. Amanda I. Seligman, *Block by Block: Neighborhoods and Public Policy on Chicago's West Side* (Chicago: University of Chicago Press, 2005).

51. Herbert J. Gans, *The Urban Villagers: Group and Class in the Life of Italian-Americans* (New York: Free Press of Glencoe, 1962).

52. Briggs, *Geography of Opportunity*.

53. William Julius Wilson, *The Truly Disadvantaged* (Chicago: University of Chicago Press, 1987).

54. Beryl Satter, *Family Properties: Race, Real Estate, and the Exploitation of Black Urban America* (New York: Metropolitan Books, 2009).

55. Paul A. Jargowsky, *Poverty and Place: Ghettos, Barrios, and the American City* (New York: Russell Sage Foundation, 1997); Paul A. Jargowsky, "Segregation, Neighborhoods, and Schools," in *Choosing Homes, Choosing Schools*, eds. Annette Lareau and Kimberly Goyette, 97–136 (New York: Russell Sage Foundation, 2014); Sean Reardon and Kendra Bischoff, "Income Inequality and Income Segregation," *American Journal of Sociology* 116, no. 4 (2011): 1092–153.

56. Robert M. Adelman, "Neighborhood Opportunities, Race, and Class: The Black Middle Class and Residential Segregation," *City & Community* 3, no. 1 (2004): 43–63; Douglas Massey and Nancy Denton, *American Apartheid: Segregation and the Making of the Underclass* (Cambridge, Mass.: Harvard University Press, 1993); Douglas S. Massey and Mary J. Fischer, "Does Rising Income Bring Integration? New Results for Blacks, Hispanics, and Asians in 1990," *Social Science Research* 28 (1999): 316–26.

57. Scott J. South, Kyle Crowder, and Erick Chavez, "Exiting and Entering High-Poverty Neighborhoods: Latinos, Blacks and Anglos Compared," *Social Forces* 84, no. 2 (2005): 873–900; Robert J. Sampson and Patrick Sharkey, "Neighborhood Selection and the Social Reproduction of Concentrated Racial Inequality," *Demography* 45 (2008): 1–29.

58. Lincoln Quillian, "Migration Patterns and the Growth of High-Poverty Neighborhoods, 1970–1990," *American Journal of Sociology* 105, no. 1 (1999): 1–37; Lincoln Quillian, "Segregation and Poverty Concentration: The Role of Three Segregations," *American Sociological Review* 77, no. 3 (2012): 354–79.

59. Mary Pattillo-McCoy, "The Limits of Out-Migration for the Black Middle Class," *Journal of Urban Affairs* 22 (2000): 225–42; Patrick Sharkey, "Spatial Segmentation and the Black Middle Class," *American Journal of Sociology* 119, no. 4 (2014): 903–54.

60. Richard Alba and Victor Nee, "Rethinking Assimilation Theory for a New Era of Immigration," *International Migration Review* 31, no. 4 (1997): 837; see also Camille Z. Charles, "The Dynamics of Racial Residential Segregation," *Annual Review of Sociology* 29 (2003): 167–207; Douglas Massey and Brendan P. Mullan, "Processes

of Hispanic and Black Spatial Assimilation," *American Journal of Sociology* 89, no. 4 (1984): 836–73.

61. Richard Wright, Mark Ellis, and Virginia Parks, "Re-Placing Whiteness in Spatial Assimilation Research," *City & Community* 4, no. 2 (2005): 111–35.

62. Richard D. Alba, John R. Logan, and Kyle Crowder, "White Ethnic Neighborhoods and Assimilation: The Greater New York Region, 1980–1990," *Social Forces* 75, no. 3 (1997): 883–912; Julie Park and John Iceland, "Residential Segregation in Metropolitan Established Immigrant Gateways and New Destinations, 1990–2000," *Social Science Research* 40, no. 3 (2011): 811–21.

63. South, Crowder, and Chavez, "Exiting and Entering High-Poverty Neighborhoods."

64. Jacob S. Rugh and Douglas S. Massey, "Segregation in Post–Civil Rights America: Stalled Integration or End of the Segregated Century?," *Du Bois Review*, 2013, doi:10.1017/S1742058X13000180; Jeremy Pais, Scott J. South, and Kyle Crowder, "Metropolitan Heterogeneity and Minority Neighborhood Attainment: Spatial Assimilation or Place Stratification?," *Social Problems* 59, no. 2 (2012): 258–81; Marta Tienda and Norma Fuentes, "Hispanics in Metropolitan America: New Realities and Old Debates," *Annual Review of Sociology* 40, no. 1 (2014), doi:10.1146/annurev-soc-071913-043315; Rima Wilkes and John Iceland, "Hypersegregation in the Twenty-First Century," *Demography* 41, no. 1 (2004): 23–36.

65. Pais, South, and Crowder, "Metropolitan Heterogeneity and Minority Neighborhood Attainment."

66. Sharkey, "Spatial Segmentation and the Black Middle Class"; Pais, South, and Crowder, "Metropolitan Heterogeneity and Minority Neighborhood Attainment"; for a review of the literature, see Mary Pattillo, "Black Middle Class Neighborhoods," *Annual Review of Sociology* 31 (2005): 305–29.

67. Camille Zubrinsky Charles, *Won't You Be My Neighbor?: Race, Class, and Residence in Los Angeles* (New York: Russell Sage Foundation, 2006); Maria Krysan, Kyle Crowder, and Michael Bader, "Pathways to Residential Segregation," in Lareau and Goyette, *Choosing Homes, Choosing Schools*, 27–63; Valerie Lewis, Michael Emerson, and Stephen Klineberg, "Who We'll Live With: Neighborhood Race Composition Preferences of Whites, Blacks, and Latinos," *Social Forces* 89 (2011): 1385–407; Jonathan Rothwell and Douglas S. Massey, "The Effect of Density Zoning on Racial Segregation in U.S. Urban Areas," *Urban Affairs Review* 44 (2009): 779–806; Rugh and Massey, "Segregation in Post-Civil Rights America"; Margery Austin Turner et al., "Housing Discrimination against Racial and Ethnic Minorities," Office of Policy Development and Research, 2012, accessed June 12, 2014, www.urban.org/.

68. Kendra Bischoff and Sean Reardon, "Residential Segregation by Income, 1970–2009," in *The Lost Decade? Social Change in the U.S. after 2000*, ed. John Logan (New York: Russell Sage Foundation, 2014).

69. See, for example, U.S. Department of Justice, Consent Order, *United States of America v. Countrywide Financial Corporation*, 2011, accessed June 12, 2014, www

.justice.gov/crt/about/hce/documents/countrywidesettle.pdf; U.S. Department of Justice, Consent Order, *United States of America v. Wells Fargo Bank, NA*, 2012, accessed June 12, 2014, www.justice.gov/crt/about/hce/documents/wellsfargocd.pdf.

70. Debbie Gruenstein Bocian et al., "Lost Ground, 2011: Disparities in Mortgage Lending and Foreclosures," Center for Responsible Lending, 2011, accessed June 12, 2014, www.responsiblelending.org; Jacob S. Rugh and Douglas S. Massey, "Racial Segregation and the American Foreclosure Crisis," *American Sociological Review* 75, no. 5 (2010): 629–51.

71. Ryan Allen, "Postforeclosure Mobility for Households with Children in Public Schools," *Urban Affairs Review* 49, no. 1 (2013): 111–40; Vicki Been et al., "Does Losing Your Home Mean Losing Your School? Effects of Foreclosures on the School Mobility of Children," *Regional Science and Urban Economics* 41, no. 4 (2011): 407–14; Jennifer Comey and Michel Grosz, "Where Kids Go: The Foreclosure Crisis and Mobility in Washington, D.C.," *NeighborhoodInfo DC Brief*, Urban Institute, Washington, D.C., accessed June 12, 2014, www.taxpolicycenter.org/; Craig Pollack et al., "A Case-Control Study of Home Foreclosure, Health Conditions, and Health Care Utilization," *Journal of Urban Health* 88, no. 3 (2011): 469–78.

72. Janet Currie and Erdal Tekin, "Is There a Link between Foreclosure and Health?," *American Economic Journal: Economic Policy* 7, no. 1 (2015): 63–94.

73. Kimberly Libman, Desiree Fields, and Susan Saegert, "Housing and Health: A Social Ecological Perspective on the US Foreclosure Crisis," *Housing, Theory and Society* 29, no. 1 (2012): 1–24.

74. Dan Immergluck and Geoff Smith, "The External Costs of Foreclosure: The Impact of Single-Family Mortgage Foreclosures on Property Values," *Housing Policy Debate* 17, no. 1 (2006): 57–79; Zhenguo Lin, Eric Rosenblatt, and Vincent W. Yao, "Spillover Effects of Foreclosures on Neighborhood Property Values," *Journal of Real Estate Finance and Economics* 38, no. 4 (2009): 387–407.

75. Ingrid Gould Ellen, Johanna Lacoe, and Claudia Ayanna Sharygin, "Do Foreclosures Cause Crime?," *Journal of Urban Economics* 74 (2013): 59–70; Thomas D. Stucky, John R. Ottensmann, and Seth B. Payton, "The Effect of Foreclosures on Crime in Indianapolis, 2003–2008," *Social Science Quarterly* 93, no. 3 (2012): 602–24.

76. Roderick W. Jones and William Alex Pridemore, "The Foreclosure Crisis and Crime: Is Housing-Mortgage Stress Associated with Violent and Property Crime in US Metropolitan Areas?," *Social Science Quarterly* 93, no. 3 (2012): 671–91; David S. Kirk and Derek S. Hyra, "Home Foreclosures and Community Crime: Causal or Spurious Association?," *Social Science Quarterly* 93, no. 3 (2012): 648–70.

77. Eric P. Baumer, Kevin T. Wolff, and Ashley N. Arnio, "A Multicity Neighborhood Analysis of Foreclosure and Crime," *Social Science Quarterly* 93, no. 3 (2012): 577–601; Danielle Wallace, E. C. Hedberg, and Charles M. Katz, "The Impact of Foreclosures on Neighborhood Disorder Before and During the Housing Crisis: Testing the Spiral of Decay," *Social Science Quarterly* 93, no. 3 (2012): 625–47.

78. Peter Dreier, "The Status of Tenants in the United States," *Social Problems* 30 (1982): 179–98.

79. Chester Hartman and David Robinson, "Evictions: The Hidden Housing Problem," *Housing Policy Debate* 14, no. 4 (2003): 461.

80. Matthew Desmond, "Eviction and the Reproduction of Urban Poverty," *American Journal of Sociology* 118, no. 1 (2012): 88–133.

81. Matthew Desmond et al., "Evicting Children," *Social Forces* 92, no. 1 (2013): 303–27.

82. Amanda Geller and Marah A. Curtis, "A Sort of Homecoming: Incarceration and the Housing Security of Urban Men," *Social Science Research* 40, no. 4 (2011): 1196–213; Melissa Latimer and Rachael A. Woldoff, "Good Country Living? Exploring Four Housing Outcomes among Poor Appalachians," *Sociological Forum* 25, no. 2 (2010): 315–33; Scott Duffield Levy, "The Collateral Consequences of Seeking Order through Disorder: New York's Narcotics Eviction Program," *Harvard Civil Rights-Civil Liberties Law Review* 43 (2008): 539–80.

83. Todd R. Clear, *Imprisoning Communities: How Mass Incarceration Makes Disadvantaged Neighborhoods Worse* (New York: Oxford University Press, 2007); Robert J. Sampson and Charles Loeffler, "Punishment's Place: The Local Concentration of Mass Incarceration," *Daedalus* 139 (2010): 20–31.

84. Desmond, "Eviction and the Reproduction of Urban Poverty," 120.

85. Chester W. Hartman, *City for Sale: The Transformation of San Francisco* (Berkeley: University of California Press, 2002); Marcus Anthony Hunter, *Black Citymakers: How the Philadelphia Negro Changed Urban America* (New York: Oxford University Press, 2013); Gans, *Urban Villagers*; Mindy Fullilove, *Root Shock: How Tearing Up City Neighborhoods Hurts America, and What We Can Do about It* (New York: Random House, 2009).

86. John Arena, *Driven from New Orleans: How Nonprofits Betray Public Housing and Promote Privatization* (Minneapolis: University of Minnesota Press, 2012); Larry Bennett, Janet Smith, and Patricia Wright, eds., *Where Are Poor People to Live? Transforming Public Housing Communities* (Armonk, N.Y.: M. E. Sharpe, 2006); Edward Goetz, *New Deal Ruins: Race, Economic Justice, and Public Housing Policy* (Ithaca, N.Y.: Cornell University Press, 2013); Pattillo, *Black on the Block*; Lawrence J. Vale, *Purging the Poorest: Public Housing and the Design Politics of Twice-Cleared Communities* (Chicago: University of Chicago Press, 2013).

87. Keisha-Khan Y. Perry, *Black Women against the Land Grab: The Fight for Racial Justice in Brazil* (Minneapolis: University of Minnesota Press, 2013).

88. Liza Weinstein and Xuefei Ren, "The Changing Right to the City: Urban Renewal and Housing Rights in Globalizing Shanghai and Mumbai," *City & Community* 8, no. 4 (2009): 407–32.

89. Nicholas Van Hear and Christopher McDowell, eds., *Catching Fire: Containing Forced Migration in a Volatile World* (Lanham, Md.: Lexington Books, 2006).

90. Briggs, *Geography of Opportunity*.

91. U.S. House Committee on Financial Services, Compilation of Basic Laws on Housing and Community Development within the Jurisdiction of the Committee on Financial Services, 107th Congr., 2d Sess., Comm. Print 108-C, 2003, accessed June 12, 2014, http://financialservices.house.gov/media/pdf/108-c.pdf.

92. Goetz, *New Deal Ruins*.

93. Michael E. Stone, "Social Ownership," in *A Right to Housing: Foundation for a New Social Agenda*, eds. Rachel G. Bratt, Michael E. Stone, and Chester W. Hartman, 240–60 (Philadelphia: Temple University Press, 2006).

94. John Emmeus Davis, ed., *The Community Land Trust Reader* (Cambridge, Mass.: Lincoln Institute of Land Policy, 2010); James Meehan, "Reinventing Real Estate: The Community Land Trust as a Social Invention in Affordable Housing," *Journal of Applied Social Science*, 2013, doi:10.1177/1936724413497480.

95. Tom Moore and Kim McKee, "Empowering Local Communities? An International Review of Community Land Trusts," *Housing Studies* 27, no. 2 (2012): 281.

96. Tracey Ross and Erik Stegman, "A Renewed Promise: How Promise Zones Can Help Reshape the Federal Place-Based Agenda," Center for American Progress, 2014, accessed June 12, 2014, http://cdn.americanprogress.org.

97. Donald F. Norris, "Prospects for Regional Governance under the New Regionalism: Economic Imperatives versus Political Impediments," *Journal of Urban Affairs* 23, no. 5 (2001): 562.

98. Loïc Wacquant, *Urban Outcasts: A Comparative Sociology of Advanced Marginality* (Cambridge, U.K.: Polity Press, 2008).

99. Peter Dreier, John H. Mollenkopf, and Todd Swanstrom, *Place Matters: Metropolitics for the Twenty-First Century*, 3rd ed. (Lawrence: University Press of Kansas, 2014); Margaret Weir, "Creating Justice for the Poor in the New Metropolis," in *Justice and the American Metropolis*, eds. Clarissa Rile Hayward and Todd Swanstrom, 237–56 (Minneapolis: University of Minnesota Press, 2011).

100. Myron Orfield, *American Metropolitics: The New Suburban Reality* (Washington, D.C.: Brookings Institution Press, 2002); Myron Orfield, "Land Use and Housing Policies to Reduce Concentrated Poverty and Racial Segregation," *Fordham Urban Law Journal* 33 (2005): 101–59; Edward Goetz, K. Chapple, and Barbara Lukemann, "The Rise and Fall of Fair Share Housing: Lessons from the Twin Cities," in Briggs, *Geography of Opportunity*, 247–65; Rolf Pendall et al., "Connecting Smart Growth, Housing Affordability, and Racial Equity," in Briggs, *Geography of Opportunity*, 219–46.

101. Martin Luther King Jr., *Where Do We Go from Here: Chaos or Community?* (Boston: Beacon Press, 1968).

102. Ron Daniels, "A Domestic Marshall Plan to Transform America's 'Dark Ghettos': Toward a Martin Luther King—Malcolm X Community Revitalization Initiative," *Black Scholar* 37 (2007): 10–13; Mary Pattillo, "Investing in Poor and Black Neighborhoods

'As Is,'" in *Public Housing and the Legacy of Segregation*, eds. Margery Austin Turner, Susan J. Popkin, and Lynette A. Rawlings (Washington, D.C.: Urban Institute Press, 2008); Eugene Robinson, *Disintegration: The Splintering of Black America* (New York: Doubleday, 2010); Billy J. Tidwell, *Playing to Win: A Marshall Plan for America* (New York: National Urban League, 1991).

Restoring Neighborhoods to the Center

Alternative Mechanisms and Institutions

DISCUSSANT: TERESA L. CÓRDOVA, UNIVERSITY OF ILLINOIS AT CHICAGO

The 2014 UIC Urban Forum centered on the topic "the return of the neighborhood as an urban strategy." What do we need to be doing at the neighborhood level to make our cities greater? Chicago is, after all, a city of neighborhoods. Many neighborhoods, however, are experiencing disinvestment and displacement. Dynamics of disinvestment and dynamics of reinvestment are two sides of the coin having to do with urban restructuring that accompanied changes in the economy following the economic crisis of the mid-1970s.[1] In cities across the country and around the world, dynamics of globalization and the movements and shifts in the flows of capital have affected what is happening in cities including the discrepancies within cities of public and private capital investments. The result is that neighborhoods are reflective of market phenomena.

At the local level, economic restructuring is played out in some neighborhoods as reinvestment coupled with displacement (gentrification). In other neighborhoods, it is played out as disinvestment and abandonment. Addressing and reversing the negative impacts of these changes requires a shift in how we view neighborhoods as well as a set of strategies that recognizes the dynamics at play, holds the purveyors of capital accountable, and builds a set of alternative strategies that provide survival mechanisms and simultaneously tackles the underlying logic that creates the conditions in the first place.

One UIC Urban Forum panel considered whether neighborhood change could occur without displacing neighbors. People move for a number of reasons, and that movement is both voluntary and involuntary.[2] A key variable, however, that affects the movement of populations and industry within and between neighborhoods is the dynamics of capital and real-estate markets that play out general principles of the economic system, accompanied by policies of the state that incentivize or subsidize that movement. A review of residential mobility literature, therefore, insists that "a discussion of residential mobility and neighborhoods that does not recognize the dominant role of capitalist market-makers and state actors misidentifies the causes of urban inequalities as being the result of individual choices and preferences, rather than the structural context within which such choices and preferences are exercised."[3]

A primary structural context to which we must pay attention is the flows of capital through the marketplace. These flows determine where and how disinvestment and reinvestment occur. The collateral damage is to the neighbors who are forced to abandon their home or forced to stay when their home has been abandoned. We forget that a neighborhood is a home when we think of it only as a market. How we view our neighborhoods determines how we will treat them. According to oral accounts, early in the process of gentrifying a neighborhood, developers come in, may use the assistance of police enforcement, chase people off corners, break down sports facilities, and put fences around parks.[4] In communities where there is disinvestment, those same resources and points of access also leave the neighborhood. The erosion of control and ownership by residents suggests that neighborhoods need to be viewed as more than a market phenomenon.

Explanations of residential mobility suggest that urban policy issues are not just about people moving in and out of neighborhoods but about people's right to stay in a neighborhood when they choose to—and when they do, to stay under conditions of economic and social viability. Neighborhoods are changing for everyone. Neighborhoods *have* changed for everyone. In a city of neighborhoods, one can ask, "what happens to the greatness of the neighborhood when the changes that have occurred are more sensitive to the flows of capital than they are to the flows of people's relationships to their neighborhoods?" There is value to the nostalgia for the relationships that have been lost in neighborhood change, because the yearning is for places that function for people and spaces that function for community. For social beings, neighborhoods continue to be important. When neighbors talk about neighborhoods, they're really talking about the sense of connection, the people they know, and the people who knew them, people they can go back to.[5] Neighborhoods are more than markets. Their significance is in

providing ties to a sense of community, a sense of belonging, a sense of connection, and a means to obtain resources. An effective urban strategy shifts
viewing neighborhoods as what is good for the market to what is good for
the people living in them.

Neighborhoods do matter. Because neighborhoods matter to people,
they matter to women, they matter to women with children, they matter to
families, they matter to immigrant communities, and they matter to young
people. Thus, there is urgency in making neighborhoods a focus of development strategies, making neighborhoods community and economic centers.
Anchor institutions, revitalized commercial districts, and access to employment, services, and medical care are among the elements of a fully functioning neighborhood. In many neighborhoods, many people don't have jobs or
means of employment. As Victor Dickson stated at a recent UIC Great Cities
Institute forum, while the structural issues are being worked on, urban strategies need to deal with the realities that people are facing in communities
where neighbors have been blocked from gaining access to employment.
"People are going to be poor if they don't have access to employment, and
so we need to have the jobs."[6]

For any number of reasons, including the scale of the problem, government responses have been inadequate in preventing displacement or
disinvestment and, in some cases, have exacerbated it through tax incentive policies and development subsidies. Instead, public funding for community development projects, including infrastructure investments, can
be directed to benefit neighborhoods if they are made central to urban
strategies. Although neighborhood advocates cannot rely on it entirely,
whether it's federal, state, or local, it is important to not give up on insisting that the public sector be a resource and be committed to neighborhood
revitalization without displacement.

The sector that represents the public interest can also play a key role as
an intermediary with the private sector. Community benefits agreements
(CBAs), for example, can be an effective mechanism for neighborhoods to
negotiate the conditions under which outside entities locate in their area.
CBAs with corporations and potential employers can help establish investment patterns and can provide a mechanism to ensure jobs to residents,
nonpolluting economic activity, respect for cultural landscape, neighborhood amenities, and an array of other benefits to a neighborhood of adjacent
commercial and industrial activities.

Vigilance on policy questions is critical, as are innovations in programs.
Multiple fronts and multiple actors are necessary to bring neighborhoods to

the center of economic development and public-policy strategies. While the obstacles are many, including the political economy and the market forces, the inclusion of alternative institutions can both counter the logic of neighborhood destruction while providing avenues of relief from the conditions the market forces have bred. It is also possible, for example, to harness collective agency and resources around collective enterprises. Given that ownership is key in the transition of neighborhoods, land trusts and land banks can be part of a strategy to stabilize neighborhoods. Worker cooperatives and the infrastructure to support them, including community banks, are valuable strategies to translate assets into employment.

Developing neighborhood-based small-business incubators is a strategy that creates self-employment opportunities and ways to increase household wealth while also serving as a mechanism to provide goods and services to a community. There are assets and talents in communities that can be tapped and turned into businesses that provide goods and services for residents to purchase. How do neighbors in gentrifying and dying neighborhoods capture their own capital—social and otherwise—and start providing local and exportable goods and services? What kind of external financial assistance ramps up the possibilities for realizing these potentials? Community banks, credit unions, and small-loan structures are options for financing local economic enterprise. Foundations, the public sector, and even private capital can put money and resources into these endeavors.

Young people in neighborhoods are especially in need, as are those whose employment options have been severely limited by policies that use any kind of criminal record as a basis for not hiring. Many young people in gentrifying and disinvested neighborhoods will find their way to higher education or high-tech jobs or both. In many cases, community-based training and work force development jobs create pathways to employment. Those efforts need continued funding.

The priority for urban strategies is to work toward developing fully functioning neighborhoods where people have more choice to stay or go. Continued accountability and assistance from the public sectors is crucial. Alternative institutions, such as land trusts, worker cooperatives, small-business incubators, and community-based financial options can be the means to build on the talents and resources of neighbors and neighborhoods to address immediate economic needs, build social cohesion, and create neighborhood vitality. The optimism is that people can stay and will want to stay. The dream is that the neighborhood is placed at a center of our urban policy and capital investment priorities.

Notes

1. Castells, M., "The Wild City," *Kapitalistate* 4, no. 5 (1976): 2–30; Fainstain, S., et al., *Restructuring the City: The Political Economy of Urban Redevelopment* (New York: Longman, 1983); Córdova, Teresa, "Community Intervention Efforts to Oppose Gentrification," in *Challenging Uneven Development: An Urban Agenda for the 1990s*, eds. P. W. Nyden and W. Wiewel, 25–48 (New Brunswick, N.J.: Rutgers University Press, 1991).

2. See Mary Pattillo's chapter in this book, "Opportunity without Moving: Building Strong Neighborhoods Where People Can Stay If They Want To."

3. Ibid.

4. Thomas, I., "Envisioning Smart Neighborhoods: Old School, New School or No School," UIC Urban Forum, Chicago, Illinois, September 18, 2014.

5. Ibid.

6. Dickson, Victor, "City on the Make: Race and Inequality in Chicago," lecture presented at the UIC Great Cities Institute, Chicago, Illinois, November 13, 2014.

People and Places

Neighborhood as a Strategy of Urban Development from the Progressive Era to Today

ALICE O'CONNOR

UNIVERSITY OF CALIFORNIA AT SANTA BARBARA

During the closing decades of the nineteenth century, U.S. cities were visibly divided places. Tree- and mansion-lined gold coasts stood aside overcrowded working-class slums as symbols of industrial capitalism's vastly disparate fortunes. Municipal plazas were key battlegrounds in increasingly violent confrontations between capital and labor. U.S. cities also became home to the networks of labor movement organizers, intellectuals, philanthropists, social-work professionals, and reform politicians who, in seeking to challenge the forces behind these vastly uneven patterns of urban development, would pitch their efforts against what they unabashedly referred to as the "evils" of Gilded Age society: monopoly power, political corruption, real-estate speculation, unregulated growth, and the endless litany of exploitive practices wrapped up in the labor question, from the low wages, unregulated hours, dangerous factory conditions, and periodic bouts of unemployment that kept so much of the largely immigrant labor force working but poor to the infamous "sweating system" that conscripted women, children, and entire families into the subbasements of the industrial labor force. Although motivated by varied and sometimes competing interests, these networks would come together around an alternative, more inclusive vision of urban development that would inform the progressive reform coalitions of the early 20th century: in which the physical infrastructure would be planned around a pluralistic vision of the common good and the value of shared public space; the industrial economy would be an engine of widely shared growth and opportunity; politics and governance would be participatory; decent affordable housing would be available as a basic right; property would be valued for social use more than for private profit; municipal services would be widely available and utilities publicly owned; and neighborhoods would be organized around the needs of families and children—for play as well as for work, safety as well as health, education, and welfare. In this vision of urban development, municipalities and regulatory commissions would bring order to the otherwise destabilizing forces of capitalism and immigration fueling economic growth in the name of the more encompassing social and civic mission to make the city what the avowedly progressive reformer Frederic Howe called "the hope of democracy."[1]

It was in this context that the idea of using neighborhood as a strategy of urban development began to gain traction in urban politics and reform circles. Challenging the embedded logic of social Darwinism and laissez-faire, early proponents of this approach rejected existing policies of privatized development and social neglect. They drew on ideas about the influence of physical and social environment on human development to argue that the slums, and the people in them, could be rehabilitated to nurture healthier, more productive, and better-adjusted citizens. More generally, they offered a positive view of immigrant neighborhoods and their role in a future of urban industry, culture, and growth. Neighborhood-based development proponents also challenged the prerogatives of private developers and propertied elites, raising issues about who should have a say in municipal improvements and how they should be financed. From the start, then, the idea of neighborhood development incorporated elements of community and class empowerment as well as social uplift. In the eyes of reformers, working-class neighborhoods would be sites of social as well as political "reconstruction," where ethnically diverse residents would organize around common interests while gaining the wherewithal to get ahead in a dynamic, modernizing economy. They would also be laboratories for what has turned out to be among the most lasting legacies of this period of progressive urbanism and reform: the wide array of more targeted neighborhood or "place-based" antipoverty interventions that, over the course of the next several decades, would be absorbed into public or private networks of social work and philanthropic practice, and ultimately into New Deal and Great Society social policy.[2]

Certainly there are echoes of this progressive reform lineage in the urban-neighborhood initiatives of the early twenty-first century—echoes made louder by the conditions within which the initiatives have taken shape. City landscapes once again reflect the gaping inequities of a vastly restructured capitalism, as Occupy Wall Street activists take on too-big-to-fail banks, immigrant and service sector workers rally for living wages, and luxury condominiums built for the global 1 percent create islands of concentrated affluence in a sea of neighborhoods destabilized by job loss and subprime foreclosure.

Variously constituted reform networks are once again positioning themselves to respond, emphasizing themes of equitable growth and environmentally sustainable development that resonate with a global conversation about the challenges of poverty in the rapidly urbanizing developing world. Invoking his early career as a community organizer "on the South Side of Chicago," from the start of his presidency Barack Obama has pledged a renewed emphasis on the problems of concentrated poverty, with federal investment in place-based interventions based on models such as the Harlem Children's Zone, which would become the basis of the administration's Promise Neighborhoods initiative.[3]

More notable than the similarities, however, is how the transformations of a century—and especially the past forty years—have reshaped the meaning, indeed the very aspirations, of neighborhood revitalization to fit the prerogatives of a new age of urban development and reform. As U.S. cities position themselves once again to be engines of growth, it is in the hopes of being at the front edge of a decidedly postindustrial "metropolitan revolution," and of attracting the innovators of the much-ballyhooed "creative class."[4] Cities thrive on the labor and cultural diversity of newly arriving immigrants from around the world, but the immigrants themselves are more and more likely to live and commute in from the outer boroughs, near-in suburbs, and satellite cities—if they work in the central city at all.[5] Poverty is becoming increasingly suburbanized, as well, even as racialized ghettos have replaced immigrant slums as the highest concentration inner-city poverty neighborhoods.[6] But by far the most significant change distinguishing the current generation of neighborhood revitalization efforts is that they are taking place within a much-altered, neoliberal framework of urban reform and development: in which private-market players establish the terms and the priorities for public investment; promoting personal responsibility, individual self-sufficiency and micro-entrepreneurialism are prevailing social policy goals; and government-supported development and antipoverty initiatives are said to have failed. Within this context, the idea of neighborhood as an urban strategy has taken on a whole new connotation: of upper-class gentrification in the urban core; ghetto dispersal led by decommissioned public housing; and "inclusionary" housing schemes that exaggerate the worst offenses of the new Gilded Age, whether by designating "poor doors" for low- and moderate-income residents of luxury buildings, or by financing "affordable" housing development with buildings that drive market rates sky-high.[7] Bottom-up, participatory neighborhood strategies have been relegated to the path of after-the-fact remediation and resistance, along with models for inclusive urban growth generated from working- and middle-class prosperity.

In what follows, I ask what we can learn from this history of neighborhood-based urban development strategies, tracing the transformations and continuities from progressive to neoliberal eras of governance and reform. Although the changing dynamics of economic and social restructuring figure centrally in this story, my focus here is on policy and politics and more specifically on the public policy and philanthropic initiatives that have targeted ailing neighborhoods for "renewal" as part of broader urban development plans. Three crosscutting themes are worth emphasizing from the start.

First is that the problems neighborhood-based urban strategies have historically tried to address are rooted in structural transformations and social inequities that originate outside the geographic boundaries of the neighborhood and that are regional, national, and global in scale. This has contributed to what is now a long-running tension in urban policy circles about whether policies should focus on rebuilding poor places or on helping poor people leave them behind, but also about whether neighborhoods can be deliberately shaped or changed to meet broader policy objectives at all. The long history of research, policy, social experimentation, and actual practice reveals that this either/or construction presents a false choice. Neighborhoods do play an independent role in structuring opportunity for individuals and families that narrowly targeted human capital investments cannot provide (or overcome as the case may be), just as improved neighborhood conditions are not enough to help families struggling with low wages and insufficient skills or access to better job opportunities. Policies have played a role in shaping neighborhood fortunes, though often indirectly and in ways that have deepened the inequities between neighborhoods. Indeed, one of the insights from taking the long view of history is that the "people vs. place" construction is itself a product of history, born of a period of highly uneven, racially segmented neighborhood development that was shaped by postwar economic growth policies that provided massive subsidies for affluent suburban neighborhoods at the expense of the deindustrialized urban core. The real challenge for what are now referred to as "place-conscious" neighborhood strategies—strategies that help people and place—is how to create equity across neighborhoods so that every place can be a source of advantage to all of its residents.[8]

The second theme is that, despite some seriously flawed policy choices, the narrative of failed government intervention is simplistic and overdrawn; as a tool in the politics of polarization and public austerity, it has done more to undermine than to assist meaningful policy learning. Beneath it is a more complex reality: of government-funded initiatives hampered by ambivalence, underfunding and cross-purpose policy commitments; of one generation's remedies meeting resistance and counter-remedy from the next; of politically opposed factions using similar policy tools for very different ends; and of disaffection with "top-down" government interventions generating unexpected alliances from across the political spectrum. But neither is this a clear-cut story of progressive policy displaced by neoliberalism's rise. Instead, the neoliberalization of neighborhood renewal grew out of a different kind of dialectic, wherein erstwhile urban liberals have come first to accommodate and then to embrace the norms and prerogatives of private development in an atmosphere of vastly diminished government support. To the extent that we are now at a turning point in thinking about the future direction of social politics, there may be opportunities to reintroduce some of the elements of progressive approaches that have been sidelined in recent decades, including ideas for more redistributive approaches to financing neighborhood initiatives, for using the tools of planning for more equitable growth, and for making neighborhoods organizing grounds for more meaningful participation in political and civic life.

The third theme is that, despite the extensive array of development strategies, financing instruments, and reform technologies this history of intervention has produced, the fortunes of neighborhoods themselves will continue to be far more profoundly affected by forces beyond their own boundaries. While this by no means suggests that neighborhood strategies are irrelevant—indeed, history has a lot to tell us about what we need to do to improve neighborhood conditions and the well-being of people in them—it does warn against setting up neighborhood interventions for failure by expecting them to accomplish things they can't achieve. The more hard-won, perennially unlearned lesson from history seems to be that sustained political commitment to economic policies that foster equitable growth, more widespread economic opportunity and fairness is a basic necessity for any given strategy's success.

NEIGHBORHOOD AS A STRATEGY OF SOCIAL BETTERMENT

In honing in on the problems of impoverished working-class neighborhoods, progressive-era reformers were tapping into some of the most acute anxieties of their times—about mass immigration, concentrated poverty, and the rise of somehow unassimilable "dangerous classes" in their midst.[9] But they were also tapping into a somewhat contradictory set of ideas and expectations about the significance and role of neighborhoods as units of social organization in the fast-expanding industrial metropolis, and more generally in negotiating the ongoing social and economic transformations that were fueling such rapid urban growth. Within this context of disruption and change, social theorists looked to neighborhoods as bastions of continuity and tradition, where city dwellers could find sociability and build community ties amid the otherwise individualizing, socially corrosive influences of competitive capitalism and urban anomie. Others, preoccupied by the prospect of mass and concentrated immigration, came to see urban neighborhoods as socially isolated and disorganized areas of cultural breakdown as newcomers from rural areas learned how to adjust—or not—to the demands of industrial capitalism and urban modernity.[10] Significantly, one could find elements of both of these views in the ecological theories of ethnic succession, conflict and competition, and assimilation developed within the much-criticized but highly influential Chicago school of urban sociology, which viewed immigrant neighborhoods as cultural enclaves with some semblance of "old-world" traditions and ties, but also as gateways for cultural transformation and assimilation to "new-world" norms.[11]

Recent historical literature puts the neighborhood question in a different light, by showing how wage-earning immigrants regarded neighborhoods as economic as much as cultural footholds in their new environs. Working-class immigrants became homeowners at much higher rates than their counterparts in Europe, for example, taking advantage of the availability of cheap land and building materials as well as community-based financing provided by building and loan associations.[12] Still, even high rates of homeownership did not necessarily make the working-class neighborhood a socially integrating or even a stabilizing environment; if anything, immigrants used homeownership as a subsistence strategy to supplement low and irregular wages in the notoriously volatile, panic- and depression-prone economy of the late nineteenth century. Meanwhile, the idea of neighborhood carried similarly mixed connotations for the growing cadres of corporate executives, professionals, administrators, and better-paid office workers who constituted the new urban middle classes. For them, neighborhood stability—and status—came to be associated with distance from the immigrant enclaves and industrial zones that housed the working classes, even at the expense of family ties.[13]

In fact, for all the significance that social theorists attached to neighborhoods as part of the natural sorting processes of urban growth and assimilation, this discourse was taking place at a time when the social geographies of

major U.S. cities were being profoundly reshaped by quite conscious practices of capital investment and speculative real-estate development that were
stratifying and fragmenting the metropolis as never before. Nowhere was this
more evident than in the newly subdivided developments that were cropping
up along privately owned railroad and transit lines outside or just within the
edges of city limits, designed to house the white, mostly native-born middle
and upper classes in an outwardly radiating hierarchy of suburban neighborhoods.[14] By the early twentieth century, rising real-estate values had priced
growing numbers of lower-skilled and otherwise less advantaged wage earners out of the home-owning market. The vast majority of wage workers lived
as tenants, in neighborhoods within easy walking or transit distance from
the factories, mills, and slaughterhouses where they worked. Nor did owner
occupancy bring the amenities associated with more affluent middle-class
neighborhoods. Although none were as densely packed as the New York
tenements made famous by photojournalist Jacob Riis in *How the Other
Half Lives*, immigrant working-class neighborhoods were seeing more and
more tenement buildings alongside dwellings that were poorly constructed,
extremely vulnerable to flood and fire, without indoor sanitation, and overcrowded with boarders that families took in to help make ends meet.[15]

Progressive reformers viewed these conditions with alarm, seeing them
as threats to public health and workers' rights but also as a product of the
rampant speculation and privatism driving urban development in ever more
fragmenting directions. Their responses laid critical conceptual and practical
groundwork for their own and future generations of neighborhood experimentation and policy, starting with the premise that neighborhoods could
be instruments of a different kind of urban development, based on the not
always compatible principles of scientific planning, social environmentalism,
shared civic identity, and participatory democracy and the more immediate
imperative to bring the social and economic landscape created by private
capital under some form of public control.[16]

Thus, as with so many of their causes, progressive reformers launched their
neighborhood initiatives with a massive outpouring of scientific social investigation to document the existence and social consequences of what in today's
terminology would be called neighborhood effects.[17] Their aim, very much in
keeping with the overarching reform spirit, was to use the tools of statistical
analysis, social mapping, and especially the community-based social survey to lay the groundwork for "scientific" or evidence-based policy reform,
and to frame a civic conversation about its necessity. In a conceptual turn
that would later be developed and widely debated in social scientific theory,

they used these investigations to reframe problems commonly attributed to personal pathology—juvenile delinquency, stunted child development, high infectious-disease and mortality rates—as signs of the social breakdown and health hazards caused by neighborhood "congestion." Progressives also used the tools of social investigation to link concentrated poverty to concentrated wealth, revealing the profits large landowners were reaping from decrepit tenements and manufacturers from the collapsing boundaries between the factory and the working-class home.[18] They made extensive use of all the then-current social media to put these connections on display, in public exhibits where reformers associated with Chicago's Hull House settlement, New York's Committee on Congestion of the Population, and the Russell Sage Foundation–funded Pittsburgh Survey would present deliberately stylized renditions of their research, replete with giant-sized charts, social problem maps, life-size mock-ups of tenement dwellings, and photographs from such renowned social documentarians as Lewis Hine.[19]

But of all the themes running through these works of investigation and display, by far the most consistent was one whose solution would take reform advocates beyond the confines of neighborhood to push for legislation ranging from wage regulation and workers' compensation to old-age insurance and mothers' pensions: that poverty was the central, defining fact of life for the wage earners who lived in Pittsburgh's steel towns, New York's tenements, and neighborhoods like Chicago's Ninth Ward—it is no coincidence that the Hull House neighborhood wage maps, along with Charles Booth's maps of poverty in London's East End slums, were among the most widely traveled exhibits of their day. It was within this broader recognition that progressive reformers singled out neighborhood conditions as a target for improvement, and not, as it would only later be designated, as a choice between so-called people- and place-based policies.

One place progressives looked for solutions was to the emerging science of urban land use planning, in the hope that a civic improvement impulse dominated by the overlapping interests of city beautifiers and business elites could be rechanneled to focus on relieving the congested living and working conditions of working-class neighborhoods. Drawing inspiration and ideas from Britain's socialist-inflected garden city movement and similar ventures in comprehensive mixed-class suburban planning, the newly established Russell Sage Foundation sponsored the development of a model community for "moderate-income" laboring families in Forest Hills, Queens, as one of its first major undertakings, anticipating that commercial developers would follow suit. Others advocated socializing development more directly through outright municipal land purchase, financed by heavy taxes on unearned profits from landownership along the lines of the widely popular single tax proposals of Henry George. Mostly, however, efforts to use planning on behalf of working-class neighborhoods revolved around a more surgical strategy of industrial deconcentration and residential dispersal using approaches adapted from German zoning practices, which relied on measures such as area-specific regulation of building type, and height and occupancy restrictions to impose social controls on an otherwise speculative development process. The hope that zoning could be used for progressive purposes was quickly dashed, however, for the simple reason that the German approach was rapidly taken up by far more powerful commercial business and real-estate interests. By the 1920s, U.S.-style zoning had been thoroughly ensconced in land use policy as a set of rules and standard operating procedures based on precepts that would prove especially detrimental to working-class neighborhood development: first, that priority should be given to protecting private real-estate values; second, that "mixing" of all sorts—by class, use, and especially by race—would lower property values; and, third, that the "right" to impose residentially exclusive zoning restrictions should be the preserve of the more affluent classes. Disillusioned, earlier progressive advocates of zoning were cynical about these developments, fearing that, except as a mechanism for clearing out unsightly slums for business development, zoning would do little to relieve neighborhood conditions at the congested core.[20]

Progressives also sought to use housing as a point of leverage for neighborhood improvement, here engaging what was—then, as now—among the most vexing and contentious problems of social policy: the failure of the commercial market to accommodate the housing needs of the industrial working class. Nowhere was this failure more visible than in the squalor social investigators were documenting in their surveys of the tenements and tenants' rights movements were organizing to protest. Varied reform coalitions had been meeting some success in passing sanitary codes and occupancy restrictions, in New York's landmark Tenement House Act of 1901, and in pushing "model" tenement construction.[21] But underlying the sensationally bad housing conditions was a deeper problem that lay beyond the reach of restrictive legislation: a crisis of affordability that was structural in nature and that would require some more direct form of intervention in the production process itself. As growing numbers of "housers" and their philanthropic allies were beginning to realize, working-class housing that was both decent and affordable to most wage earners was impossible to produce in the speculative for-profit market, and difficult under any circumstances in which private investors expected a return. The problem was exacerbated by land values driven up by speculative development, widening the gap between the incomes of even better paid workers and rising housing costs. Working in alliance with sympathetic businessmen and philanthropists, progressive housers began to pursue scattered experiments in "social housing" in the decades leading up to the Great Depression, including outright philanthropic funding as well as limited dividend, cooperative, and publicly subsidized nonprofit housing development. Though limited in scope and even more so in the volume of units they produced, these experiments anticipated the later emergence of a more institutionalized nonprofit sector to meet the persistent need for housing affordable to low-wage workers. In the aftermath of World War I, when growing demand sent real-estate values skyrocketing once again, even commercial developers began to join the call for more substantial public subsidy for working-class housing, although there was no agreement on what form it should take.[22]

A distinctively progressive neighborhood strategy reached its fullest expression in various efforts to organize or rehabilitate neighborhoods from within. It would also find its most lasting institutional innovation in the form of the neighborhood social settlement house. From the beginning, the settlement idea was laced with ambiguity and tension that future neighborhood-based initiatives would continue to navigate. Here again, the tension was not so much about an opposition between people and places or about what a properly "organized" neighborhood should provide. It was about how an organized neighborhood should function in a pluralist democracy—as an agent of rehabilitation and uplift, cultural assimilation, neighborhood empowerment, or some combination of all three. Based on the approach pioneered by upper-class Christian Socialists at London's Toynbee Hall, the social settlements were conceived as a way to bridge the social divide that was creating these tensions. They were also intended as a self-conscious leap forward—and critique—of an older tradition of "scientific" charitable neighborliness, in which upper-class "friendly visitors" would bestow gratuitous advice about the values of hard work, independence, proper child rearing, and household budget management while lobbying to eliminate public relief for the "undeserving poor." Rather than bestowing advice from afar, the recent college graduates who were typically drawn to the U.S. settlement house movement set up residence in those neighborhoods, in houses that were meant to serve as all-purpose neighborhood centers with a full complement of social welfare, recreational, and training services. Residents also thought of themselves as engaged in an ongoing social experiment, and the neighborhoods they lived in as laboratories for building bonds of mutual trust and civic engagement, both within the neighborhood and across the socially divided metropolis. Although more than an element of paternalism initially motivated these ventures, and the suspicion that they were mere agents of Americanization was ever-present, over time the most prominent settlements took on an ethos of participatory democracy and began to steer their activities toward neighborhood advocacy and political organizing.[23]

Much of the activism and experimentation launched by the progressives would continue well into the following decades, but the outbreak of war in 1914 sapped much of the reform energy of the movement. It also ushered in a period of intensified anti-immigrant activism that led to the passage of sweepingly restrictive federal legislation in 1924 and that, along with the migrations of African Americans to northern and midwestern cities and of Mexicans to the Southwest, changed the demographic face and the spatial politics of inequality in the postwar metropolis. Progressives could point to many accomplishments, but much of the urban agenda, including its neighborhood components, remained unfinished.

The period nonetheless left a lasting policy legacy. Progressive reform intellectuals laid critical conceptual groundwork for framing neighborhood social conditions as at once part of the problem and part of the solution to urban inequality. They identified the basic elements of the policy toolkit that neighborhood builders would deploy for decades to come, in planning, housing, social work, and participatory democracy. They played a key role in brokering policy networks and political coalitions. In this and other ways, they established the basic architecture of ideas, interventions, and aspirations that would last well into the New Deal and that would be replicated in some fashion in each of the subsequent generations of neighborhood initiatives. Progressives expected to do a lot for and with working-class neighborhoods in their efforts to build a better city, but they expected a lot of those neighborhoods, as well, from forging a sense of solidarity among diverse residents to providing an environment of respite from the grind of industrial labor, and of organizing to demand a fairer distribution of the fruits of working-class labor.

Still, critical questions remained unresolved or unaddressed, and these, too, form an important part of the period's legacy, if only because they point to the issues that would be the main points of contention in the decades ahead. First was the question of how neighborhood-based development should be financed, especially when the residents were so readily dismissed by unsympathetic observers as alien, unproductive, and wont to become dependent.

The second issue was the question of how the public interest would be defined, especially where state power was exercised to regulate property rights. The third issue was the growing significance of race as factor in neighborhood stratification, reflected in the proliferation of racial covenants, blockbusting, and incidents of racial violence in the wake of African American and Mexican migrations. Finally was the issue that would come to the fore with the collapse of capitalism during the Great Depression, of what, if any, role the federal government would play in alleviating urban poverty and restoring ailing cities to growth.

NEIGHBORHOOD AS A STRATEGY OF ECONOMIC GROWTH

The policy environment for neighborhood-based urban strategies underwent significant changes during the New Deal and especially in the immediate postwar decades. The fate of cities and urban neighborhoods became increasingly tied to the federal government and to Keynesian economic growth politics, which in the United States meant managing the economy more through fiscally stimulated growth than through planning or redistributive social-welfare spending; generating and distributing a growing share of the nation's wealth through housing construction and mortgage finance; and brokering a city's ability to garner federal funds through the formation of pro-growth political coalitions that brought reform-minded housers, social workers, and policy intellectuals into sometimes reluctant alliances with local machine politicians, organized labor, business groups, and private builders and developers. In the absence of federal planning and in the context of a welfare state that provided most social assistance through a two-tiered system of income supports, funding for neighborhoods would be channeled almost exclusively through housing. It was in this context that postwar neighborhood "renewal" became a strategy of urban development that relied heavily on bricks-and-mortar spending, that was principally shaped by the priorities and the interests of business and private developers, and that at its most ambitious aimed to refashion the industrial working-class city as a modern middle-class, ultimately postindustrial metropolis.[24]

Key strands of the progressive neighborhood idea would continue to play a role in this shifting policy landscape. Neighborhood-based activism continued and if anything grew more radicalized throughout the Depression and postwar years, giving rise to a number of robust tenants' rights movements and, in Chicago, to the distinctive style of political organizing cultivated in Saul Alinsky's Back of the Yards Neighborhood Council (established in 1939)

and Industrial Areas Foundation (1940) and in the street corner anti-delin-
quency initiatives developed out of Chicago School sociology. City planners
found jobs in the local housing authorities that were charged with overseeing
the location and construction of public housing according to the provisions
of the Housing Act of 1937. Progressive housing networks figured centrally
in debates leading up to that landmark legislation, and teamed with labor
to build architecturally innovative, community-oriented projects for workers. Many of their ideas about incorporating child care and social services,
designing buildings around open and accessible spaces, and encouraging
tenant association would find their way into public housing projects such
as the widely admired Harlem River Houses in New York.[25] This expansive
vision of community-friendly public housing was part of postwar growth
politics as well, finding expression in ambitious projects designed to incorporate public housing into a modernized urban landscape and to serve the
needs of a diverse working class for decent affordable housing in a welcoming community environment.[26] A well-functioning system of public housing
was an essential part of the infrastructure for economic growth, proponents
argued, that would bring further private investment to poor neighborhoods
while helping workers in their own economic advancement.

Still, the influence of these ideas would be diluted by the politics of housing
at the federal level, by the growing vigilance of politicians eager to capitalize
on fears of "socialized" housing, and by the way race, and racially segregationist norms specifically, factored into this and every other element of postwar
policy.[27] In the years following the original authorizing legislation, public
housing opponents would succeed in imposing ever-stricter limitations on
income eligibility and per capita space allocations, making it less attractive, and less available, to working-class families of moderate means. They
deployed race at every turn, from insisting that public housing not "upset"
segregated racial distributions to red-baiting Federal Housing Authority
(FHA) officials charged with establishing standards of racial fairness and
protecting the interests of racial minorities.[28] Such tactics only reinforced the
segregationist norms already embedded in FHA guidelines for everything
from slum clearance to determining eligibility for mortgage loans.

Local real-estate developers, for their part, pushed to shift the emphasis
away from public-housing construction altogether, recognizing that federal funds for slum clearance offered a rich public subsidy for potentially
valuable downtown real estate that could be developed for more profitable
purposes.[29] These aims were largely realized in urban renewal, as the policy
established by the Housing Acts of 1949 and 1954 came to be known, which

promised to clear out the slums and revive the downtown economy by attracting new businesses and middle-class residents back into the urban core. The 1949 legislation specified that a designated proportion of cleared land be used for "residential purposes" and that the bill include provisions for relocating displaced residents to "decent, safe, and sanitary housing." As private developers were quick to discover, however, "residential purposes" did not necessarily mean housing for the poor.[30] In subsequent amendments, the balance between housing construction and redevelopment was steadily shifted, as Congress lightened the requirement that cleared land be used for housing construction and created incentives for hospital construction and university expansion instead.[31] Evaluation studies also confirmed that relocation requirements were minimally enforced. The bill's provisions for resident consultation and cooperative planning, another distant holdover from progressivism, were also meaningless in practice.[32] Taking advantage of the vague provisions of the 1954 act, many cities used funding to start investing in postindustrial growth areas, including culture, the knowledge economy, major hospital complexes, providing jobs and, often, housing for an expanding white-collar workforce while displacing working-class neighborhoods with new construction. Urban rebuilders also aggressively sought federal subsidies for highway building, with similar results. By the late 1950s, public housing advocates had come to see the program as little more than a generous public buy-out of land for private real-estate interests. Public housing became increasingly crowded with families displaced by development. Among African Americans, it became widely known as Negro removal.

At the same time, as much by accident as by design, urban renewal became an important site of protest and ultimately of participatory planning and policy learning. In street protests, architectural forums, and in consultations organized by local housing officials, public-housing residents drew attention to what critics depicted as the soul-destroying impact of modernist high-rise architecture, pointing out that once-celebrated innovations such as superblock construction were actually isolating tenants from the street life of their neighborhoods and displacing small businesses. These sentiments would be echoed and more broadly applied in Jane Jacobs's influential critique of centrally planned, modernist development, *The Death and Life of Great American Cities*.[33] But unlike Jacobs, public-housing residents also protested practices that were concentrating poverty and segregation, starting with the use of racist land use planning guidelines to declare minority and working-class neighborhoods "blighted" and subject to eminent domain. And in raising concerns about the white and white-collar orientation of the development that was breaking up their neighborhoods, street protests over urban renewal were also making clear that the struggles over urban renewal went beyond residential housing and beyond what the neighborhood could provide, to the problem of jobs and working-class opportunities in the changing urban economy.[34]

Thus, buried within urban renewal's sad legacy were important insights that, before they appeared on the radar of federal policymakers, were circulating through the channels of experience and activism that would shape coming efforts to make neighborhood renewal a strategy for more equitable urban development: by putting the soul of the neighborhood back into city planning; creating jobs for a postindustrial working class; using neighborhoods as a source of unity and political empowerment rather than racial and class polarization; and resisting the federally supported tides of suburbanization and urban deindustrialization that were threatening the economic viability of working-class neighborhoods even as urban renewal's slum-clearing federal bulldozers were breaking them up.

NEIGHBORHOOD AS A STRATEGY OF EMPOWERMENT

Neighborhood strategies of urban development entered a new phase in the mid-1960s, as liberal policymakers in the Kennedy and Johnson administrations responded to citizen activism by bringing the "human face" of poverty into liberalism's ongoing bricks-and-mortar approach, and by pledging to fight rather than uphold segregationist norms in housing policy.[35] They were also reacting to growing concern about the volatile mix of poverty, political disfranchisement, racism, crime, and police-community relations that would erupt in violent confrontations in and around ghettoized neighborhoods throughout the decade. But neighborhood strategies were also part of the rise of Great Society liberalism and of the expanding array of federal social-welfare policies and agencies devoted to ending poverty and racial injustice. Urban neighborhoods would take on a new role in this expansion of federal purpose, especially in the arsenal of the War on Poverty. No longer strictly targets for renewal, they would become sites for resident participation and political empowerment. They would also find new sources of federal support in the Department of Health Education and Welfare, the newly established (1965) Department of Housing and Urban Development (HUD), and the Office of Economic Opportunity (OEO), where neighborhoods would be part of the administration's pledge to fight poverty with the "maximum feasible participation" of the poor.

To the degree there was any single idea of empowerment in the War on Poverty, it was in the legislative requirement that local agencies include representation from poor people in developing antipoverty initiatives as part of the federal Community Action Program. Underlying that mandate was a lingering ambiguity—about whether empowering poor people meant giving them a voice in planning social services or in political decisions about how resources should be allocated—that picked up on longstanding tensions in progressive social politics and would continue to thread through War on Poverty programs.[36] In actuality, the distinction was more nominal than real, as would soon be apparent in the local outcry against any kind of meaningful, let alone "maximum feasible" participation of poor people, especially African Americans, in programs that might challenge local power structures.[37] This was especially the case with the federally funded Community Action Program, which came to encompass a number of "national emphasis" programs such as Head Start and the Legal Services Program, but at its core was a special grants program that invited localities to develop their own antipoverty strategies that would be awarded OEO grants only if they showed evidence of inclusive planning—and an alternative to the status quo. Although the program would provide grants to well over a thousand local Community Action agencies and seed innovative programs that last to this day, it was the constant target of political attack and budget cutbacks. It also had limited leverage over the kinds of resources that might stimulate job opportunities in increasingly ghettoized central cities.[38]

Model Cities was established in 1966 in part to respond to both of these pressures, although the way the program unfolded indirectly validated Community Action's empowerment strategy. Based on an ambitious plan proposed by United Auto Workers president Walter Reuther for a six-city demonstration combining bricks-and-mortar urban renewal with comprehensive social services, job training, and middle- and working-class jobs, the ultimate legislation was spread out over nearly two hundred communities, with less than half the recommended budget, and put under the direct supervision of local mayors' offices, effectively circumventing the possibility of unsanctioned community participation. The Special Impact Program (SIP), authorized by an amendment to the Economic Opportunity Act sponsored by Senator Robert F. Kennedy, took its basic program structure, the community development corporation (CDC), from the radical economic development strategies coming up through the black power movement, which aimed to establish an alternative economic base from which to challenge the dominant white corporate power structure. Continuing a partnership that had started in the early planning stages of the War on Poverty, the SIP program made its first major grant to the substantially deradicalized Bedford Stuyvesant Support Corporation, a Ford Foundation project set up at Senator Kennedy's behest to seed economic development in the neighborhood by drawing in white corporate investment capital. Although presented as a neighborhood-based and controlled enterprise, the Bedford Stuyvesant program came under criticism for its initially bifurcated "inside/outside" governing structure, which left the most important financial decisions to a board of white business investors created as a liaison to corporate finance. While that structure was eventually dropped under pressure from the "inside" African American leadership (headed by Franklin A. Thomas, who became the first African American president of the Ford Foundation), CDCs would continue to occupy an uneasy space between communities struggling for autonomy and economic justice and the corporate and foundation support they would come to rely on for economic development funds.[39]

By the late 1960s, the Johnson administration had amassed a complex array of neighborhood interventions that promised empowerment through more comprehensive, better-integrated social services, physical and human renewal, local economic development, and community-based political organizing. Expanding the scope of President John F. Kennedy's 1961 antidiscrimination executive order, the Fair Housing Act of 1968 added another significant dimension to federal capacity to combat neighborhood poverty and promote equitable urban growth. For all their promise and ambition, however, the Great Society community empowerment programs were limited in scope and lacked the serious funding or targeted job creation capacity to alter the racial and economic apartheid of the American ghetto. Nor did they have much political clout within an administration that considered economic growth, full employment, and human capital investments to be its chief weapons in the War on Poverty. Reacting to their limited "measurable-outcome" results, hard-headed Great Society policymakers began to view efforts to revive and empower urban neighborhoods through the lens of a debate that had originally taken shape around the problem of rural poverty, asking whether the aim of policy should be to invest in poor places or to help people to leave them.[40] This debate would only become more sharply defined as conditions in poor urban neighborhoods deteriorated in the 1970s and 1980s.

A more nuanced view was emerging from community experience, however, that called into question what looked from the top to be a people/place divide. From the standpoint of people who had been utterly disenfranchised from local decision making about the distribution of essential services and opportunities, it was clear that the War on Poverty's community-based programs were providing immeasurable support for local activism and institution building, creating jobs and political openings for thousands of neighborhood residents, and opening community health centers, neighborhood service organizations, law centers, community development corporations, Head Start centers, and local action agencies. These initiatives also gave rise to a whole new network of nonprofit providers and intermediary organizations that would play a sustaining role in the community development movement in decades to come.

The community level view also confirms that the overriding limitations on neighborhood empowerment had as much to do with what they were up against as with the administration's ambivalence or inadequate financial support. Official resistance, locally entrenched discrimination in employment, rising unemployment in African American inner-city neighborhoods, and racially biased local police practices were all powerfully disenfranchising forces. So was the "other" war, in Vietnam. These overlapping forces of disenfranchisement were dramatically displayed in the uprisings that broke out in several cities during the 1960s, as local protests against police brutality and, more deeply, systemic inequality grew violent and sustained. Tensions reached a height in July 1967, when conflict sparked by a police raid of an after-hours bar during a party for local servicemen turned several blocks at the center of Detroit's African American community into a virtual armed encampment for all the world to see. President Johnson sent in federal troops to restore order. He also appointed the twelve-member National Advisory Commission on Civil Disorders, chaired by Illinois governor Otto Kerner, to investigate why cities were burning nationwide. The commission report was a searing indictment of the institutionalized white racism that was tearing the nation into "two societies, one black one white—separate and unequal." It also gave expression to a concern that seems naive in retrospect, though it reflected the deep-seated racial anxieties that would remain the defining, if sometimes hidden, issue in the ongoing "people vs. place" discussion: the concern that "gilding the ghetto" through the massive, place-based investments in housing, social services, and neighborhood jobs the report called for would become an excuse for avoiding what the report viewed as the more difficult task of opening up the segregated suburb to provide African Americans with a meaningful choice about where they wanted to live.[41] As it turned out, neither side of the binary would be pursued with the resources and vigor the Kerner Commission (along with leading civil rights organizations) deemed necessary. Instead, the proviso against "gilding the ghetto" would be used by subsequent administrations as a counsel of disinvestment and neglect.

NEIGHBORHOOD AS A STRATEGY OF LOCAL CONTROL

The 1970s brought significant change as local actors responded to shifts in the infrastructure of federal support for urban neighborhoods and in the policy environment for urban development more generally. These shifts were connected to the political realignments that had led to the 1968 election of Richard Nixon as president and would help him to push through a "new federalist" policy agenda that gave local governments more discretion in allocating funds, shifted support for public housing from construction to vouchers, treated civil rights enforcement with "benign neglect," and eliminated the flagship programs of the War on Poverty. Nixon's "law-and-order" rhetoric also highlights the trend that would later harden into a much more aggressive policy of "governing [the ghetto] through crime."[42] Although overall spending held steady after the passage of the Community Development Block Grant (CDBG) legislation in 1974, fewer federal resources went to poor urban neighborhoods as part of the "stage-theory" or "triage" approach to budget allocations adopted by budget officials, and as requirements for local participation in planning were eliminated. Equally significant was the retreat from the Great Society's government-centered sense of public purpose—or obligation—this represented, a sentiment that cut across partisan lines. The consequences played out in many arenas, but nowhere more than in the profoundly altered relationship between the federal government and urban America captured in President Gerald R. Ford's infamous (headline-making—"Ford to City: Drop Dead!") refusal to provide federal bail-out funds for New York City when it was on the verge of fiscal collapse. The Carter administration took steps to repair relations and restore funding, although it did not alter the general trend toward devolution and self-help. But the push for local control over urban development was not just coming from changes at the top. It was also coming from a number of neighborhood-based groups steeped in the values of participatory democracy and the politics of resistance, and as eager to resist the encroachments of liberal urban renewal as they were to keep corporate America in check.

Reflecting these conflicting pulls, the devolution to neighborhood control played out in complicated ways that revealed localism's promise and limitations as a strategy of urban development. In a number of cities, localism helped give rise to a resurgence of progressive reform politics, based on commitments to racial and economic diversity, integration, and inclusive economic growth, and on coalition-building strategies in which neighborhood-based organizing and policy advocacy played a key role. Working-class neighborhoods became important sites of grassroots activism in the coalition-building process, where newly established groups such as National People's Action (NPA) and the Association of Community Organizations for Reform Now (ACORN) joined the Industrial Areas Foundation (IAF) to use common neighborhood concerns as an organizing base for building solidarity across racial and ethnic lines. Using the direct-action tactics Saul Alinsky had made famous in his 1945 manifesto *Reveille for Radicals*, these groups staged protests for better municipal services and against the development vision of the downtown-friendly "growth machine."[43] They joined up with local civil rights groups to push back against "panic pedaling" in transitional neighborhoods, demand local enforcement of the open-occupancy provisions of the 1968 Fair Housing Act, and expose redlining in the commercial lending industry in local campaigns that generated the drive for the passage of the Community Reinvestment Act of 1977.[44] In the late 1960s, civil-rights activists and public-housing tenants scored a major victory in their paired antidiscrimination suits against the Chicago Housing Authority and the Federal Housing Administration brought under the name of public-housing tenant Dorothy Gautreaux, when the courts held the agencies responsible for the racially concentrated distribution of public housing.[45] On these and a variety of quality of life issues, neighborhood activists also found common cause with the clusters of middle-class professionals, artists, and intellectuals who were moving into and, more controversially, beginning to gentrify older neighborhoods with neglected housing stock. Under the leadership of self-styled reform Democrats who had come up through civil rights and women's movement politics, these neighborhood-based groups came together in electoral coalitions that posed serious challenges to entrenched political machines. By the late 1970s and early 1980s, progressive reform coalitions were beginning to score victories in traditional machine strongholds like Boston, Chicago, Cleveland, and Pittsburgh, as well as in cities with more established progressive traditions like Portland, Oregon, San Francisco, and New York, based on platforms that promised more balanced and environmentally friendly approaches to growth, affordable housing funded by downtown developer fees, neighborhood empowerment for planning and service allocation purposes, racial and gender equity in the municipal workforce and in awarding contracts, community review boards to keep police forces in check, and a commitment to preserving historic spaces and buildings.[46]

Devolution to local control also provided the framework for a different, in some ways competing strand of reform politics as local officials, federal agencies, and, especially, liberal foundations set out to build the financial, institutional, and broader policy infrastructure for an approach to urban development based on the concept of "neighborhood revitalization." While sharing progressive commitments to racial integration and economic inclusion, this approach remained more firmly rooted in traditionally downtown-centered growth coalitions and actively sought cooperation with local corporations and developers. Its proponents also took a decidedly more top-down approach to policy planning and implementation, putting much greater emphasis on promoting sound management and technical expertise in community-based organizations than on looking to them to promote neighborhood empowerment. The impact was especially apparent in the so-called second generation of CDCs and related community economic development organizations, which drew substantially expanded support and technical assistance from foundation-organized social investment loan funds, or program-related investments, starting in the late 1960s, and from financial intermediaries such as the federally funded loan and technical assistance pool that would later become known as NeighborWorks, the Local Initiatives Support Corporation (LISC) created by the Ford Foundation in 1981, and the Enterprise Foundation, which was established in 1983 with funding from the developer James Rouse.[47] Foundations teamed up with federal agencies to invest in building up expertise on the dynamics of neighborhood change and more specifically on how neighborhood revitalization could work as a strategy of urban development, much of which found its way into a massive high-profile report produced by President Carter's National Commission on Neighborhoods, released in 1979.[48] Thanks to these efforts, by the early 1980s, neighborhood revitalization stood on what looked to be a solid if modest edifice of financial and institutional support, anchored in a politically neutralized (though hardly apolitical) network of funders, nonprofit developers, and professionals geared to broker the relationship between poor communities and corporate capital. National People's Action and other grassroots organizing groups had also begun to build up their research and technical capacity, focusing especially on training local groups to use the Community Reinvestment Act to pressure banks into lending in their neighborhoods.[49] Although Carter's much-anticipated comprehensive urban neighborhood initiative fell short on the legislative front, entrepreneurial neighborhood revitalizers could still find federal and state support for their efforts, from tax incentives for historic preservation to funds from the tellingly titled Neighborhood Self-Help Development Act of 1978.[50] For the moment, anyway, even the weight of expertise seemed to be on their side, as scholars developed models for "managed" integration and gradual gentrification and grew more vociferous in challenging the validity of neighborhood "triage" as a theory of urban planning.[51]

And yet, the various inroads that made local control seem like a viable, even a progressive urban-development strategy also pointed to the powerful countervailing forces these initiatives were up against. As municipal coffers were drained under the impact of federal cutbacks, recurring recession, industrial job loss, and ongoing, federally subsidized white middle- and working-class suburbanization, working-class neighborhoods became flashpoints in racially charged struggles over school decentralization, busing, and crime, and in racially charged class conflicts over the displacement effects of gentrification. Few issues were more volatile than the location of public housing, as the Gautreaux plaintiffs were to find in their frustrated efforts to get the Chicago Housing Authority to build scatter-site housing within city limits, and the suburbs remained stubbornly resistant to integrated housing of any kind.[52] Thus, even as grassroots localism generated hope for a progressive vision of urban development, devolution left cities with fewer resources to follow through, especially in the face of deindustrialization and ongoing resistance to racial integration. These tensions would continue to play out in coming decades as the federal retreat from the city became more pronounced. They exposed the fault lines that would allow a rising generation of reformers to usher in a whole new era of policy and experimentation, in which the fate of the city and its neighborhoods would be tied to the market in a way they hadn't been since before the Great Depression.

NEIGHBORHOOD AS A STRATEGY
OF PRIVATIZED URBAN DEVELOPMENT

The turn to the market in the 1980s was not a new development; it continued the devolutionary trends started a decade earlier. It did mark a major turning point for neighborhood-based urban strategies (as for all social and economic policy), however, as part of the political counterrevolution that swept Ronald Reagan into the presidency, based on the pledge to reverse the tide of big-government activism ("government is not the solution to our problem; government is the problem") and to use deregulated markets as instruments of social and economic reform.[53] The shift was immediately apparent in the administration's earliest budgets, which proposed massive cuts in taxes and social welfare spending, pushed for privatization of public services, and called for across-the-board deregulation and tax incentives to stimulate capital investment. It was also apparent in Reagan's new federalism, which took devolution to new lengths in its push toward local, voluntary, and individual responsibility for social provision. And it was evident in the president's ratcheted-up approach to the "law-and-order" politics introduced during the Nixon administration and Reagan's more sweeping rollback of civil rights enforcement. The result was a much-altered policy environment for neighborhood-based development initiatives, in which the role of government was to advance rather than to countervail or soften the blows of market interests—or even to acknowledge the possibility of market failure at all—and the ultimate goal was to restore private control over whatever was left of public obligation. Reagan-era policies left cities bereft of direct federal funds for development as well—Reagan cut the HUD budget by 50 percent and CDBG spending by 60 percent over the course of his eight years in office, citing the need to end the "dependency" of cities and their residents—and channeled support for low-income housing through vouchers for individuals and tax incentives (the Low Income Housing Tax Credit, or LIHTC) for builders instead. The administration proposed tax- and regulation-free "enterprise zones" as the centerpiece of its urban revitalization strategy, and a combination of privatization, demolition, and tenant ownership as its "attack on federal housing." Both proposals failed, due in part to revelations of massive corruption at HUD, but they would be taken up again—unsuccessfully—by HUD Secretary Jack Kemp in the George H. W. Bush administration.[54] Privatized development was also all the rage in conservative movement circles, where movement-oriented think tanks and journals were actively promoting a "new urban paradigm" based on principles—of individual self-reliance, choice, and public austerity as the road to private wealth—that essentially turned the progressive idea on its head.[55]

Although the administration's most ambitious market-unleashing proposals failed, its urban policies quickly trickled down to the local level, for the most part with the intended effect. Once again, neighborhoods became key sites of reform activism and policy experimentation, this time based on an agenda that was broadly neoliberal in its "free-market" approach to economic development and social provision but that also drew on the interventionist strain of so-called compassionate conservatism in its moralistic treatment of the poor. In a notable departure from standard practice, conservative foundations took up an old progressive tradition to treat low-income neighborhoods as laboratories for privatized and "faith-based" social provision in welfare, teen pregnancy prevention, and, especially, school choice. They also invested heavily in promoting the gospel of "broken-windows" policing.[56] Conservatives held up business improvement districts (BIDs)—where commercial property owners agree to special assessments to pay for privately contracted street cleaning, garbage collection, security, and nuisance prevention—as models of public-private enterprise and efficiency that could cut through union rules and government red tape. Critics saw them as examples of government-sanctioned social exclusion and the privatization of public space.[57] Notably, BIDs relied on methods of financing civic improvements—special assessments—that progressive reformers had rejected as both inefficient and undemocratic three-quarters of a century before.[58] CDCs were also lauded as models of public-private enterprise, but more tellingly as examples of the creative use of "corrective capitalism" to bring poor communities into the economic mainstream.[59]

Whether mediated by public-private partnerships or not, privatized development tied neighborhood fortunes to the increasingly visible hands of financial and speculative real estate markets. City officials looking to spur a downtown renaissance used tax breaks, special concessions, eminent domain, and began experimenting with mechanisms such as historic preservation and tax increment financing (TIF) districts to lure corporate developers and investors. Their efforts produced a central-city boom in "festival" marketplaces, retail malls, commercial offices, and luxury hotels, and a surge of speculative development—yuppification—in once more gradually gentrifying neighborhoods. In the absence of federal support, cities also grew more reliant on debt markets for capital improvements.[60] CDCs and the growing network of intermediaries and investment funds set up to support them grew adept at leveraging the LITC to draw for-profit developers into what was becoming a more businesslike business of residential development in low-income communities—in the process becoming more businesslike, and focused on housing production, themselves.[61] Still, neither of these privatized neighborhood-based development strategies could address the ongoing loss of manufacturing and overall labor market restructuring that were draining cities of decent-paying working-class jobs and leading to neighborhood concentrations of long-term unemployment.

By the mid-1990s "new urban paradigm" enthusiasts were declaring privatized development an unmitigated success, and celebrating New York's Rudy Giuliani, Philadelphia's Ed Rendell, and Steven Goldsmith of Indianapolis as shining examples of mayors whose municipal service cutbacks, business-friendly tax incentives, antiunionism and get-tough crime and welfare policies were putting their cities back on a path of growth.[62] The social map of urban America presented a different picture, of not just uneven but polarized—and polarizing—development in the rapid growth of racially segregated concentrated-poverty neighborhoods. These otherwise abandoned neighborhoods were where the law-and-order politics of privatized development would leave its heaviest imprint. The Bush administration's response to the outbreak of civil unrest in South Central Los Angeles in 1992 was telling in this regard, and especially so in contrast to the response advocated a quarter century earlier in the Kerner Commission report. In the so-called post–civil rights era, civil disorder in racially segregated urban neighborhoods sparked an influx of federal dollars under the auspices of a Department of Justice antidrug program known as Weed and Seed, whose unfortunate name and uneven implementation spoke volumes about how federal policy makers perceived the problems of inner-city race and poverty—and what would be the first, often the only, line of response in the decades to come.[63]

NEIGHBORHOOD AS A STRATEGY OF TRANSFORMATION

The policy environment for neighborhood revitalization continued to move in neoliberalized directions in the Clinton and George W. Bush administrations. As the centerpiece of his "new covenant" with urban America, Bill Clinton's Empowerment Zone/Enterprise Community initiative folded community participation requirements and interagency coordination into what was basically a variation on the enterprise zone idea: tax incentives for private investment meant to make designated neighborhoods more competitive in the global economy. While managing to restore some funding for low-income housing supplements, the Clinton administration also continued the emphasis on promoting self-sufficiency and enforcing tough behavioral sanctions on public-housing tenants, an emphasis reinforced by Clinton's controversial signing of the welfare-ending Personal Responsibility and Work Opportunity Reconciliation Act of 1996. In contrast, the administration's crime bill injected comparatively massive amounts of funding into drained city coffers, most of it targeted to added law enforcement and community policing—and contributed to a huge increase in African American incarceration rates with its "three strikes" and felony drug provisions and added funding for prison construction.[64] Meanwhile, ignoring warning signs from the 1987 stock market crash and the savings and loan crisis of the late 1980s and early 1990s, both Clinton and Bush accelerated the financial deregulation initiated during the Carter years, in what was becoming a bipartisan trend. Caught up in the romance of mortgage-backed securitization and the expanding market for subprime loans, both administrations made homeownership the real centerpiece of their low-income housing policy, while continuing to move the federal government out of the business of providing public housing by implementing the planned demolition of the most "severely distressed" projects under the Homeownership and Opportunity for People Everywhere Act of 1992 (HOPE VI).[65]

In this neoliberalized policy environment—of exuberant faith in the market and diminished expectations of what government could or should provide—local policymakers and practitioners began to embrace the idea of neighborhood "transformation" as a strategy of urban development in the 1990s. Versions of that idea inspired a number of ambitious initiatives that took place along—and in some cases contributed to—the ever more bifurcated lines of late-twentieth- and early-twenty-first-century capitalism. Those initiatives underscored how disconnected from a sense of *public* purpose and capacity the idea of neighborhood initiative had become.

Thus, one version of neighborhood transformation has led to gentrification on an unprecedented scale, as entrepreneurial city officials redoubled their downtown redevelopment campaigns to capitalize on the residential real estate and hi-tech booms, as well as the investment income of the global 1 percent.[66] Although examples exist of more deliberate mixed-income gentrification strategies that aim to avoid displacement, what remain for the most part market-driven upscaling campaigns have put lower-income residents, renters, and local businesses at a substantial structural disadvantage against rising property values, disapproving newcomers, and distant landlords eager to raise rents.[67] The ongoing implementation of HOPE VI has also raised concerns about what neighborhood "transformation" will mean for former tenants. Of the tens of thousands of displaced families, a relatively small percentage has returned to benefit from mixed-income replacement housing; most have moved from one poor neighborhood to another. The overall stock of affordable public housing has shrunk, while cleared neighborhoods have been open for private gentrification that continues to drive rents higher.[68]

A more complex, studied version of neighborhood transformation informed the community change initiatives undertaken by a large network of foundations, technical support and policy-oriented intermediaries, and various community-based stakeholders that began to come together in the early to mid-1990s to launch a number of redevelopment projects in low-income communities across the country. Significantly, these initiatives positioned themselves as a new, better-informed generation of place-based intervention, at the very moment when HUD was planning its own ambitious experiment, called Moving to Opportunity, designed to help poor people escape the disadvantages associated with living in poor places by moving them into safer, better-off neighborhoods in the hope that they would find more opportunities to get ahead.[69] Neighborhood change initiatives could bring about broader transformations, proponents argued, as long as interventions were comprehensive in their approach, attentive to strengthening internal community capacity and social bonds, and as long as they were clear about their goals and underlying "theories of change." A 2010 evaluation offered a partial validation of these views: twenty years of community-based work had brought improvements in individual well-being and neighborhood life, the report concluded, especially in neighborhoods with strong traditions of resident participation, democracy building, and community organizing. It had also brought billions of dollars of added philanthropic investment, and substantial new expertise to help put it to work. But comprehensive community change efforts had not transformed the economic prospects of low-income people and places in any meaningful way; for that, the evaluations concluded, they would need to look beyond the neighborhood as a site for social investment and concentrate instead on finding ways to connect poor neighborhoods to regional networks of economic opportunity, planning and political organizing.[70] Notably, the "people" side of the experimental balance sheet—the Moving to Opportunity program—produced similarly mixed, tempered, and untransformative results.

In practice, then, the concept of neighborhood transformation has been more vigorously—and with far more public resources—pursued as a strategy for attracting speculative investment and high-end development than for development that sustains thriving working- and middle-class communities. Putatively "transformative" interventions in high-poverty neighborhoods, in this context, have been reduced to a set of poor, artificially bifurcated people-versus-place choices that, precisely because they are designed to work within rather than to countervail the structural sources of stratification, are bound to fall short of their rhetorical aspirations.

WHAT KIND OF A CITY CAN NEIGHBORHOOD STRATEGIES CREATE?

Barack Obama's election in 2008 changed the policy environment for neighborhood organizing and initiative in significant ways, not in the least by raising hopes that his presidency would be transformative for urban America by restoring the long-since-eroded relationship with federal government established in the New Deal and expanded during the Great Society. In light of his personal ties to urban neighborhoods and community organizing, Obama's election also raised hope for a revival of the progressive idea of neighborhoods as sites of movement building for economic and social democracy. That prospect has proved elusive to say the least, as municipalities continue to endure the ongoing fallout from the Great Recession, partisan paralysis, federal "austerity," and the decidedly top heavy—and partial—shape of the postrecession economic recovery. Although history might not point us to easily replicable models for equitable development, it does remind us that current patterns of increasingly *in*equitable development are rooted in a legacy of past and ongoing policy choices that are subject to political scrutiny, challenge, and change. It also highlights the enduring relevance of key insights from within the historically progressive tradition of activism and reform that serve as useful starting points for making neighborhood reinvestment a strategy of equitable urban development today.

One is that neighborhoods can't "fix" the structural inequities we refuse to confront on a more systemic level, which is where policies of devolution have left us today. Equitable neighborhood revitalization strategies need to be embedded in a broader political and policy agenda aimed at generating jobs that pay living wages; producing decent affordable housing; enforcing antidiscrimination law and otherwise combating exclusionary practices of all kinds; and establishing a stable system of municipal finance—based in progressive taxation—that generates revenues to invest in the public infrastructure all neighborhoods rely on to thrive.

A second insight is that urban neighborhoods have long been and remain places where people cultivate lasting social ties that are vital to human development. But they are also places where people of diverse backgrounds cultivate political ties that enable them to exercise power and demand accountability from elected officials and that make neighborhoods venues for participatory democracy.

Third is that the very things that make urban neighborhoods "livable" for the working (and middle) classes cannot and never have been provided for by relying on the for-profit market—chief among them affordable housing. Nor have strategies that promise "trickle-down" or "trickle-out" from tax-incentivized high-end development ever worked to the benefit of low-income and working-class neighborhoods.

The final insight is that just as making neighborhoods a strategy of equitable and inclusive urban development is going to require much more than tinkering around the edges of contemporary approaches, so too will it require a much greater openness to ideas and momentum generated from community-based organizing and coalition building with otherwise organized constituencies. Along with the more concrete elements of a strategy that addresses the challenges of jobs, affordable housing, social infrastructure, and public finance, organizing an equitable growth coalition begins from a sustained and inclusive public conversation about what makes a city livable, sustainable, and empowering for its diverse but ultimately interdependent inhabitants, very much in the spirit of public purpose with which the neighborhood idea was articulated more than a century ago.

Notes

1. Frederic C. Howe, *The City: The Hope of Democracy* (New York: Scribner's, 1905).

2. Robert Halpern, *Rebuilding the Inner City: A History of Neighborhood Initiatives to Address Poverty in the United States* (New York: Columbia University Press, 1995); Alice O'Connor, "Swimming against the Tide: A Brief History of Federal Policy in Poor Communities," in *Urban Problems and Community Development*, eds. Ronald F. Ferguson and William T. Dickens, 77–137 (Washington, D.C.: Brookings Institution Press, 1999); Alyosha Goldstein, *Poverty in Common: The Politics of Community Action during the American Century* (Durham, N.C.: Duke University Press, 2012).

3. Office of the President-Elect, "Urban Policy Agenda: The Obama-Biden Plan," at http://change.gov/agenda/urbanpolicy_agenda/, accessed May 26, 2015.

4. Bruce Katz and Jennifer Bradley, *The Metropolitan Revolution: How Cities and Metros Are Fixing Our Broken Politics and Fragile Economy* (Washington, D.C.: Brookings Institution Press, 2013); Richard Florida, *The Rise of the Creative Class: Revisited* (New York: Basic Books, 2012).

5. Alan Ehrenhalt, *The Great Inversion and the Future of the American City* (New York: Knopf, 2012); Audrey Singer, Susan Hardwick, and Caroline Brettell, *Twenty-First Century Gateways: Immigrant Incorporation in Suburban America* (Washington, D.C.: Brookings Institution Press, 2008); Michael B. Katz and Kenneth Ginsburg, "Immigrant Cities as Reservations for Low-Wage Labor," unpublished paper, April 2014, copy in author's possession.

6. Patrick Sharkey, *Stuck in Place: Urban Neighborhoods and the End of Progress Toward Racial Equality* (Chicago: University of Chicago Press, 2013); Robert J. Sampson, *Great American City: Chicago and the Enduring Neighborhood Effect* (Chicago: University of Chicago Press, 2012).

7. Ginia Bellante, "On the Upper West Side, a House Divided by Income," *New York Times*, July 25, 2014, at www.nytimes.com, accessed October 22, 2014.

8. Manuel Pastor and Margery Turner, "Reducing Poverty and Economic Distress after ARRA: Potential Roles for Place-Conscious Strategies," Urban Institute Research Report, March 2010, at www.urban.org/research/, accessed October 22, 2014.

9. Charles Loring Brace, *The Dangerous Classes of New York and Twenty Years' Work among Them* (New York: Wynkoop and Hallenbeck, 1872).

10. Lewis Mumford, "The Neighborhood and the Neighborhood Unit," *Town Planning Review* 24, no. 4 (1954): 256–70.

11. Dorothy Ross, *The Origins of American Social Science* (Cambridge: Cambridge University Press, 1991).

12. Kenneth T. Jackson, *Crabgrass Frontier: The Suburbanization of the United States* (New York: Oxford University Press, 1985); Margaret Garb, *City of American Dreams: A History of Home Ownership and Housing Reform in Chicago, 1871–1919* (Chicago: University of Chicago Press, 2005).

13. Richard Sennett, excerpt from *The Uses of Disorder*, reprinted in *The Community Development Reader*, eds. James DeFilippis and Susan Saegert, 174–80 (New York: Routledge, 2012).

14. Jackson, *Crabgrass Frontier*, 87–137; Garb, *City of American Dreams*, 117–47.

15. Gail Radford, *Modern Housing for America: Policy Struggles in the New Deal Era* (Chicago: University of Chicago Press, 1996). See also Jacob A. Riis, *How the Other Half Lives: Studies among the Tenements of New York* (New York: Charles Scribner's Sons, 1890).

16. Sam Bass Warner, *The Private City: Philadelphia in Three Periods of Its Growth* (Philadelphia: University of Pennsylvania Press, 1968).

17. John Louis Recchiuti, *Civic Engagement: Social Science and Progressive-Era Reform in New York City* (Philadelphia: University of Pennsylvania Press, 2007).

18. Eileen Boris, *Home to Work: Motherhood and the Politics of Industrial Homework in the United States* (Cambridge: Cambridge University Press, 1994); Elizabeth Beardsley Butler and Paul Underwood Kellogg, *Women and the Trades, Pittsburgh, 1907–1908* (New York: Charities Publication Committee, 1909); Margaret F. Byington, *Homestead: The Households of a Mill Town* (New York: Charities Publication Committee, 1910).

19. Alice O'Connor, *Social Science for What? Philanthropy and the Social Question in a World Turned Rightside Up* (New York: Russell Sage Foundation, 2007).

20. Radford, *Modern Housing for America*, 29–37; Daniel T. Rodgers, *Atlantic Crossings: Social Politics in a Progressive Age* (Cambridge, Mass.: Belknap Press of Harvard University Press, 1998), 181–87; David M. P. Freund, *Colored Property: State Policy and White Racial Politics in Suburban America* (Chicago: University of Chicago Press, 2007), 45–92.

21. Lawrence J. Vale, *From the Puritans to the Projects: Public Housing and Public Neighbors* (Cambridge, Mass.: Harvard University Press, 2000).

22. Radford, *Modern Housing for America*, 29–57; Rodgers, *Atlantic Crossings*, 187–208.

23. Recchiuti, *Civic Engagement*; Halpern, *Rebuilding the Inner City*; Garb, *City of American Dreams*.

24. Roger Biles, *The Fate of Cities: Urban America and the Federal Government, 1945–2000* (Lawrence: University Press of Kansas, 2011); Samuel Zipp, *Manhattan*

Projects: The Rise and Fall of Urban Renewal in Cold War New York (Oxford: Oxford University Press, 2010).

25. Radford, *Modern Housing*, 147–76.

26. Zipp, *Manhattan Projects*.

27. Ira Katznelson, *When Affirmative Action Was White: An Untold History of Racial Inequality in Twentieth-Century America* (New York: W. W. Norton, 2005); Freund, *Colored Property*.

28. Biles, *Fate of Cities*, 32–38; Arnold R. Hirsch, "Less than Plessy: The Inner City, Suburbs, and State-Sanctioned Residential Segregation in the Age of Brown," in *The New Suburban History*, ed. Kevin Michael Kruse and Thomas J. Sugrue, 33–56 (Chicago: University of Chicago Press, 2006).

29. Marc A. Weiss, "The Origins and Legacy of Urban Renewal," in *Federal Housing Policy and Programs: Past and Present*, ed. Paul J. Mitchell, 253–76 (New Brunswick, N.J.: Rutgers University Center for Urban Policy Research, 1985).

30. Ibid., 256–72.

31. Guian A. McKee, *The Problem of Jobs: Liberalism, Race, and Deindustrialization in Philadelphia* (Chicago: University of Chicago Press, 2008); Margaret Pugh O'Mara, *Cities of Knowledge: Cold War Science and the Search for the Next Silicon Valley* (Princeton, N.J.: Princeton University Press, 2005).

32. James Q. Wilson, ed., *Urban Renewal: The Record and the Controversy* (Cambridge, Mass.: MIT Press, 1966).

33. Jane Jacobs, *The Death and Life of Great American Cities* (New York: Random House, 1961).

34. Zipp, *Manhattan Projects*; Matthew Countryman, *Up South: Civil Rights and Black Power in Philadelphia* (Philadelphia: University of Pennsylvania Press, 2006); McKee, *Problem of Jobs*.

35. Jon C. Teaford, *Rough Road to Renaissance: Urban Revitalization in America, 1940–1985* (Baltimore, Md.: John Hopkins University Press, 1990), 168–99; Hugh Davis Graham, *The Civil Rights Era: Origins and Development of National Policy, 1960–1972* (New York: Oxford University Press, 1990).

36. For a more extensive discussion of the genesis of the ideas informing community action in the War on Poverty, see Alice O'Connor, *Poverty Knowledge: Social Science, Social Policy and the Poor in Twentieth Century U.S. History* (Princeton, N.J.: Princeton University Press, 2001).

37. Annelise Orleck and Lisa Gayle Hazirjian, *The War on Poverty: A New Grassroots History, 1964–1980* (Athens: University of Georgia Press, 2011).

38. McGee, *Problem of Jobs*.

39. Alice O'Connor, "The Ford Foundation's Gray Areas Program," *Journal of Urban History* 22, no. 5 (1996): 586–625; Karen Ferguson, *Top Down: The Ford Foundation, Black Power, and the Reinvention of Racial Liberalism* (Philadelphia: University of Pennsylvania Press, 2013).

40. Elissa Minoff, "Free to Move? The Law and Politics of Internal Migration in Twentieth-Century America," PhD diss., Harvard University, 2013.

41. National Advisory Commission on Civil Disorders, *Report of the National Advisory Commission on Civil Disorders* (New York: Bantam Books, 1968), 396–408.

42. Jonathan Simon, *Governing through Crime: How the War on Crime Transformed American Democracy and Created a Culture of Fear* (Oxford: Oxford University Press, 2007).

43. John R. Logan and Harvey Molotch, *Urban Fortunes: The Political Economy of Place* (Berkeley: University of California Press, 1987); Barbara Ferman, *Challenging the Growth Machine: Neighborhood Politics in Chicago and Pittsburgh* (Lawrence: University Press of Kansas, 1996); Saul Alinsky, *Reveille for Radicals* (Chicago: University of Chicago Press, 1945).

44. Amanda Seligman, *Block by Block: Neighborhoods and Public Policy on Chicago's West Side* (Chicago: University of Chicago Press, 2005), 183–207; Beryl Satter, *Family Properties: How the Struggle over Race and Real Estate Transformed Chicago and Urban America* (New York: Metropolitan Books, 2009).

45. Andrea M. K. Gill, "Moving to Integration? The Origins of Chicago's Gautreaux Program and the Limits of Voucher-Based Housing Mobility," *Journal of Urban History* 38, no. 4 (2012): 662–86.

46. Peter Dreier, John H. Mollenkopf, and Todd Swanstrom, *Place Matters: Metropolitics for the Twenty-First Century* (Lawrence: University Press of Kansas, 2001); Suleiman Osman, *The Invention of Brownstone Brooklyn: Gentrification and the Search for Authenticity in Postwar New York* (Oxford: Oxford University Press, 2011).

47. Halpern, *Rebuilding the Inner City*, 127–48; Alexander von Hoffman, "The Past, Present, and Future of Community Development in the United States," in *Investing in What Works for America's Communities: Essays on People, Places, and Purpose*, ed. Nancy O. Andrews and David J. Erickson (San Francisco: Federal Reserve Bank of San Francisco and Low Income Investment Fund, 2012), available at http://econpapers .repec.org, accessed October 22, 2014.

48. Michael J. White, *American Neighborhoods and Residential Differentiation* (New York: Russell Sage Foundation, 1988), 9–14; National Commission on Neighborhoods, *People, Building Neighborhoods: Final Report to the President and Congress* (Washington, D.C.: Government Printing Office, 1979).

49. James DeFilippis, "Community Control and Development: The Long View," in DeFilippis and Saegert, *Community Development Reader*, 28–35; Margaret Weir, "Power, Money and Politics," in *Urban Problems and Community Development*, eds. Ronald F. Ferguson and William T. Dickens, 139–92, (Washington, D.C.: Brookings Institution Press, 1999); Ferman, *Challenging the Growth Machine*.

50. DeFilippis, "Community Control and Development," 30–32.

51. John Metzger, "Planned Abandonment: The Neighborhood Life-Cycle Theory and Urban Policy," *Housing Policy Debate* 11, no. 1 (2000): 7–40.

52. Gill, "Moving to Integration?"; Christopher Bonastia, *Knocking on the Door: The Federal Government's Attempt to Desegregate the Suburbs* (Princeton, N.J.: Princeton University Press, 2006).

53. Ronald Reagan, "Inaugural Address," January 20, 1981, at www.presidency.ucsb.edu.

54. Biles, *Fate of Cities*, 250–66.

55. Alice O'Connor, "The Privatized City: The Manhattan Institute, the Urban Crisis, and the Conservative Counterrevolution in New York," *Journal of Urban History*, 34, no. 2 (2008): 333–53.

56. Alice O'Connor, "Bringing the Market Back In: Philanthropic Activism and Conservative Reform," in *Politics and Partnerships: The Role of Voluntary Associations in America's Political Past and Present*, ed. Elisabeth Stephanie Clemens and Doug Guthrie, 121–50 (Chicago: University of Chicago Press, 2010).

57. Lorlene Hoyt and Devika Gopal Agge, "The Business Improvement District Model," *Geography Compass* 1, no. 4 (2007): 946–58; M. Steel and M. Symes, "The Privatization of Public Space?" *Local Government Studies* 31, no. 3 (2005): 321–34.

58. Robin L. Einhorn, *Property Rules: Political Economy in Chicago, 1833–1872* (Chicago: University of Chicago Press, 1991).

59. Neal R. Pierce and Carol F. Steinbach, *Corrective Capitalism: The Rise of America's Community Development Corporations* (New York: Ford Foundation, 1987).

60. Jason Hackworth, *The Neoliberal City: Governance, Ideology, and Development in American Urbanism* (Ithaca, N.Y.: Cornell University Press, 2007), 150–53; Jon C. Teaford, *The Twentieth-Century American City*, 2nd ed. (Baltimore, Md.: Johns Hopkins University Press, 1993), 152–61; Rachel Weber and Sarah O'Neill-Kohl, "The Historical Roots of Tax Increment Financing, or How Real Estate Consultants Kept Urban Renewal Alive," *Economic Development Quarterly* 27, no. 3 (2013): 193–207.

61. Lehn Benjamin, Julia Sass Rubin, and Sean Zeilenbach, "Community Development Financial Institutions: Expanding Access to Capital in Under-Served Markets," *Journal of Urban Affairs* 26, no. 2 (2004): 177–95.

62. O'Connor, "Privatized City"; Michael B. Katz, *The Price of Citizenship: Redefining the American Welfare State* (New York: Metropolitan Books, 2001), 104–20.

63. Michael deCourcy Hinds, "Experts Are Critical of Bush Anti-Drug Program," *New York Times*, July 20, 1992, www.nytimes.com, accessed October 22, 2014.

64. Biles, *Fate of Cities*, 318–47; Michelle Alexander, *The New Jim Crow: Mass Incarceration in the Age of Colorblindness* (New York: New Press, 2010): 55–57.

65. On the original thinking and ongoing debates about HOPE VI, see Henry Cisneros and Lora Engdahl, *From Despair to Hope: HOPE VI and the New Promise of Public Housing in America's Cities* (Washington, D.C.: Brookings Institution Press, 2009).

66. Hackworth, *Neoliberal City*, 123–49.

67. Mary E. Pattillo, *Black on the Block: The Politics of Race and Class in the City* (Chicago: University of Chicago Press, 2007); Mark Davidson, "Critical Commentary: Gentrification in Crisis Towards Consensus or Disagreement?," *Urban Studies* 48, no. 10 (2011): 1987–96.

68. Peter B. Edelman, *So Rich, So Poor: Why It's So Hard to End Poverty in America* (New York: New Press, 2013), 121–23.

69. Xavier de Souza Briggs, Susan J. Popkin, and John Goering, *Moving to Opportunity: The Story of an American Experiment to Fight Ghetto Poverty* (New York: Oxford University Press, 2010).

70. Anne C. Kubisch et al., *Voices from the Field III: Lessons and Challenges from Two Decades of Community Change Efforts* (Washington, D.C.: Aspen Institute, 2010).

Varieties of Neighborhood Capitalism

Control, Risk, and Reward

DISCUSSANT: RACHEL WEBER,
UNIVERSITY OF ILLINOIS AT CHICAGO

The title of this session set up a face-off between neighborhoods and capitalism, with the implication that government often acts as a referee between the two. Rather than view place and economy in opposition, or to treat neighborhoods as static and capital as footloose, I instead argue for a perspective that sees neighborhoods as dynamic places punctuated by the movement of capital into and out of them. Such a perspective would also recognize the multitude of neighborhood-based capitalisms. These forms stretch out along a continuum tethered at two extremes. At one extreme is what I believe the UIC Urban Forum organizers were trying to evoke and provoke with the notion of wills battling souls: finance capitalism. On the other end lies a more democratic mode of community capitalism.

This dichotomy, while crude and filled with a variety of in-between configurations, puts into sharp relief the fact that neighborhood capitalisms vary in several important respects. The assemblages of individuals, organizations, and institutions controlling capital inflows and outflows differ. These gatekeepers seek different kinds of returns on their investments within different time frames. They also do different things with the profits they make from their investments.

The community capitalism model seeks maximum local control over investment. Residents, small-business owners, and neighborhood groups channel capital toward renovations of the existing commercial and residential stock, fight for tax revenues for neighborhood amenities such as schools and parks, and raise money to fix infrastructure. In general, these neighborhood-based actors seek modest financial returns or anticipate nonfinancial ones that indicate resident usage, enjoyment, and human development. If financial returns are generated, they are recycled back into the community—instead of going to a distant investor's stock portfolio. Community capitalism emphasizes long-term stewardship over short-term appreciation. This philosophy contrasts sharply with the one highlighted in the 1997 Brookings report—confusingly, also titled *Community Capitalism*—that served as a rallying cry during the Clinton era for profit-oriented businesses to recognize the untapped economic potential of the inner city.[1]

The kinds of democratic initiatives for community capitalism to which I refer have their origins in the local self-reliance movements of the 1960s and 1970s that Alice O'Connor references in her paper for the UIC Urban Forum.[2] These include neighborhood health clinics but also housing-, worker-, and consumer-owned cooperatives, land trusts, and community development financial institutions (CDFIs).[3] Today they include well-known CDFIs, such as Accion in Chicago or the Reinvestment Fund in Philadelphia (which make micro-loans to small entrepreneurs in underserved markets), and also under-the-radar cooperatives that provide green cleaning, catering, printing, and bike repair services. The goal of these organizations is to generate and recycle funds in neighborhoods to enhance civic ties and provide existing residents with more production, consumption, and leisure opportunities. They operate on the premise that locally owned businesses have higher economic multipliers and are potentially less footloose or vulnerable to sudden relocation than those controlled by absentee owners.[4]

The jury is still out on newer variations of what many have called the sharing economy. For instance, crowdfunding models have emerged as a means of organizing public service provision and funding community economic development that circumvent the state and conventional lenders. Kickstarter and other platforms embrace social-network technologies to distribute responsibility for financing socially desirable investments to "the crowd."[5] They have the potential to bring together the laudable goals of self-reliance and community building. On the other hand, they also potentially exploit charitable impulses, commodify social networks, and transfer a portion of the locally raised funds to large corporations who provide the infrastructure and financing for these new platforms.

The finance capitalism model at the other extreme of the continuum of neighborhood capitalisms is more familiar. The actors and institutions range in size from small-scale home-flippers to private equity funds like BlackRock Inc., which purchased Stuyvesant Town, twenty thousand rent-stabilized apartments in Manhattan, with the intention of "deregulating" them to market rates.[6] In these cases, absentee investors who often possess little local knowledge enter a neighborhood with the intention of speculating on near-term appreciation. Under this model, the goal is to sniff out and "unlock" hidden cash flows. Financial capitalism often causes dislocation and conflict, partly because in order to unlock these hidden cash flows, investors try to capitalize on difference—differences between what old and new buildings generate in income, or differences between what existing and new residents can pay for housing, goods, and services. That incremental difference—that is, the gain from a sale, fees from the securitization of debt—is appropriated and distributed at geographic scales far from the location where it was generated.

Finance capitalism typically produces assets that are more large-scale and visible than community capitalism. Its engagement with neighborhoods results in new construction, chain stores, and fee-based infrastructure—as opposed to rehabilitated structures or job training, small-business loans or education. Investors like the visibility of mega-projects, which lead to spillovers in property value and registers in the next property reassessment. In order to cover the expense of new construction, developers and investors seek large amounts of other people's money, both equity and debt finance, to underwrite their interventions. The scale of projects therefore requires that external, conventional sources of funding participate in the neighborhood development process.

These oversimplified models also represent pathways that local governments can take as intermediaries between capital and place and as stewards of perhaps the largest source of collectively produced wealth: taxes.

Governments have the capacity to open up public funds to more democratic forms of neighborhood investment and focus on improving the lot of existing residents and businesses, rather than future, potential ones. Take the example of participatory budgeting (PB), which began in Porto Alegre, Brazil, where up to 20 percent of the municipal budget is now distributed through an assessment of community needs and vote by fifty thousand individuals, including the city's poorest residents. PB has been adopted in several U.S. cities since 2009, and is a more democratic, inclusive, and, some would argue, effective way to make spending decisions than relying on elected officials. In PB Chicago, for instance, aldermen in participating wards put their discretionary capital improvement money up for public deliberation and vote. In the 2012–13 cycle, neighborhood residents voted to fund street and sidewalk repairs, bike lanes, playground and park improvements, street lights, new trees, murals, a dog park, showers at a public beach, and several other community projects.

Unfortunately, it is still more common for municipal governments to swing in the other direction, toward finance capitalism. In addition to paying for retiree benefits, many cities are struggling with legacy costs from capital projects provided in the past that were not fully paid for at the time of delivery. Decreasing population, property values, and incomes mean that traditional sources of revenue cannot be tapped to pay for improvements that might allow them more control over their futures. Under fiscal stress from all directions, local governments have looked for new cash flows to monetize instead of new ways for communities to generate and control capital. The city of Chicago's experience with tax increment financing (TIF, monetizing property tax increment), as well as the leasing of its infrastructure to private investment consortia (monetizing tolls and parking fees), demonstrates the frequency with which such options are pursued. After structuring the financing so that absentee investors are the primary partners, cities feel obligated to market places, subsidize projects, and pass regulations that will increase those cash flows that have the most potential to grow. Neighborhoods where revenue streams are less forthcoming are likely to be bypassed in the competition for resources and public investment.

Cities have come to see financial returns as an ends rather than a means to achieving the goal of neighborhood improvement. Financial rationality has become deeply entrenched as the governing logic—the language, the conceptual frame, and the discursive field—through which the concept of neighborhood is now understood.[7] The common experiences of neighbors and the civic rationale for proximity and colocation are often less important to cities than a neighborhood's status as an asset from which rents can be extracted.[8] The outcomes that once represented the substantive ends of neighborhood development (solidarity, quality of life) are now seen as means to bolster financial values. When cities take this approach, it is not surprising that their policies end up providing few long-term benefits to existing residents. Worse, they displace them or leave them to struggle for the souls of their neighborhoods.

Although we find instances of both models in major cities like Chicago, their preferences are clear from looking at the numbers. In 2013, for example, $4 million of aldermanic menu money was dedicated to PB. In contrast, the city of Chicago's 151 TIF districts generated $422 million in revenue that year.

These projects are not even in the same league. If we expect governments to do more than pave the way for financial capitalism to take hold in neighborhoods, we need to organize to push them back toward the other side of the continuum.

Notes

1. American Assembly and the Brookings Institution, *Community Capitalism: Rediscovering the Markets of America's Urban Neighborhoods* (Washington, D.C.: Brookings Institution, 1997); Porter, Michael E., "New Strategies for Inner City Economic Development," *Economic Development Quarterly* 11 (1997): 11–27.

2. O'Connor, Alice, "Neighborhood as a Strategy of Urban Development from the Progressive Era to Today," paper presented at the UIC Urban Forum, Chicago, Illinois, September 14, 2014; see also her chapter in this book.

3. Shuman, Michael, *Going Local: Creating Self-Reliant Communities in a Global Age* (New York: Routledge, 2000); Gunn, Christopher Eaton, and Hazel Dayton Gunn, *Reclaiming Capital: Democratic Initiatives and Community Development* (Ithaca, N.Y.: Cornell University Press, 1991).

4. Markusen, Ann, and Greg Schrock, "Consumption-Driven Urban Development," *Urban Geography* 30, no. 4 (2009): 344–67.

5. Ashton, Philip, and Rachel Weber, "Hordes with Cash: Capital Circuits and the Legal-Regulatory Constitution of the Crowd," paper presented at Urban Planning and Policy Symposium, "The Crowd, the Cloud, and Urban Governance," University of Illinois at Chicago, April 20, 2015.

6. Wei, Lingling, and Mike Spector, "Tishman Venture Gives Up Stuyvesant Project," *Wall Street Journal*, January 25, 2010.

7. Lake, Robert, "The Financialization of Urban Policy in the Age of Obama," *Journal of Urban Affairs* 37 (2015): 75–78.

8. Smith, Janet L., "Neighborhoods Matter . . . Neighborhood Matters," paper presented at the UIC Urban Forum, Chicago, Illinois, September 14, 2014; see also her chapter in this book.

Cities, Schools, and Social Progress

The Impact of School Reform Policies on Low-Income Communities of Color

PEDRO A. NOGUERA

NEW YORK UNIVERSITY

Jane Jacobs, the widely respected urban planner, scholar, and activist, once pointed out that cities are organic spaces that evolve and transform over time.[1] Like forests, prairies, and marshlands, the ecosystems of cities are subject to constant change, transforming in response to local political, economic, and social trends as well as broader changes occurring in the society at large.[2] While cities are by no means invulnerable to changes triggered by the natural environment (e.g., climate change, earthquakes, hurricanes), human initiatives are more often the primary sources of change in the urban landscape.

For example, Yardley Street in the South Bronx has served as the backdrop for presidents, starting with Carter, who used it to talk about urban decay. Reagan then used it to talk about how tax incentives could spur development, and Clinton used it to make commentary on possibilities for urban renewal in the United States.[3] Each presidential visit offered a new opportunity to make a point about the role of public policy in alleviating poverty, stimulating economic growth, or stabilizing low-income urban communities. The fate of communities like the South Bronx, one of the poorest in the nation, has been influenced by economic growth and decline, shifts in population that occur as a result of immigration, gentrification and the return of the middle class to certain blocks (real-estate agents call it SoBro), and changes engineered by policy makers and planners who decide to erect new housing, a highway, or a hospital.

At times, the pace of change may seem gradual, occurring almost imperceptibly across decades, such as when a major city like New Bedford, Buffalo, or Flint ceases to be a major hub of industry and commerce, and gradually becomes a substantially smaller, economically depressed city that is a shadow of its formerly vibrant and vital self. At other times, change can be dramatic and rapid, such as when a major new corporation arrives (e.g., Google in San Francisco) or departs (e.g., General Motors in Detroit), bringing with it profound shifts in population, employment, housing values, and quality of life. In almost all cases, the changes that dramatically alter the character and landscape of a city also produce beneficiaries who gain from new jobs, parks, and transportation, as well as those whose fortunes decline as they are pushed out or left behind to contend with a diminished quality of life. More often than not, it is the nonwhite urban poor—African Americans, Latinos, new immigrants, and others, who have endured the negative consequences of change.

For many years, urban public schools were the one aspect of cities that were least likely to change. Certainly, the composition of urban schools has been dramatically altered over time by shifts in population brought about by "white flight" and the arrival of new immigrants. But, even when the population served changed, schools provided urban communities with a sense of continuity and stability through their steady presence. Such stability has been important to many communities, but in those that are economically and socially marginal, the ones William Julius Wilson described as "no zones"—no banks, no supermarkets, no libraries, or post offices—public schools have been especially important.[4] In blighted neighborhoods, even when middle-class homeowners, banks, and private industry have fled, public schools have generally remained, providing an anchor and source of stability for those left behind. To be certain, they remained not necessarily because they performed well or succeeded in carrying out their mission—educating children—but because for as long as there were families with children present, schools have been required to serve them. In this way, public schools, even flawed and troubled ones, have often managed to provide a degree of continuity that creates a semblance of order important to communities characterized by disorder and disarray.

In recent years, the stability once provided by public schools to urban neighborhoods has become a thing of the past as a new generation of reformers has undertaken the task of radically transforming the character of public schools. Typically, the reformers have rationalized changes that have been promoted as being necessary to improve the performance of schools with long track records of failure. However, in their zeal to overhaul public education, the reformers have often displayed little attention or regard to how their work has affected the communities where these flawed but stable institutions were located.

In many respects, the federal No Child Left Behind (NCLB) law enacted in 2001 was the starting point for the current period of reform.[5] Although it could be argued that the nation has been in a perpetual state of education reform since the Soviet Union launched *Sputnik*, none of the policy measures adapted to reform public education have been as far-reaching or profound as NCLB.[6] In fact, the impact of NCLB may well prove to be as significant to the character of U.S. education as the *Brown v. Board of Education* decision of 1954 and the enactment of the Elementary and Secondary Education Act (Title I) in 1964, both of which have widely been regarded as watersheds of U.S. public education policy.[7] NCLB influence has been attributed to the fact that it significantly expanded the federal role in education and ushered in a new series of reforms under the banner of standards-based accountability.[8] Since the enactment of NCLB, states have adopted high-stakes assessments to monitor student achievement and, in recent years, have embraced a series of new reforms for the purpose of accelerating the pace of change. Some of these measures include school choice, charter schools, mayoral control, portfolio management, and most recently, the common-core standards.[9] While many of these policies have been directed at public education generally, their most profound impact has been on cities where the need for change has been seen as greatest.[10] A smaller number of cities have also created and significantly expanded the number of community schools; schools that provide a full range of services to children and families, including social services and after-school programs.[11] While there have been numerous studies documenting and analyzing the impact of reform on schools, relatively little research and scholarship has been devoted to the way this agenda has affected urban neighborhoods.[12]

As I show in the pages ahead, the reforms that are occurring in U.S. cities today are dramatically changing the character of schools and the communities they serve. In this chapter I explore how the reform strategies pursued in New York and Tulsa-Union have affected the character of the communities where they have been targeted. I focus in particular on mayoral control, school closures, the expansion of charter schools, and the expansion of community schools because they provide an interesting lens through which to compare and contrast the changes that are occurring in urban communities as a result of school reform.

As I present this analysis, I try to remain aware that school reform has not been the only political, environmental, or economic trend that is altering the character of cities. In New York and Tulsa-Union, gentrification, immigration, deindustrialization, and the machinations of local politics, have played major roles in transforming neighborhoods. However, I focus on school reform because while considerable attention has been focused on understanding how communities are affected by these trends, comparatively less attention has been directed to the impact of education reform. Throughout this analysis, I consider how school reform is affecting community well-being, a term most often associated with public health, because it makes it possible to assess how the quality of life experienced by the poor and economically vulnerable has been affected by the current wave of school reform policies.[13]

The experience of New York and Tulsa-Union (Tulsa-Union is a school district encompassing the southeastern part of Tulsa and the city of Broken Arrow) provides a useful context for illuminating the impact of different aspects of the current reform agenda. Whereas New York has been an experimental laboratory for what is now referred to as "market-based reform," Tulsa-Union have been at the forefront of the community-schools movement, which has expanded access to early childhood and after-school programs and a variety of school-based social services. The differences in the paths taken allow for a rich comparative analysis that sheds further light on the social consequences of education reform.

In addition, throughout this chapter I make the race and class impact of policy central to the analysis. I do so because the communities where these reforms have been carried out are largely comprised of low-income African Americans, Latinos, and new immigrants. As I show, understanding the social and political dynamics between local residents and the largely white political and economic elites who have championed and implemented education reforms is essential for shedding light on how the politics of education reform is influencing conditions in impoverished communities and affecting the character of the modern U.S. city. In post–civil rights America, race is often unmentioned in policy discourse in part to maintain a facade of color blindness.[14] Given the clear evidence of widening racial disparities in education and throughout U.S. society, it is increasingly important not only to dispel the facade of post-racialism but to directly examine the race and class implications of public policy.[15]

THE URBAN EDUCATION DILEMMA

In 1988, education scholar Gene Maeroff wrote an important article titled "Withered Hopes, Stillborn Dreams: The Dismal Panorama of Urban Education." In this unrestrained indictment of educational policy he wrote, "the educational reform movement has proven largely irrelevant to urban minority students' needs. Dropout prevention programs have bestowed meaningless diplomas, while side-stepping the *root causes* of failure and underachievement." He then cited an array of data to document the extent of the problems afflicting urban schools, including high dropout rates, low math and reading scores, incidents of violence, and dilapidated facilities. In discussing what he regarded as the "root cause" of pervasive failure—racial segregation and deeply entrenched inter-generational poverty—he points out that none of the educational policies pursued at the federal, state, or local level were addressing these issues.[16]

Undoubtedly, a similar article on the current state of urban education in the United States could be written today, and it would not differ markedly from the picture Maeroff described nearly thirty years ago. Despite numerous reforms, graduation rates in the fifty largest cities have risen only slightly to 53 percent in the last twenty years.[17] While several cities have experienced improved performance on the National Assessment for Educational Progress (NAEP), SAT and ACT scores have remained largely stagnant.[18] Moreover, even cities such as Boston, Charlotte, Houston, and Miami that have been awarded the Broad Prize for excellence in urban education and are frequently cited as bright spots among large urban school districts, disparities in academic performance between cities and surrounding suburbs largely remain.[19]

Of course, the problem is related not merely to geography. In many U.S. cities, there are a certain number of high-performing public schools. However, more often than not, these successful schools screen out the most disadvantaged children and often serve a more privileged student population. There are also high-performing urban public schools that serve low-income students.[20] However, these are few in number, and their existence is insufficient to offset the "dismal panorama" described by Maeroff. In fact, nearly all of the schools recognized by state departments of education as "failing" or in need of improvement are composed of low-income, African American, and Latino students.[21] Despite the wave of reform ushered in by the adoption of NCLB, it largely continues to be the case that, wherever poor children are concentrated, the quality of education they receive is poor and school failure is the norm.[22]

Of course, pervasive failure in urban education is not a new phenomenon. In 1961, former Harvard University president James B. Conant made observations that mirror those of Maeroff in his *Slums and Suburbs*. After describing the deplorable conditions he found in what he called "slum schools," Conant writes that "we are allowing a social dynamite to accumulate in our large cities." He adds that "the continuation of this situation is a menace to the social and political health of the large cities."[23] Like Maeroff, Conant recognized that addressing social and economic conditions in the communities where "negro" children resided was essential if schools were to be improved. Writing in 1961, before the riots that erupted in cities throughout the United States later in the 1960s, he seems almost prophetic. Conant recognized that the harsh conditions in the "negro slums" were generating "social dynamite." Like Maeroff, he also understood that the problem of urban education could not be addressed without confronting racial segregation and concentrated poverty in inner-city neighborhoods, a recognition that is scarcely mentioned by reformers today.[24]

In subsequent years, the task of explaining the underlying causes of the nation's urban education dilemma has been taken up by scholars like Michelle Fine in *Framing Dropouts*, who describes a pattern of indifference and neglect in the management of urban schools that results in some students being pushed out of school.[25] Others, such as author Jean Anyon, have documented how deeply entrenched political corruption, nepotism, and patronage have made it possible for a small number of politicians and contractors to extract financial benefits from urban school systems while allowing deeply flawed schools to remain in disarray.[26] In *Getting What We Ask For*, sociologist Charles Payne went a step further, showing how the gaps between policy and practice produced a system where those with power and authority cast blame on those who work in schools, or the children and families that are served, while simultaneously distancing themselves from the disorder and dysfunction in the school systems they are ostensibly responsible for.[27]

More recently, several studies have attempted to explain why the current wave of school reform has yielded so little progress in improving the nation's urban schools. In an important longitudinal study on Chicago public schools, Anthony Bryk and his colleagues analyzed how schools responded to the various reform strategies that were implemented over a ten-year period.[28] Bryk and colleagues showed how concentrated poverty frequently overwhelmed schools and contributed to their failure. The authors also identified five essential ingredients that were present in schools experiencing improvement that was sustained over time.[29] Finally, in a 2014 book, Joseph McDonald analyzes reforms carried out in several major cities over a thirty-year period. Like Payne, he finds a lack of attention to addressing school climate and culture, and, like Bryk and colleagues, he finds insufficient attention to the "essential ingredients" of change. McDonald goes further in pointing out that as poverty and inequality have increased in urban districts it is increasingly important for reforms to address the social needs of children:

The continuing practice of urban school reform must take seriously the impact of poverty on schools. This need not be, and should not be, about excusing poor performance by students, teachers, schools, or districts. Nor should it be based on the faulty idea that poor children in general cannot learn at high levels . . . schools serving deeply disadvantaged neighborhoods, where social capital is low, are often distracted from efforts to build sufficiently strong academic systems by the poverty that accompanies a significant proportion of their children to school every day. What reformers need to do, following the model of Geoffrey Canada, James Comer, and others, is to take this problem into account in their formulation of theories of action, and they also need to raise and deploy extra resources to deal with it.[30]

Among the existing studies of urban education, my own book, *City Schools and the American Dream*, is one of few that attempt to link problems related to school performance directly to the social context of urban areas. Focusing on urban schools in the Bay Area of northern California, I posit that the interaction of factors that are external to schools, namely concentrated poverty, political indifference toward the plight of poor neighborhoods, and weak social capital within them, helped to produce school failure, a phenomenon that throughout the United States is intimately associated with the race and class of students.[31] These external conditions contribute to the development of internal dynamics within schools that become manifest in the form of structural barriers (e.g., tracking, teacher assignment, inequities in resources allocated by administrators) and the development of cultural patterns (e.g., low teacher expectations, differential discipline practices) that negatively influence school performance and undermine academic outcomes among low-income students of color. Several authors have argued that inequality and poverty are the primary causes of lower school and student performance.[32] While my argument does not dispute this contention, it differs from these and others by recognizing the dynamic created by the interaction of the external and internal factors and their role in perpetuating and maintaining race and class disparities in achievement.[33]

In *City Schools* I also argue that while the external-internal dynamics were different in high wealth cities like San Francisco and Berkeley, the outcomes for low-income students of color were remarkably similar to those obtained in high-poverty cities like Oakland and Richmond, despite the fact that the former spent considerably more per student than the latter. In that book I conclude that student and school performance was inextricably connected to how individuals and groups accessed power and resources both within and outside of schools. For this reason, academic outcomes for students were much more likely to be related to their race and class and where they lived with respect to the race-class composition of their neighborhood, than the school district they attended. Schools, like other public services and institutions (e.g., hospitals, police departments, public transportation) respond to the needs of communities based to a large degree on the power and social capital they exert.[34]

Placing Race and Class at the Center

Though urban schools were not the focus of their analysis, both William Julius Wilson and Loic Waquant came to similar conclusions about the persistence of poverty in their studies of economically marginalized urban communities.[35] In a far-reaching study of poverty in African American communities in Chicago, Wilson showed that deindustrialization led to the loss of economic opportunities and social isolation in inner-city neighborhoods.[36] He also showed that, as the economy changed, social problems such as crime, violence, and teen pregnancy increased. Wilson argued that local institutions such as public schools were limited in their ability to counter the adverse conditions in the urban environment. For Wilson, the problem was rooted in a political economy that produced social isolation and concentrated poverty, and alleviating these conditions had to be the focus of reform.

Drawing on a historical framework to illuminate how ghetto communities emerged, Wacquant went a step further than Wilson. He argued that the emergence of ghettos was directly tied to a larger political project of racial exclusion and control, what he termed a "deadly symbiosis." Writing several years before Michelle Alexander produced her seminal work, *The New Jim Crow*, to explain the advent of mass incarceration, Wacquant argued that prisons eventually replaced the ghetto as an even more efficient means to control and exploit a population brought for cheap labor that was now regarded as unnecessary and an impediment to social progress.[37] For Wacquant, the failure of urban public schools was a manifestation of these historic trends (he points out that they weren't "failing" when they served the white working class), and that now they often generate what he termed negative social capital by undermining the communities they are supposed to serve because they operate without a sense of accountability to local residents. In contrast with what might be termed "positive" social capital, which is frequently characterized as a resource that can be deployed to further group or individual interests, "negative" social capital weakens bonds between individuals by sowing distrust and the abandonment of local public institutions.[38]

While their work has focused primarily on an explanation of persistent poverty rather than the failure of school reform, in their attention to political economy Wilson and Wacquant provide a basis for understanding the social context where policies pursued in the name of education reform have been launched. As I show, most of have these policies, with the notable exception of the community-school model being implemented in Tulsa-Union, have focused exclusively on what was happening within schools while deliberately ignoring how the social context interacts with the operation of schools. As a result, not only have the current reform policies failed to deliver the positive changes that were promised, they have actually contributed to the instability and deterioration of the poorest and most marginal neighborhoods in several cities. In the pages ahead I show how the reform strategies pursued in New York and Tulsa-Union have affected the quality of life in poor neighborhoods, in the hope that these case studies can illustrate how the interplay between the local social context and the current wave of school reform.

THE IMPACT OF SCHOOL REFORM ON
NEW YORK AND TULSA-UNION

The two cases I have chosen for this analysis provide an interesting vantage point from which to study how cities are being affected by the current wave of reform. To some degree, the choice is arbitrary; there are very few U.S. cities that have not experienced some degree of change as a result of the current reform movement. In fact, both of the chosen cities have undergone similar reforms: major changes in the way school districts are administered, school choice, and the rapid expansion of charter schools, new teacher evaluation systems, and so on. However, the contexts in which these reforms have occurred make these two cases interesting if nothing else. In New York, the billionaire Mayor Michael Bloomberg committed to overhauling the nation's largest school system with technocratic efficiency. In one of the nation's reddest states (Oklahoma), a different strategy has been pursued in Tulsa-Union, one that might be criticized as a form of socialism were it not occurring in America's heartland, led by Republic political leaders, and funded by oil wealth.

In both cases, I focus on different aspects of the current reform agenda: mayoral control, school closure and the rapid expansion of charter schools in New York, the embrace of universal preschool and community schools in Tulsa-Union. Again, I spend less time examining the reforms themselves, instead devoting attention to their impact on the cities and local communities where they occurred. In this way I hope to illuminate who gains or loses (and how) when schools are reformed in these ways. Assessing the impact of education reform on the urban communities they were intended to benefit is a topic that has rarely been addressed by those who study school reform. Even among the increasingly strident advocates who frequently rationalize their actions as necessary to breathe new life into a failed enterprise (public education), and in many cases describe their efforts as part of the "civil rights movement of the twenty-first century," rarely do they consider the effects of their policies and actions on the communities where they have been carried out.

REMAKING SCHOOLS IN NEW YORK CITY

The election of Michael Bloomberg just two months after the terrorist attacks on September 11, 2011, was heralded as a major change for New York City and its politics. Bloomberg succeeded Rudolf Giuliani, a polarizing figure who gained national prominence in the wake of 9/11. Giuliani alienated large segments of the African American and Latino communities, who regarded him as indifferent at best and in many cases hostile to the needs of their communities, while simultaneously embracing repressive policing tactics. Although Bloomberg was also (at the time) a Republican in a largely Democratic city, he presented himself as an independent and impartial businessman, a technocrat who would use the skills he acquired in business to solve the problems plaguing this large and unruly city.

From the very beginning, Bloomberg made it clear that he intended to focus on reforming the city's public schools, which he derided as subpar and inefficient. His first move was to petition the state legislature for control of the system, contending that the system could be managed more effectively if power was taken away from the democratically elected board of education. Next, following an extensive public search for a chancellor to lead the nation's largest school system, during which the mayor made clear his intention to hire a noneducator, he chose a former member of the Clinton Justice Department, attorney Joel Klein, who had made his name leading a lawsuit against the technology giant Microsoft in a high-profile antitrust case. Like Bloomberg, Klein made it clear from the start that his goal was not to merely tinker with the system but to redesign, shake up, and totally transform it. Klein described the stability created by labor-management cooperation as "the elixir of the status quo," a state of affairs he claimed was producing rampant failure.[39]

Initially, many of the changes launched by Bloomberg and Klein focused on how the system would be managed. Larger administrative regions replaced the community school districts that had been in place for decades. In a 2003 public meeting to assess the state of the city, Bloomberg announced that the forty community district superintendents would be replaced, calling them "notorious bureaucratic dinosaurs."[40] A new leadership academy was established, designed to train principals and other administrative leaders in corporate managerial techniques with support from General Electric and its former CEO Jack Welch. Soon after, Klein announced that under the new accountability system schools would be graded based on how well their students performed.

In a move rich with symbolism, the headquarters of the board of education was moved from its offices in Brooklyn, which Bloomberg referred to as a "rinky dink candy store," to the old Tweed Courthouse adjacent to City Hall, changing the name to the Department of Education (DOE). Following a cue from Bloomberg's financial information firm, private offices were replaced with cubicles, ostensibly for the purpose of fostering communication among the managers in charge of the mammoth system. The changes were more than cosmetic. A new breed of managers—young, smart, mostly white, and often upper middle-class—was running the new system, replacing a more diverse cadre of senior educators. More than a few had MBAs but no more than two or three years of teaching experience, despite their impressive administrative titles and major new responsibilities.

When the financial crisis of 2008 hit New York City, Bloomberg engineered a third term for himself, despite the two-term limit stipulated in the city's charter.[41] Claiming that only a leader with his financial acumen could steer city government through the economic crisis, during the campaign he and Klein boldly asserted that the gains achieved by his administration in public education were nothing short of remarkable. According to DOE data, graduation rates and test scores were rising, and the so-called achievement gap was closing.[42] In the months before the election, over 80 percent of the city's schools received an A or B on the DOE's evaluation system, although many of the gains asserted by the DOE evaporated when the state education department recalibrated the test scores; in fact, very little progress had been achieved.[43] Coincidently, this sobering news from the state was delivered only after Bloomberg had secured his third term, which he used to claim a mandate for continuing his brand of education reform.

The school ratings were particularly important because they provided the justification for one of the administration's most far-reaching education policies. As a strategy for stimulating further improvement, Bloomberg and the DOE began shutting down schools deemed to be failing based on their accountability system. By the end of his third term in 2013, Bloomberg and the DOE had closed 160 schools. This was by far one of the most radical and controversial of the measures undertaken by the Bloomberg administration in their effort to reform public education. Despite presenting evidence that the schools selected for closure were failing according to the criteria established by the DOE (e.g., test scores, graduation rates), in many cases, teachers, students, and parents from these schools rallied to keep them open. At meetings of the Panel on Educational Policy (PEP), the body authorized to approve the closures (the majority of PEP members are appointed by the mayor and the remainder by each of the five borough presidents), each vote for closure became more contentious and generated more opposition. Despite the chancellor's clear and compelling case that the schools were failing and therefore in need of closure, large numbers of people turned out to plead for the schools to remain open.

A closer analysis of where the "failing" schools were located and who was served by them reveals an unambiguous, distinct pattern. A disproportionate number of the schools targeted for closure were in the poorest neighborhoods of the city. For example, in Brooklyn neighborhoods such as Brownsville, Bedford-Stuyvesant, East New York, and Bushwick, most of the middle and high schools received a rating of D or F.[44] Closer analysis of the schools targeted for closure also revealed that even those not in poor neighborhoods were disproportionately serving the most disadvantaged students—English language learners, students with learning disabilities, and poor students generally. A 2009 report by Parthenon, a private consulting firm, commissioned by the NYC Department of Education, showed that the city's "failing schools" had been required to enroll a disproportionate number of "high-need" students. The report suggested that the problem was related to the fact that many selective public and charter schools were allowed to screen or counsel out the most disadvantaged children. The report found that "nearly 80 percent of variance among individual schools performance can be explained by a few factors, amongst which, enrollment size and concentration of low level students (both ELA and Math) are the most important."[45] The DOE assured parents that superior new schools would replace the schools that were closed. However, because of the school choice system that was implemented in 2003, there was no guarantee that children from the neighborhoods affected by closures would have access to these schools. Furthermore, the phase-out plan adopted by the DOE ensured that none of the students in the schools designated as failing would have access to the new schools.[46]

Neighborhood Effects

A study conducted by Manpower Research and Development Corporation (MDRC) found that many of the newly created schools in fact performed better than the schools they replaced.[47] However, a report by Norman Fruchter from the Annenberg Institute, *Is Demography Still Destiny?*, found that the creation of new schools did not alter the dynamic of school failure in the city's poorest neighborhoods.[48] Table 1 shows the strong correlation between low rates of college readiness and the racial composition of schools and neighborhoods in Brooklyn and the Bronx.

The neighborhoods with lowest rates of college readiness also happen to be the poorest neighborhoods in New York City. According to a report by the Community Service Society in 2013, these neighborhoods had unemployment rates for African American men that were well over 50 percent before the recession of 2008. Additionally, in contrast to the gentrifying neighborhoods in other parts of the cities, these areas continued to have high rates of crime and violence.[49] As part of the Bloomberg-Klein strategy, new charter schools were established in some of these neighborhoods. Yet, despite evidence suggesting that many of the charter schools outperformed DOE schools in the same neighborhoods, achievement indicators for children in those neighborhoods showed no improvement.[50] Although Bloomberg and Klein claimed that the purpose of their reforms was to benefit those who had been poorly served in the past, the evidence showed that schools in high-poverty neighborhoods had

Table 1. Rates of College Readiness and the Racial Composition of Schools and Neighborhoods in Brooklyn and the Bronx

High Schools	College-Ready Students	Blacks/Latinos in Student Population
East New York	12%	96%
Ocean Hill	12%	99%
North Baychester	12%	93%
Edenwald	12%	93%
Melrose	12%	100%
Hunt's Point	12%	100%
East Tremont	12%	98%
Mount Hope	11%	98%
Bathgate	11%	95%
Brownsville	11%	100%
Crotona Park	11%	99%

Source: Fruchter, N. M., M. Hester, C. Mokhtar, and Z. Shahn, *Is Demography Still Destiny? Neighborhood Demographics and Public High School Students' Readiness for College in New York City* (Providence, R.I.: Annenberg Institute for School Reform, Brown University, 2012), 6.

not improved despite the fact that so many of the schools designated as failing had been closed.[51]

In March 2010, State Supreme Court Justice Joan B. Lobis temporarily halted the closing of nineteen schools, ruling that the DOE had not provided adequate analysis and information to the public related to the impact that the closings would have on communities. However, the court's ruling was only a temporary setback for Mayor Bloomberg and Chancellor Klein, who pressed ahead and managed to close dozens more schools before the mayor left office. All of the nineteen schools served an extremely high proportion of at-risk students. An average of 94 percent of students in the schools were African American or Latino, 10 percent were designated as having limited proficiency in English, 18 percent were in special-education programs, and 11 percent were overage for their grade level.[52] In the high schools that the DOE wanted to close, a large number of students had entered the ninth grade below grade level in reading and math. Finally, many of the targeted schools had received high numbers of "over-the-counter students": transfer students who enroll in school long after the school year has begun. A large number of these students have weak academic preparation or significant periods of interrupted formal education. According to Judge Lobis, there was no evidence that the schools the DOE wanted to close had been provided with the resources needed to support the students they had been required to serve.

Despite the court ruling, Bloomberg managed to continue pursuing his reform agenda until the day he left office. He also maintained that schools had improved under his leadership. He pointed to graduation rates that rose to 64 percent during his twelve years in office, ignoring data collected by the City University of New York (CUNY) Institutional Research Center that found 80 percent of New York City graduates admitted to CUNY colleges were required to enroll in remedial courses, effectively repeating classes they were supposed to have taken and passed while in high school. Bloomberg also maintained that his support for choice and charter schools had significantly increased the supply and availability of good schools in the city, ignoring the fact that several studies showed the new charter schools were under-enrolling English language learners, the undocumented, homeless children, and students with special needs.[53]

The school closure strategy also exposed a crucial weakness in Bloomberg and the DOE's approach to reform. Throughout his twelve years in office, neither he nor Klein ever made it clear how their strategy would lead to better schools for the most disadvantaged students in the most marginalized neighborhoods. As the Parthenon study of 2009 showed, a disproportionate number of students in the schools targeted for closure were English-language learners, students with severe learning disabilities, and students who were already academically behind when they entered high school. Despite imposing a grade retention policy in fourth, sixth, and eighth grades for students who failed to perform beyond the lowest level on standardized tests, the Bloomberg administration never offered an explanation or conducted an evaluation to find out why so many students were still entering high school at the lowest level of achievement. They also did little to address the high turnover of teachers at schools in the poorest neighborhoods and did little to support or stabilize these high rates.[54]

McDonald and his colleagues write about the Bloomberg-Klein stance toward low-income communities: "Bloomberg and Klein did little to support or increase grassroots civic capacity. Indeed, they tended to spurn grassroots civic capacity as unsophisticated at best and corrupting at worst. Although they instituted a system of parent coordinators for every school, they also disempowered the community school boards and offices that had been the principal channel for parental voice and participation. Moreover, the continual restructuring of district offices and the geographical diffusion of the support organizations left parents and other community stakeholders confused about who held the power to address their questions, concerns, and grievances."[55] Given the administration's stance toward community engagement, it is hardly surprising that community concerns and needs were rarely considered as relevant to the reform agenda in New York City.

A DIFFERENT PATH FOR TULSA-UNION

Lying in northeastern Oklahoma, Tulsa is a midsize city (forty-sixth largest in the United States), and together with surrounding areas outside the city limits has just under a million people, making it the second largest metropolitan area in the state. Since Tulsa's founding in the late nineteenth century, the region's economy has been highly dependent on oil production, and residents often refer to it as the "oil capital of the world." Tulsa had been home to a community known as the Black Wall Street, one of the most prosperous African American communities in the United States in the late nineteenth century.[56] Located in the Greenwood neighborhood, the area was destroyed by fire and mob violence in 1921, during what is now commonly referred to as the Tulsa Race Riot, one of the nation's worst acts of racial violence and civil disorder. After sixteen hours of rioting on May 31 and June 1, as many as three hundred people, mostly blacks, were killed; over eight hundred people were admitted to local hospitals with injuries; and an estimated ten thousand people were left homeless as a result of fire.[57] Efforts to obtain reparations for survivors of the violence have been unsuccessful, though the city and state later acknowledged the violence and devastation and supported the erection of a memorial to the victims.

The schools in the Union Public School District in Tulsa County are more diverse than those in New York City, which were recently identified as among the most segregated in the nation.[58] Of the nearly forty thousand students enrolled in Tulsa in 2014 approximately 27 percent are Caucasian, 26 percent are African-American, 30 percent are Hispanic, 6 percent are Native American, and just over 1 percent are Asian American. Approximately 79 percent of students in the school district qualify for free or reduced-price lunch.[59] With just over fifteen thousand students, Union Public Schools also serve a relatively diverse student population: 5.6 percent Native American, 14.7 percent African American, 7.5 percent multiracial, 7 percent Asian, 65 percent Caucasian, and 25 percent Hispanic. Approximately 3,620 students are bilingual or live in a home where a language other than English is spoken. Like Tulsa, the vast majority of children served by Union Public Schools come from households in poverty (80 percent).[60]

In 2007, the Tulsa Area Community Schools Initiative (TACSI) was established through the Tulsa Metropolitan Human Services Commission (MHSC). Although the focus of the initiative is to provide services to children and families through the public schools, it is administered by the Community Service Council of Greater Tulsa (CSC) rather than the school districts and is guided by a community steering committee. A management team leads the TACSI Resource Center at CSC, with leaders from the two participating school districts (Union and Tulsa) represented but not in control. The structure was designed to foster a sense of shared accountability among district and civic leaders in the two cities and to engage key institutions in supporting the implementation and support of TACSI. TACSI is a participant in the national Coalition for Community Schools, a consortium that provides support to similar initiatives throughout the United States.[61] TACSI currently partners with over 150 community organizations that together develop social and educational capacity within schools and provide resources to support the social and psychological needs of children. The goal of the partnership is to create opportunities for "increased stability in families and in communities, as well as provide rich experiences for children."[62]

TACSI claims to serve more than nine thousand students and families each year, covering all elementary schools in low-income neighborhoods throughout the Tulsa area. Its stated goal is to build a "web of innovative programs, services, and opportunities to support the success of students and to promote healthy families and engaged communities."[63]

Figure 1 shows the locations of community schools in Tulsa-Union. It is important to note that not only do nearly all of the elementary schools operate as full-service community schools, but they also provide a broad array of services, including early childhood education, health services and health education, mental health and social services, youth development and recreation, after-school support programs, and family and community engagement initiatives.

Tulsa-Union is not alone in embracing the concept of building a social safety net for children. Since 1988, the state of Oklahoma has made early childhood education available to all children through public funding. According to Skip Steele, a Republican member of the Tulsa City Council, "This isn't a liberal issue. This is about investing in our kids. It just makes sense."[64]

The Oklahoma early childhood initiative was made possible in part by the financial contributions of George B. Kaiser, a Tulsa billionaire who made his money in the oil industry. Kaiser claims that he became an advocate and investor in early childhood education after becoming aware of research in neuroscience that shows the impact of early interventions on the development of

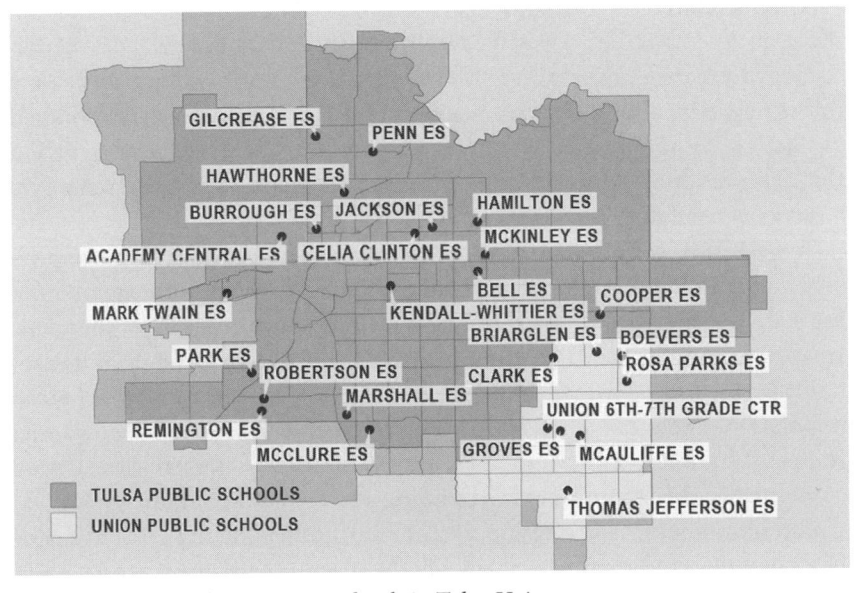

Figure 1. Location of community schools in Tulsa-Union

the brain. Because of his prominence and money, politicians were willing to listen to the evidence he presented and the moral argument he made: that all children should have access to early learning opportunities.

In addition to community schools, Tulsa-Union has embraced the Obama administration's Promise Neighborhood initiative to advance its efforts to combat poverty in the poorest areas. The initiative is based in the Kendall-Whittier and Eugene Field sections of Tulsa, where 30 percent of the households have incomes that fall below the poverty line and 46 percent of residents are Latino, the fastest-growing ethnic group in the metropolitan region. The theory of change described in the Promise Neighborhood proposal focuses on making early childhood education available for every three-year-old combined with interventions designed to strengthen the economic and physical health of low-income parents to reduce intergenerational poverty. The effort is financed by a combination of public and private funds and is not dependent on support from the federal government.

The Promise Neighborhood initiative is part of a larger strategy being pursued throughout the Tulsa-Union metropolitan area to use education as a central part of the strategy for countering poverty and boosting economic development in poor neighborhoods. The plan appears to be registering some progress. Community schools, the opening of several new recreation and arts centers, the expansion of job training opportunities through adult education programs offered by local universities, and several new housing developments in several of the poorest neighborhoods are all part of the Tulsa-Union strategy to reduce poverty. In contrast with the rhetoric espoused by many in the new education reform movement and the strategy that was pursued by Michael Bloomberg in New York City, there is an explicit recognition that schools alone cannot combat poverty and that a more comprehensive strategy is needed.[65]

Tulsa-Union continues to face significant challenges with respect to poverty and the quality of life in poor communities. Although unemployment rates are relatively low (5 percent), poverty rates have risen in recent years. In 2012, 35 percent of all children under the age of five came from households in poverty.[66] Poverty rates are highest among the fast-growing Latino population, and relatively few Latinos have been employed in professional roles in the public sector, where advocacy for services is most likely to occur. Nonetheless, the commitment to building a safety net for children in Tulsa-Union sets its reform strategy apart from most others taking place in major U.S. cities today. Only time will tell whether or not the strategy is successful in meeting the educational needs of students and enhancing the quality of life in the neighborhoods where they and their families reside.

CONCLUSION

New York and Tulsa-Union provide interesting contexts from which to compare and contrast the ways in which the education reform strategies being pursued are impacting poor, urban communities. Though school improvement and higher levels of academic achievement have been embraced as goals by both cities, the strategies employed to realize these goals have been markedly different. By analyzing the differences in these strategies and assessing their impact on the schools and communities that have been targeted by the initiatives, it is possible to make explicit how cities generally and low-income neighborhoods specifically are affected by different approaches to education reform.

During the Bloomberg years (2002–13), New York became the showcase for what is now termed market-based reform.[67] Private foundations, hedge fund companies, banks, and wealthy individuals embraced the Bloomberg strategy and contributed significant sums of money to support it. The Bill and Melinda Gates Foundation alone contributed over $1 billion to the development of dozens of new schools throughout New York City.[68] Bloomberg and Chancellor Joel Klein took a no-holds-barred approach as they pursued their reform agenda and swiftly dismissed all critics as defenders of the status quo. In a striking contrast to the strategy pursued in Tulsa-Union (and supported by at least one oil billionaire there), poverty was treated as an unimportant issue in New York. In fact, a 2010 editorial by Klein and his allies in the *Washington Post* lays out their position: "In the debate over how to fix American public education, many believe that schools alone cannot overcome the impact that economic disadvantage has on a child, that life outcomes are fixed by poverty and family circumstances, and that education doesn't work until other problems are solved. This theory is, in some ways, comforting for educators. . . . Problem is, the theory is wrong. It's hard to know how wrong but plenty of evidence demonstrates that schools can make an enormous difference despite the challenges presented by poverty and family background."[69]

To their supporters, such assertions were encouraging because they suggested that poverty would not be an obstacle to the success of the Bloomberg reform agenda. However, as poverty and homeless rates rose in New York City, particularly during and after the recession of 2008, it became increasingly clear that the idea that poverty could be ignored was not only naive but in some ways even callous. In 2012, child poverty rates in New York City rose to their highest level in over a decade. While the child poverty rate for the United States rose to 22 percent, in New York City it rose to over 31 percent.[70]

While Bloomberg and Klein may not be responsible for the rise in poverty, their steadfast refusal to acknowledge the problem or to direct additional help to the schools that were serving the greatest number of poor children left many schools across the city foundering.

Ironically, while the "no-excuses" strategy was popular in a politically liberal city like New York, Republican controlled Tulsa-Union was constructing a safety net for poor children, a strategy that evoked memories of the War on Poverty policies of Lyndon B. Johnson. Like the reforms carried out in New York City, the Tulsa-Union strategy was backed with funding from a private philanthropist but guided by local community leaders who established TACSI. Ironically, Bloomberg enthusiastically supported the Harlem Children's Zone developed by Geoffrey Canada, an antipoverty program that provided a broad array of academic and social services to six thousand poor children in central Harlem. Yet, he and the DOE refused to adopt similar strategies at the schools located at the poorest neighborhoods in the city despite clear evidence that these schools were experiencing the highest degree of failure. During the Bloomberg years, the only strategy put forward to address their struggles was closure.

In Tulsa-Union, the commitment to create community schools in high-poverty neighborhoods was combined with a willingness to develop partnerships with community-based organizations that would take the lead in providing some services (particularly after school programs) and conducting outreach to families. According to community activists like Frances Jordan Rakestraw, the executive director of the Greenwood Cultural Center, and attorney Hannibal Johnson in Tulsa, community schools opened the door to "parents and community leaders who care about the welfare of our children. It has given us a sense of ownership over our schools and a way to be involved."[71] While private foundations provide the bulk of the funding to support the initiative, the board directing TACSI consists of a diverse cross section of community members who have deep roots in the communities where the programs are based. However, the rapidly growing Latino population is the one community that is significantly underrepresented in leadership of the Tulsa-Union reform initiative. According to district leaders, this is an issue that they are working on and hope to address in the near future.

Poor communities in New York and Tulsa-Union continue to be beset by enormous hardships and challenges. Angie Avery, a community activist with the community-schools network in Tulsa, told me that a recent food giveaway in Tulsa generated lines with hundreds of people. "We knew there were lots of people who were living on the edge but we had no idea how many. Given the lines we saw I can only imagine how many families with children must be going hungry on a regular basis. We're doing a lot to help them but we have to do more."[72]

The same could be said of New York. In what was considered a repudiation of Bloomberg and his policies, New York voters elected Bill de Blasio mayor in 2013. De Blasio was seen as the anti-Bloomberg: an unabashed progressive who promised to focus on reducing poverty and inequality once elected. Like public officials in Tulsa-Union, de Blasio campaigned on a promise that he would make access to preschool universal and bring an array of social services into public schools to help address social issues related to poverty. While it is far too early to assess the effectiveness of his education policies or their impact on low-income communities, there is no doubt that public schools in New York City are now on a different course.

Bipartisan support for community schools is now beginning to emerge in the U.S. Congress. A bill introduced in July 2014 by House Minority Whip Steny Hoyer (D-MD) and Rep. Aaron Schock (R-IL), called the Full-Service Community Schools Act, was referred to committee in November 2014 and no action has yet been taken as of this writing. The press release in support of the bill noted: "the bill authorizes funding for full-service community schools, which . . . can be found in nearly 100 places across the country, from Oakland, CA and Cincinnati, OH to Lincoln, NE and Albuquerque, NM. If authorized, this bill would increase the number of places implementing community schools across the country, and enlist communities as key partners for student success."[73] If this bill were to have been passed by the highly polarized Congress, it could very well have signaled a major shift in the direction of education reform nationally.

The race-class dynamics of education reform in New York and Tulsa-Union also provide an interesting basis for comparison. In New York, a top-down approach was taken in which reformers from City Hall and the DOE determined how the failing schools in the poorest communities would be fixed. The approach taken was highly paternalistic because the architects assumed they alone possessed the technical expertise needed to address the chronic school failure. In Tulsa-Union, not only was poverty identified as a central focus of reform, but community partners also were embraced as partners in the effort. As a result of this effort, individuals from marginalized neighborhoods in Tulsa-Union described themselves as "empowered and engaged" in the school reform work, while in New York most neighborhood activists found themselves protesting decisions made about their schools by powerful elites.

McDonald reminds us in his *American School Reform* that the history of educational policy in the United States over the last thirty years has been characterized by sweeping reform initiatives that have been offered periodically as a means to overhaul and elevate U.S. education to new heights.[74] When promoted by elected officials, the reforms have typically been offered as a means for the nation to maintain its competitive advantage. I have described David Tyack and Larry Cuban's analysis "as an elusive march toward utopia."[75] They point out that the grand promises of reform that are typically issued each time a new administration assumes office have often ignored the underlying social and economic challenges that impact education: "Leaders inside and outside of education generally share a common vision of scientific management as a blueprint for re-organizing the school system. Such approaches avoid intractable problems such as social inequality and racial discrimination and place unrealistic expectations upon schools."[76] Sociologist Charles Payne, in his critique of major school reform initiatives carried out in Chicago from 1995 to 2006, has made a similar point. He asks: "So much reform . . . why so little change?"[77] For poor people in urban communities throughout the United States, that question continues as pertinent as ever.

Notes

1. Jane Jacobs, *The Death and Life of Great American Cities* (New York: Random House, 1961).

2. Manuel Castells, *The City and the Grassroots: A Cross-Cultural Theory of Urban Social Movements* (Berkeley: University of California Press, 1983).

3. Paul Grogan and Tony Proscio, *Comeback Cities: A Blueprint for Urban Neighborhood Revival* (Boulder, Colo.: Westview Press, 2001); Robert Worth, "Guess Who Saved the South Bronx? Big Government," *Washington Monthly* 31, no. 4 (1999): 26–33; Howell Raines, "Reagan, in Speeches, Doesn't Let the Facts Spoil a Good Anecdote or Effective Symbol," *New York Times* (1980), www.nytimes.com, October 19.

4. William Julius Wilson, *The Truly Disadvantaged: The Inner City, the Underclass, and Public Policy* (Chicago: University of Chicago Press, 1987).

5. Jal Mehta, *The Allure of Order* (Cambridge: Oxford University Press, 2013).

6. On unending education reform since the 1960s, see David Tyack and Larry Cuban, *Tinkering toward Utopia: A Century of Urban School Reform* (Cambridge, Mass.: Harvard University Press, 1995).

7. Tyack and Cuban, *Tinkering toward Utopia*.

8. Mehta, *Allure of Order*.

9. Joseph McDonald et al., *American School Reform: What Works, What Fails, and Why* (Chicago: University of Chicago Press, 2014); Michael Fullan and Alan Boyle, *Big City School Reform: Lessons from New York, Toronto and London* (New York: Teachers College Press, 2014).

10. Pauline Lipman, *The New Political Economy of Urban Education: Neo-Liberalism, Race and the Right to the City* (New York: Routledge, 2011).

11. J. G. Dryfoos, J. Quinn, and C. Barkin, *Community Schools in Action: Lessons from a Decade of Practice* (New York: Oxford University Press, 2005).

12. On the impact to schools, see Steven Brill, *Class Warfare: Inside the Fight to Fix America's Schools* (New York: Simon and Schuster, 2011); Fullan and Boyle, *Big City School Reform*; McDonald et al., *American School Reform*.

13. On public health, see S. L. Syme, "Social Determinants of Health: The Community as Empowered Partner," *Preventing Chronic Disease: Public Health Research, Practice, and Policy* 1, no. 1 (2004): 1–4.

14. Dorinda J. Carter Andrews and Frank Tuitt, eds., *Contesting the Myth of a 'Post Racial Era': The Continued Significance of Race in U.S. Education* (New York: Peter Lang, 2013).

15. On racial disparities, see Prudence Carter and Kevin Wellner, eds., *Closing the Opportunity Gap: What America Must Do to Give Every Child an Even Chance* (Oxford: Oxford University Press, 2013).

16. Gene Maeroff, "Withered Hopes, Stillborn Dreams: The Dismal Panorama of Urban Education," *Phi Delta Kappan* 69, no. 9 (1988): 37–39, 16.

17. America's Promise Alliance, *Building a GradNation* (Washington, D.C.: America's Promise Alliance, 2014).

18. P. Barton and R. Coley, *The Black-White Achievement Gap: When Progress Stopped* (Princeton, N.J.: Education Testing Service, 2009).

19. Council of Great City Schools, *Beating the Odds: Analysis of Student Performance on State Assessments* (Washington, D.C.: Council of Great City Schools, 2014).

20. K. Chenoweth, *It's Being Done: Academic Success in Unexpected Schools* (Cambridge, Mass.: Harvard Education Press, 2010).

21. U.S. Department of Education, *Evaluation Brief. Schools Identified as in Need of Improvement Under Title I: Recent Evidence from the National Longitudinal Survey of Schools* (Washington, D.C.: U.S. Department of Education, 2013).

22. A. Wade Boykin and Pedro Noguera, *Creating the Opportunity to Learn: Moving from Research to Practice to Close the Achievement Gap* (Alexandria, Va.: ASCD, 2011).

23. James B. Conant, *Slums and Suburbs: A Commentary on Schools in Metropolitan Areas* (New York: McGraw-Hill, 1961), 2.

24. Richard Rothstein, *Class and School* (Washington, D.C.: Economic Policy Institute, 2004).

25. Michelle Fine, *Framing Dropouts: Notes on the Politics of an Urban Public High School* (Albany, N.Y.: SUNY Press, 1988).

26. Jean Anyon, *Ghetto Schooling: A Political Economy of Urban Educational Reform* (New York: Teachers College Press, 1997).

27. Charles Payne, *Getting What We Ask For: The Ambiguity of Success and Failure in Urban Education* (Santa Barbara, Calif.: Greenwood Publishing, 1984).

28. A. S. Bryk et al., *Organizing Schools for Improvement: Lessons from Chicago* (Chicago: University of Chicago Press, 2010).

29. According to Bryk et al., the five essential ingredients needed for school improvement are an instructional guidance system, continuous professional capacity building, a student-centered learning climate, strong parent and community partnerships, and strong leadership.

30. McDonald et al., *American School Reform*, 143.

31. Pedro Noguera, *City Schools and the American Dream: Reclaiming the Promise of Public Education* (New York: Teachers College Press, 2003).

32. Rothstein, *Class and School*; Barton and Colcy, *The Black-White Achievement Gap*; Diane Ravitch, *The Death and Life of the Great American School System* (New York: Basic Books, 2010).

33. Noguera, *City Schools and the American Dream*.

34. J. S. Coleman, *Foundations of Social Theory* (Cambridge, Mass.: Belknap Press of Harvard University Press, 1998); C. N. Stone et al., *Building Civic Capacity: The Politics of Reforming Urban Schools* (Lawrence: University of Kansas Press, 2001); Noguera, *City Schools and the American Dream*.

35. Wilson, *Truly Disadvantaged*; Loic Waquant, "Deadly Symbiosis: When Ghetto and Prison Meet and Mesh," *Punishment and Society* 3, no. 1 (2001): 95–133.

36. Wilson, *Truly Disadvantaged*.

37. Michelle Alexander, *The New Jim Crow: Mass Incarceration in the Age of Colorblindness* (New York: New Press, 2010).

38. On positive capital, see Coleman, *Foundations of Social Theory*. On negative capital, see L. Wacquant, "Negative Social Capital: State Breakdown and Social Destitution in America's Urban Core," *Netherlands Journal of Housing and the Built Environment* 13, no. 1 (1998): 25–40.

39. J. Klein, "The Failure of American Schools," *Atlantic*, April 26, 2011.

40. Allison Gendar, "Shaking Up the City Schools Bloomberg Vows a Better Education," *New York Daily News*, January 16, 2003.

41. David Chen and Michael Barbarao, "Bloomberg Wins 3rd Term as Mayor in Unexpectedly Close Race," *New York Times*, November 3, 2009.

42. Paul Hill, "Bloomberg's Education Plan Is Working: Don't Ditch It," *Atlantic*, October 22, 2013.

43. Jennifer Medina, "State's Exams Became Easier to Pass, Education Officials Say," *New York Times*, July 19, 2010.

44. Schott Foundation, *A Rotting Apple: Education Redlining in New York City Schools* (Cambridge, Mass.: Schott Foundation, 2012).

45. New York City Department of Education, *NYC Secondary Reform Selected Analysis* (Boston: Parthenon Group, 2009).

46. The DOE school closure plan called for schools to shrink gradually over time by not allowing new cohorts of ninth graders in the case of high schools, or sixth graders in the case of middle schools, to enroll. A report by the Annenberg Institute found that teacher and student attrition at the schools subjected to phase out was

higher than at other schools because all who could found ways to "abandon the sinking ship." Annenberg Institute, *The Way Forward: From Sanctions to Supports* (New York: New York City Working Group, 2012).

47. Howard S. Bloom, Saskia Levy Thompson, and Rebecca Unterman, *Transforming the High School Experience* (New York: Manpower Research and Development Corporation, 2010).

48. Norm Fruchter et al., *Is Demography Still Destiny? Neighborhood Demographics and Public High School Students' Readiness for College in New York City* (Providence, R.I.: Annenberg Institute for School Reform, Brown University, 2012), http://annenberg institute.org/, accessed May 27, 2015.

49. Community Service Society, "Statement on the Latest New York City Poverty Rates," press release, Community Service Society, 2013.

50. Annenberg Institute, *Way Forward*.

51. Schott Foundation, *Rotting Apple*.

52. Pedro Noguera, "Closing Schools Won't Fix Them," *City Limits*, July 1, 2010.

53. Stephanie Banchero and Caroline Porter, "Charter Schools Fall Short on Disabled," *Wall Street Journal*, June 19, 2012.

54. Schott Foundation, *Rotting Apple*.

55. McDonald et al., *American School Reform*, 51.

56. Scott Ellsworth, "Tulsa Race Riot," Oklahoma Historical Society, 2009.

57. A. G. Stulzburger, "As Survivors Dwindle, Tulsa Confronts Past," *New York Times*, www.nytimes.com, accessed June 20, 2011.

58. Kucsera, J., with G. Orfield, *New York State's Extreme School Segregation: Inequality, Inaction, and a Damaged Future* (N.p.: Civil Rights Project/Projecto derechos civiles, March 2014), accessed May 25, 2015, http://civilrightsproject.ucla.edu.

59. Tulsa Public Schools, Tulsa Public Schools—District Summary, no date, http://www.tulsaschools.org/, accessed May 25, 2015.

60. "Welcome to Union Public Schools!," *Union Public Schools*, http://www.unionps.org/, accessed May 28, 2015.

61. "Coalition for Community Schools," Institute for Educational Leadership, www.communityschools.org/, accessed May 25, 2015.

62. "TACSI: Tulsa Area Community Schools Initiative," *Community Service Council*, http://csctulsa.org/, accessed May 25, 2015.

63. Ibid.

64. Nicholas Kristoff, "Oklahoma: Where Learning Starts Early," *New York Times*, November 13, 2013.

65. Rebecca Hollis, "Schools Alone Cannot Counter Poverty: They Need a Community," *Oklahoma Policy Institute*, 2014, http://okpolicy.org/, accessed May 25, 2015.

66. Community Service Council, "Who Is Tulsa: The Changing Population of the City of Tulsa and Tulsa County," Tulsa, OK, 2012.

67. Lipman, *New Political Economy of Urban Education*; Fullan, *Big City School Reform*.

68. Diane Ravitch, "Bill Gates and His Silver Bullet," *Forbes Magazine*, November 19, 2008.

69. J. Klein, M. Lomax, and J. Muraguia, "Poverty Is Not the Issue," *Washington Post*, April 9, 2010.

70. S. Roberts, "Poverty Rate Is Up, and Income Gap Is Wide in New York City, Census Data Shows," *New York Times*, September 19, 2013.

71. Hannibal Johnson, interview with the author, June 2014.

72. Angie Avery, interview with the author, June 20, 2014.

73. Coalition for Community Schools and Institute for Educational Leadership, "Bipartisan Bill Introduced to Expand Community Schools," July 23, 2014.

74. McDonald et al., *American School Reform*.

75. Pedro A. Noguera and Lauren Wells, "The Politics of School Reform: A Broader and Bolder Approach to Newark," *Berkeley Review of Education* 2, no. 1 (2011).

76. Tyack and Cuban, *Tinkering toward Utopia*, 46.

77. C. Payne, *So Much Reform, So Little Change: The Persistence of Failure in Urban Schools* (Cambridge, Mass.: Harvard Education Press, 2008).

Other References

Dryfoos, J. "Schools as Places for Health, Mental Health, and Social Services." *Teachers College Record* 94, no. 3 (1993): 540–67.

Fruchter, Norman. *Urban Schools, Public Will: Making Education Work for All Our Children.* New York: Teachers College Press, 2007.

Fruchter, N. M., M. Hester, C. Mokhtar, and Z. Shahn. 2012. *Is Demography Still Destiny? Neighborhood Demographics and Public High School Students' Readiness for College in New York City.* Providence, R.I.: Annenberg Institute for School Reform at Brown University, 2012. http://annenberginstitute.org/. Accessed May 27, 2015.

Greenberg, M., and Schneider, D. *Environmentally Devastated Neighborhoods: Perceptions, Policies, and Realities.* New Brunswick, N.J.: Rutgers University Press, 1996.

LaShaw, A. "The Radical Promise of Reformist Zeal: What Makes Inquiry for Equity Plausible?" *Anthropology and Education* 41, no. 4 (2010): 323–40.

Oakes, J. *Keeping Track: How Schools Structure Inequality.* 2nd ed. New Haven, Conn.: Yale University Press, 2005.

Rothstein, R. "Out of Balance: Our Understanding of How Schools Affect Society and How Society Affects Schools." *The Spencer Foundation 30th Anniversary Essay.* Chicago: Spencer Foundation, 2002.

Sampson, R. J., Raudenbush, S. W., and Earls, F. "Neighborhoods and Violent Crime: A Multilevel Study of Collective Efficacy." *Science* 277 (1997): 918–23.

Tabb, W. *The Political Economy of the Black Ghetto.* New York: W. W. Norton, 1970.

The Janus-Faced Neighborhood School

DISCUSSANT: ELIZABETH S. TODD-BRELAND,
UNIVERSITY OF ILLINOIS AT CHICAGO

Groups on opposing sides of education debates have used the rhetoric and ideology of "the neighborhood school" to achieve very different ends. The iconic neighborhood school was a school that children could easily walk to from their home—a school that served a defined attendance area within a community, without additional special admissions policies. Since the mid-twentieth century, groups with conflicting interests—including white segregationists and racial moderates, black and white antibusing supporters, and African Americans struggling for community control and funding equalization—have advocated for preserving neighborhood schools. In contemporary education reform debates, opponents of the market-based privatization of public education have again worked to defend and improve neighborhood schools. Understanding the drastically different ideological and rhetorical uses of neighborhood schools reveals how urbanites' understanding of "the neighborhood" was profoundly shaped by histories of racial discrimination and structural inequality and exposes an enduring tension between the ideals of desegregation and efforts to maintain neighborhood schools.

In the wake of the 1954 *Brown v. Board of Education* decision, segregationist white southerners responded to court-ordered desegregation with massive resistance, while moderate white southerners in metropolitan areas asserted their desire to support local neighborhood schools. Maintaining neighborhood-based school attendance areas allowed for nominal integration near borders between black and white communities and token integration by some middle-class blacks. These plans, predicated on the neighborhood school, relied on neighborhood residential segregation to prevent widespread comprehensive integration.[1]

In northern cities with high levels of residential segregation, school officials also used the defense of neighborhood schools to maintain school segregation. In Chicago during the 1960s, black parents and community activists increasingly questioned why black students were warehoused in overcrowded schools but barred access to open seats in nearby predominantly white schools. To alleviate these inequities, parents and community members demanded the desegregation of Chicago Public Schools. Superintendent

Benjamin Willis was insistent that maintaining neighborhood schools was the best way to ensure quality education. Willis used this commitment as a justification for his opposition to desegregation.[2] Rather than move black students from overcrowded black schools into empty seats in predominantly white schools, Willis built portable temporary classrooms for overcrowded black schools.[3] These policies relegated black students to separate and unequal segregated schools.

In the late 1960s, in a peculiar convergence of rhetoric and politics, groups of white and black parents used the symbol of the neighborhood school in antibusing movements. In cities with extreme residential segregation, busing was often proposed as a means to desegregate schools.[4] Mothers Support Neighborhood Schools, a group of white women in San Francisco, rallied in 1969 against a proposed busing plan, claiming it threatened the sanctity of neighborhood schools. Despite using the rhetoric of a commitment to neighborhood schools, surveys revealed that whites' aversion to busing plans for desegregation actually reflected white parents' opposition to plans that required their children to travel to attend predominantly black or Latino schools.[5]

At the same time, groups of African American parents were also voicing their opposition to busing. In an effort to appease white parents, one-way busing plans were established that required black students to be bused into white schools in white communities but did not require white students to be bused into black communities. Black parents contended that limited one-way busing plans put an unfair burden on black students, reinforced ideas of black inferiority, and ignored the majority of black students who were left behind in under-resourced schools within black communities. Increasingly, black parents argued that, like white children, their children were entitled to receive a quality education at schools in their own neighborhoods. They insisted that quality education should include more black teachers and administrators and a curriculum that incorporated black history and culture. These demands formed the foundation of black movements for community control of schools in the 1960s and 1970s. Rather than continue the fight for desegregation, black activists sought control of the public institutions serving their neighborhoods. Black education reformers pursued strategies to achieve quality education within predominantly black schools in black neighborhoods.[6]

Debates over neighborhood schools have surfaced again in contemporary urban education reform struggles. Since the early 2000s, school systems in Chicago, Cleveland, Denver, Detroit, Kansas City, New York City, St. Louis, and other large cities have shuttered many traditional neighborhood public schools in predominantly black and Latino neighborhoods. Simultaneously, these school systems allowed privately managed charter schools to open, often in the very same communities where neighborhood public schools were closed. In contrast to traditional neighborhood public schools, many charter schools admit students using a lottery system and do not always require that students live in nearby neighborhoods. As privately managed schools, charter schools often lack oversight by, and accountability to, the people living in those communities, prompting local protests and concerns over the privatization of public education. In this context, saving and improving neighborhood schools has become a rallying cry for opponents of charter schools, school choice programs, and market-based school reform policies.[7]

Here, history offers an interesting lesson about language, ideology, and strategy. Grassroots community organizations and progressive education reformers have repurposed the rhetorical defense of neighborhood schools, used in different ways by both segregationists and black community control activists, to make claims for a more equitable distribution of resources in cities' most under-resourced and racially isolated communities. Establishing engaged, well-resourced, high-performing neighborhood schools as anchors in communities would go a long way toward improving education in urban neighborhoods. However, as I have argued, the history of the rhetoric and ideology of neighborhood schools has been rife with contradiction. Rather than center future struggles on the neighborhood school as a solution to urban inequities, in and of itself, it is important to be vigilant that strategies that center on neighborhood schools also align with policies that promote racial and economic justice more broadly.

Notes

1. The *Brown* case declared that "separate educational facilities are inherently unequal." In *Brown II*, a year later, the court ordered local districts to implement the 1954 decision with "all deliberate speed." In Virginia, Georgia, Arkansas and other southern states, government officials pursued closing entire public school systems and redistributing public school resources to private white segregationist academies, rather than desegregate existing public schools. "History of Brown v. Board of Education," *United States Courts*, accessed June 30, 2014, www.uscourts.gov/; Matthew D. Lassiter, *The Silent Majority: Suburban Politics in the Sunbelt South* (Princeton, N.J.: Princeton University Press, 2007), 13–14; Kevin M. Kruse, *White Flight: Atlanta and the Making of Modern Conservatism* (Princeton, N.J.: Princeton University Press, 2007), 131–60, 169–72.

2. In Chicago during the 1950s, schools in black communities were often over-crowded, in poor physical condition, and lacked adequate teaching supplies. Many of these schools operated on double shifts to accommodate overcrowding, resulting in students attending school for half-day shifts and sharing books and other teaching resources. Barbara A. Sizemore, *Walking in Circles: The Black Struggle for School Reform* (Chicago: Third World Press, 2008), 42; John Hall Fish, *Black Power/White Control: The Struggle of the Woodlawn Organization in Chicago* (Princeton, N.J.: Princeton University Press, 1973), 175–76; John L. Rury, "Race, Space, and the Politics of Chicago Public Schools: Benjamin Willis and the Tragedy of Urban Education," *History of Education Quarterly* 39, no. 2 (1999): 117–42, 124–26.

3. Willis took a color-blind approach to racial issues in the schools, claiming that because the school system did not keep track of racial statistics, he was not in a position to address accusations of race-based inequality in the city's schools. Michael Homel, "The Politics of Public Education in Black Chicago, 1910–1941," *Journal of Negro Education* 45, no. 2 (1976): 179–91, 183; Dionne Danns, *Something Better for Our Children: Black Organizing in Chicago Public Schools, 1963–1971*, Studies in African American History and Culture (New York: Routledge, 2003), 26.

4. Gary Orfield, *Must We Bus? Segregated Schools and National Policy* (Washington, D.C.: Brookings Institution, 1978); James T. Patterson, *Brown v. Board of Education: A Civil Rights Milestone and Its Troubled Legacy* (Oxford: Oxford University Press, 2001), 178–81; Jeanne Theoharis, "'I'd Rather Go to School in the South': How Boston's School Desegregation Complicates the Civil Rights Paradigm," in *Freedom North: Black Freedom Struggles Outside the South, 1940–1980*, ed. Jeanne Theoharis and Komozi Woodard, 125–52 (New York: Palgrave McMillan, 2003).

5. Russell Rickford, "Integration, Black Nationalism, and Radical Democratic Transformation in African American Philosophies of Education, 1965–74," in *The New Black History: Revisiting the Second Reconstruction*, ed. Manning Marable and Elizabeth Kai Hinton, 287–317 (New York: Palgrave Macmillan, 2011), 289–90; Orfield, *Must We Bus?*, 115–18, 250.

6. Danns, *Something Better for Our Children*, 66–71; Dionne Danns, *Desegregating Chicago's Public Schools: Policy Implementation, Politics, and Protest, 1965–1985* (New York: Palgrave Macmillan, 2014), 19–27; Rickford, "Integration, Black Nationalism, and Radical Democratic Transformation in African American Philosophies of Education, 1965–1974," 289–90; Joseph Cronin, *The Control of Urban Schools: Perspective on the Power of Educational Reformers* (New York: Free Press, 1973), 182–83. For more on community control, see Joy Williamson, "Community Control with a Black Nationalist Twist: The Black Panther Party's Educational Programs," in *Black Protest Thought and Education*, ed. William H. Watkins, 137–57 (New York: Peter Lang, 2005); Jerald Podair, *The Strike That Changed New York: Blacks, Whites, and the Ocean Hill-Brownsville Crisis* (New Haven, Conn.: Yale University Press, 2002); Jane Anna Gordon, *Why They Couldn't Wait: A Critique of the Black-Jewish Conflict over Community Control in Ocean Hill–Brownsville (1967–1971)* (New York:

Routledge, 2001); Daniel Perlstein, *Justice, Justice: School Politics and the Eclipse of Liberalism* (New York: Peter Lang, 2004); Clarence Taylor, ed., *Civil Rights in New York City: From World War II to the Giuliani Era* (New York: Fordham University Press, 2011); Marilyn Gittell et al., *Local Control in Education: Three Demonstration School Districts in New York City* (New York: Praeger, 1972).

7. Michael Fabricant and Michelle Fine, *Charter Schools and the Corporate Makeover of Public Education: What's at Stake?* (New York: Teachers College Press, 2012); Pauline Lipman, *The New Political Economy of Urban Education: Neoliberalism, Race, and the Right to the City* (New York: Routledge, 2011). Monica Martinez, "Learning Deserts," *Phi Delta Kappan* 92, 5 (2011): 72–73.

Migrant Civil Society
and the Metropolitics of Belonging

NIK THEODORE

UNIVERSITY OF ILLINOIS AT CHICAGO

NEW URBAN LANDSCAPES OF MIGRATION

In July 2014, President Barack Obama conceded that efforts to enact comprehensive immigration reform had failed, marking the fourth time in eight years that a congressional impasse prevented significant reforms to the nation's immigration system. Reforming immigration laws is a federal matter. The U.S. Supreme Court has repeatedly affirmed the federal government's plenary authority, granting sole power to the legislative and executive branches to regulate all aspects of immigration. But despite clear directives from the court, there are signs that the locus of immigration policy making may be changing.

Increasingly, state and local governments are enacting a variety of policies related to immigration. At one end of the political spectrum is a set of local policies aimed at immigrant integration. These policies establish programs to expand access to public services, such as legal aide, employment assistance, and social services, or they otherwise seek to regularize the status of immigrants through measures such as municipal identification cards. The objectives of these policies include promoting social cohesion and improving health, employment, education, and public-safety outcomes for residents. At the other end of the spectrum are policies with overtly restrictionist objectives. They seek to deny unauthorized immigrants access to public services, such as education and health care; penalize landlords and employers who rent housing to or hire undocumented immigrants; and institute English-only laws governing municipal affairs. Some laws have gone so far as to criminalize first responders, social workers, community organizers, and members of the general public who knowingly provide assistance to undocumented immigrants. Many such laws have been found to be unconstitutional and have been struck down in federal court. But these court rulings have not staunched the spread of "illegal immigration relief acts," as they are commonly known. Model legislation has moved from jurisdiction to jurisdiction and has been introduced in every region of the country.

The congressional impasse on immigration reform has not meant that the federal government has been inactive in this policy domain. Deportation figures have climbed, surpassing the two million mark during the Obama presidency; the number of border patrol agents has never been higher; the Secure Communities and 287(g) programs have enlisted local police in immigration enforcement; and, in a development that the Obama administration has characterized as a humanitarian crisis, more than sixty thousand youths were apprehended at the Mexico-U.S. border in just a four-month period in 2014, leading the administration to pursue expedited deportations of minors. Immigrant communities have responded to these developments by escalating their political engagement through mass demonstrations, civil disobedience, litigation, consumer boycotts, legislative advocacy, media campaigns, and community organizing. These activities have, at times, been incorrectly described by journalists as "spontaneous" bursts of dissent, thereby inadvertently underplaying the foundational role that civil society actors have played in laying the groundwork for social activism, scripting political narratives, mobilizing popular sentiments, and galvanizing public support.[1] Community organizations, particularly those that have been established by immigrants, are now a major political force in the United States, articulating the interests of a growing immigrant population.

This chapter examines the shifting landscape of immigration politics in the United States, with a focus on how municipal governments and civil-society organizations have sought to meet the challenges that attend to the growing immigrant populations in urban areas. New urban landscapes of migration are made at the intersection of four meso-level dynamics: (1) migration flows, which can alter the demographic composition of a local populace; (2) the nature of the political climate within municipalities, including the partisan leanings of the electorate, which can profoundly shape the local context of migrant reception; (3) the structure of economy, particularly its industrial and occupational makeup, which shapes labor demand and affects working conditions; and (4) the characteristics of a city's civil society, which can act both as a local political force that affects policy outcomes and as a service provider that can help immigrants manage their everyday needs.

The chapter begins by examining recent patterns of immigration to urban areas and what these have meant for the demographic composition of cities and suburbs. The second section briefly considers the contested local politics of immigration reform in light of the federal government's repeated failure to enact comprehensive immigration reform legislation. Advocates and opponents of stricter immigration laws increasingly contend that the local scale is where opportunities are greatest for resolving many of the problems resulting from the nation's "broken immigration system." However, local immigration politics has been no less polarized than at the national level, and municipalities have adopted diametrically opposed stances on immigration issues. Moreover, the local political climate in large part determines the field of play for immigrant groups by dictating whether these organizations will be required to adopt a defensive stance against punitive policies or whether there is scope to pursue innovative initiatives to enhance immigrant incorporation. The third section explores the maturation of "migrant civil society," both as a political force and as a service provider. Civil-society organizations have stepped into the fray of contentious immigration politics, advocating for more inclusive policies at the federal, state, and local levels. The final section summarizes some of the key policies and programs that have been adopted by cities, often at the urging of or in partnership with immigrant-serving organizations, with the goal of facilitating immigrant social, economic, civic, and political incorporation.

IMMIGRANT GATEWAYS, NEW AND OLD

Migration to the United States has been increasing steadily since the 1970s, rising especially sharply during the 1990s and into the 2000s (fig. 1). As of 2012, the United States was home to an estimated 40.8 million immigrants—13 percent of the total population. Approximately 11.7 million of these immigrants are in the country without authorization, slightly down from a peak of 12.2 million in 2007.[2]

These figures do not reveal the complexity of the demographic shifts that have occurred. Migration flows have always been geographically uneven, and the unprecedented wave of migration that occurred in the 1990s and 2000s was no exception. Currently, more than two-thirds of all immigrants,[3] and 60 percent of unauthorized immigrants,[4] reside in just six states: California,

Figure 1. Number of Immigrants Living in the United States, 1950–2010

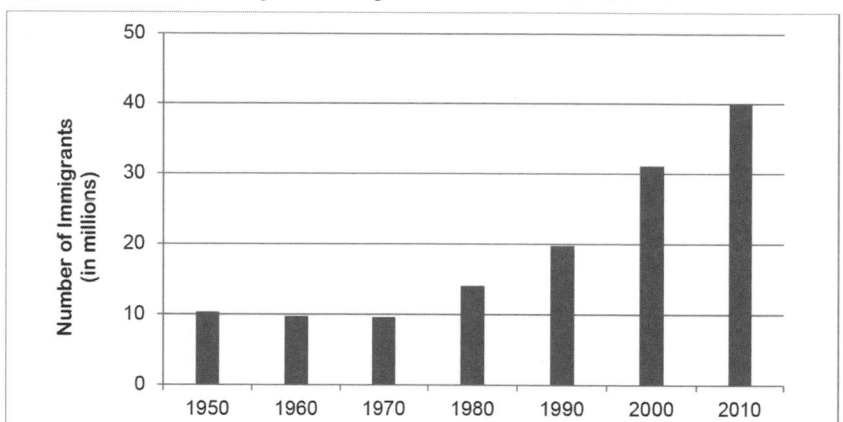

Source: Migration Policy Institute tabulation of data from the U.S. Census Bureau's 2012, 2011, and 2010 American Community Surveys and 1970, 1990, and 2000 decennial census data. All other data are from Campbell J. Gibson and Emily Lennon, U.S. Census Bureau, Working Paper No. 29, *Historical Census Statistics on the Foreign-Born Population of the United States: 1850 to 1990* (Washington, D.C.: U.S. Government Printing Office, 1999).

Florida, Illinois, New Jersey, New York, and Texas. However, during the 1990s, the share of the nation's immigrants living in these states declined for the first time.[5] In large part due to booming job markets outside traditional port-of-entry cities, new gateway cities emerged as key destinations for recent immigrants. The resulting pattern of migration is now more diverse, both in terms of the metropolitan areas in which immigrants have settled and the communities within those areas where they now live. This section explores each of these dimensions in turn.

Audrey Singer has developed a useful typology of gateway cities that places immigrant ports of entry in historical context (table 1). *Former gateways*, like Buffalo, Cleveland, and Milwaukee, were important destinations for immigrants in the early years of the twentieth century but have seen little foreign migration in the last seventy years. *Continuous gateways*, like Chicago, New York, and San Francisco, witnessed large migration flows in the early 1900s and again after 1970. Having experienced modest levels of foreign in-migration in the early part of the century, *post–World War Two gateways*, like Los Angeles, Houston, and Miami, became major immigrant destinations after 1970. *Emerging gateways*, among them Atlanta, Dallas, and Las Vegas, saw their immigrant populations rise sharply after 1990. *Re-emerging gateways*,

Table 1. A Typology of Migrant Gateway Metropolitan Areas

Former	Continuous	Post–World War II	Emerging	Re-Emerging	Pre-Emerging
Baltimore	Bergen-Passaic, N.J.	Fort Lauderdale	Atlanta	Denver	Austin
Buffalo	Boston	Houston	Dallas	Minneapolis–St. Paul, Minn.	Charlotte, N.C.
Cleveland	Chicago	Los Angeles	Fort Worth	Oakland	Greensboro-Winston-Salem, N.C.
Detroit	Jersey City	Miami	Las Vegas	Phoenix	Raleigh-Durham, N.C.
Milwaukee, Wisc.	Middlesex-Somerset-Hunterdon, N.J.	Orange County, Calif.	Orlando	Portland, Oreg.	Salt Lake City
Philadelphia	Nassau-Suffolk, N.Y.	Riverside–San Bernardino, Calif.	Washington, D.C.	Sacramento	
Pittsburgh	New York	San Diego	West Palm Beach, Fla.	San Jose, Calif.	
St. Louis	Newark			Seattle	
	San Francisco			Tampa	

Former: Above national average in percentage foreign-born 1900–1930, followed by percentages below the national average in every decade through 2000
Continuous: Above-average percentage foreign-born for every decade 1900–2000
Post–World War II: Low percentage foreign-born until after 1950, followed by percentages higher than the national average for the remainder of century
Emerging: Very low percentage foreign-born until 1970, followed by high proportions in the post-1980 period
Re-Emerging: Similar pattern to continuous gateways: Foreign-born percentage exceeds national average 1900–1930, lags after 1930, then increases rapidly after 1980
Pre-Emerging: Very low percentages of foreign-born for the entire 20th century
Source: Audrey Singer, *The Rise of New Immigrant Gateways* (Washington, D.C.: Brookings Institution, 2004).

like Denver, San Jose, and Seattle, were home to large numbers of immigrants in the early 1900s, saw their share of foreign-born population decline throughout much the century, and then experienced large-scale in-migration after 1990. And finally, *pre-emerging gateways*, like Austin, Charlotte, and Salt Lake City, had small immigrant populations in 1980 but experienced rapid in-migration in the 1990s.

Turning to the changing residential location of immigrants within metropolitan areas, Manuel Pastor has critiqued the contemporary relevance of the "spatial assimilation model" that has guided scholarship on immigrant settlement patterns for decades.[6] With roots in the urbanization theories of the Chicago School, the predominant model of spatialized assimilation posits that immigrant households will initially locate in disadvantaged areas of central cities. As these households experience upward economic mobility, they will relocate from these immigrant enclaves to more prosperous neighborhoods and then to suburban areas. This model appears to have been fairly well-suited to the waves of European migration of the early and mid-twentieth century. But, as Pastor argues, federal immigration policy changes disrupted immigrant settlement patterns. In particular, the 1986 Immigration Reform and Control Act (IRCA), which granted amnesty to undocumented immigrants, provided new opportunities for residential mobility. Immigrants responded by moving to states such as Georgia, North Carolina, and Nevada, where job opportunities were abundant.[7] Likewise, formerly undocumented immigrants could bypass the traditional port-of-entry neighborhoods of central cities—where tightly knit social networks would insulate them from heightened exposure to immigration authorities—and move to suburban locales in search of jobs and better-quality, lower-cost housing. Pastor notes, however, that amnesty did not allow for unfettered movement among immigrants, especially nonwhite immigrants. Discrimination in housing markets led the new residential locations to be stratified by race, nationality, and class, leading to immigrant population clustering in some cities and suburbs, while other areas received few, if any, recent migrants.

For immigrants, there are at least two potential benefits to the increased, though still constrained, geographic dispersion of foreign-born populations. The first is economic. Because recent migrants tend to cluster in a relatively small number of industries and occupations, economic competition can be reduced through geographic dispersal.[8] Industry and occupation clustering, particularly in industries with high rates of workplace violations, can depress immigrant workers' wages and erode long-term economic security.[9] Residential mobility can open up new opportunities for immigrants to break out of occupational niches where wages have stagnated as a result of intense job competition.[10]

A second benefit is political. Pastor argues that "in some 'new' places . . . there is less deep-rooted and historic hostility to immigrants, and this can make immigrant integration a less politically explosive topic."[11] Of course, the reverse can hold as well; some of the cities with the most virulent anti-immigrant politics have experienced only modest migration flows. There are other drawbacks, as well. In an era of dwindling government support for human services—cutbacks in social assistance, job training, and housing assistance, especially for immigrants—community organizations have come to play an increasingly important role in helping households manage the vagaries of urban life. In areas that have recently experienced immigrant population growth, this sector may be ill-equipped to meet the needs of specific populations.[12]

The context of reception for recent immigrants is significant for a host of reasons. It shapes immigrants' opportunity structures in terms of employment, health, education, and civic life, and therefore directly influences their quality of life over the short and long term. Michael Jones-Correa writes that "urban areas provide immigrants' first sustained experience of government and its institutions in America—its role in policing, housing, health care, education, and the job market. These impressions are formative and lasting. Participation in a local context provides immigrants with the tools and skills of citizenship that lead to the management of their relationships with their neighbors—and that serve as a gateway into participation in the larger national polity."[13] For reasons elaborated more fully later in this paper, cities' histories of migration can strongly influence the character of local immigration politics, as well as the conditions of reception encountered by immigrants. Where migration flows have been long established, it is common for a robust set of pro-immigrant civil-society actors to occupy a prominent place in local politics and civic life and to have developed organizational capacities for meeting the service delivery needs of immigrant populations. Conversely, where large migration flows have been more recent, local civil society may be underdeveloped, and immigrants' interests may have less influence on the tenor of local politics. In these cities, the context of reception—and immigrants' first sustained experience of government and its institutions in the United States—may prove unwelcoming, even hostile.

RESCALING IMMIGRATION POLICY

State and municipal government responses to immigration have been as polarized as the immigration reform debate itself. In 2010, the state of Arizona became, in some quarters, the standard-bearer for nonfederal immigration policymaking. At the same time, the state was widely vilified for its spate of restrictionist policies, many of which were ultimately ruled unconstitutional. Arizona moved to adopt new laws that criminalize undocumented immigrants while expanding the roles of state and local police in enforcing immigration laws, and for policy makers in more than two dozen states, it became a legislative model.[14] While it justifiably received the most scrutiny, Arizona is just one of hundreds of states and localities that have enacted immigration-related laws in recent years, an indication that in the absence of comprehensive reform, the locus of immigration policy making is shifting to the state and local levels.

Since at least the late 1880s, the federal government's plenary power over immigration policy has been reaffirmed through cases that have tested the limits of governmental authority over immigration matters.[15] The courts have found numerous state and local immigration laws to be in violation of the U.S. Constitution, since many of these sub-federal initiatives are preempted by the federal government's plenary power or violate individuals' civil rights and liberties. Although the U.S. Supreme Court and lower courts have consistently upheld the federal government's exclusive authority over immigration policy, state and local governments are not prevented from enacting legislation that pertains to immigrants and to immigrant incorporation. This crucial distinction—between immigration policy and immigrant affairs—has emboldened lawmakers to test the limits of sub-federal authority and to pursue immigration-related legislation and locally scaled immigration policy.

According to the National Conference of State Legislatures, immigration-related matters have recently been an area of concerted state-level legislative activity.[16] In 2010, for example, every state legislature that was in regular session considered bills pertaining to immigrants or immigration, and from 2007 to 2012, more than 8,300 immigration-related bills were introduced in state legislatures across the country. Many of these bills could be classified as pro-immigrant, such as bills that expand health and education programs for immigrants and their children. But anti-immigrant reforms are being pursued with increasing vigor.[17] State and local governments have enacted numerous "illegal immigration relief acts" that seek, among other things, to impose penalties on landlords who rent living quarters to unauthorized immigrants and on employers who hire undocumented workers. Surprisingly, perhaps, "the *restrictionist* responses of local governments to undocumented immigration are largely unrelated to demographic pressures in terms of increases in the number of recent immigrants or the proportion of Spanish-speaking households" (original emphasis).[18] Instead, these local responses are more strongly associated with political partisanship and community activism (such as protests and rallies), with the former offering the greatest explanatory power in statistical models. So while a number of new immigration gateways have emerged since the 1990s, restrictionist measures are not typically pursued by those municipalities. Instead, the immigration backlash often occurs in places where there have been just modest levels of in-migration by the foreign born.

Illegal immigration relief acts are the policy expression of the attrition strategy: the notion that if policy makers are able to make life sufficiently miserable for undocumented immigrants, they will "self-deport." According to proponents, the attrition strategy is premised on the idea that by deterring the settlement of new illegals, by increasing deportations to the extent possible, and, most importantly, by increasing the number of illegals already here who *give up and deport themselves*, the United States can bring about an annual decrease in the illegal-alien population. . . . The point, in other words, is not merely to curtail illegal immigration, but rather to bring about a steady reduction in the total number of illegal immigrants who are living in the United States. The result would be a shrinking of the illegal population to a manageable nuisance, rather than today's looming crisis. (emphasis added)[19]

The attrition strategy seeks to enlist unauthorized immigrants in their own removal from the United States. Having failed to forge an effective political coalition at the federal level capable of enacting their preferred legislative proposals, restrictionists have resorted to immigration reform by stealth through their attempts to materially degrade conditions of everyday life for immigrants through state and local legislation and administrative procedures. This rescaling of immigration control has been accompanied by a new politics of immigration at the state and local levels.

However, even if taken strictly on its own terms, the attrition strategy is a failed public policy. Many of the recently enacted laws that have been inspired by notions of "attrition through enforcement" (as the strategy is also called) have been ruled unconstitutional by U.S. courts. In addition, studies of migration flows from several states where the attrition strategy has been most prominent show little evidence of out-migration of unauthorized immigrants.[20] However, illegal immigration relief acts and other restrictionist measures clearly have had an impact on community life, and these impacts are felt well beyond the jurisdictions where restrictionist policies have been enacted. These policies have contributed to rising levels of fear and mistrust in immigrant communities nationwide, including fears of law enforcement authorities, public officials, and public institutions.[21] In this context, civil society, and in particular community-based organizations, faith-based groups, and advocacy coalitions, have special importance in the lives of immigrants, serving as trusted allies that provide collective resources to help immigrants navigate hostile environments.

THE COMING AGE OF MIGRANT CIVIL SOCIETY

Immigrant rights groups have been active participants in the contested politics of immigration reform. In areas where restrictionist policies have been adopted, these organizations have lobbied to overturn these policies, contested anti-immigrant laws in court, and helped immigrants contend with the everyday challenges these laws pose. In areas that have been more welcoming to immigrants, a range of civil society actors, such as community-based organizations, faith-based groups, labor unions, and advocacy organizations, have partnered with state and municipal governments to deliver services, design programs, and strengthen protections for immigrants.

With the increase in immigration to the United States over the past several decades, many community organizations have modified their programmatic foci to better serve recent arrivals, while countless new organizations have been established specifically to address the challenges faced by a growing foreign-born population.[22] Building on the work of scholars studying the civil-society organizational forms being created by migrants,[23] Nik Theodore and Nina Martin have argued that a distinct segment of civil society had emerged through these efforts.[24] This "migrant civil society"—community organizations, social movements, hometown associations, churches and faith-based organizations, social clubs, and other organized groups that represent the interests of migrants and operate between markets, households, and the state—plays an increasingly important role in mediating the myriad dislocations and conflicts brought about by mass migration. The organizations and social actors that comprise migrant civil society share a number of unifying characteristics: (1) their mission directs them to address the social, economic, and political concerns that are crucial to the well-being of immigrants; (2) they engage in a range of activities (e.g., citizenship classes and immigrant rights advocacy) that are dedicated to immigrants' needs and concerns; and (3) a substantial share of their clients and constituents are immigrants and their families. In addition, many of these organizations have been established by immigrants themselves, and immigrants often take on a central role in agenda setting, programming, and matters of governance.

Although migrant civil-society organizations share many features with broader civil society, they remain distinctive in that many of their core activities are framed in terms of the wellbeing of immigrant populations. Issues such as citizenship and naturalization, redressing workplace abuses suffered by undocumented migrants; restoring the social safety net for noncitizens, and engaging in transnational activities, such as development projects abroad, charitable giving, and cultural exchanges, have come to define the work of these organizations.[25] Furthermore, because migrant civil-society actors represent the concerns of immigrants to society at large, the various entities that constitute migrant civil society can usefully be conceptualized as a distinct political force, one that has exhibited the ability to act collectively to voice constituents' concerns. In addition to forging political alliances, many of these organizations have stepped in to fill the void created by the withdrawal of public services to immigrants that has occurred in many cities; such organizations provide emergency services, housing assistance, job training programs, and otherwise assist immigrants who are in need.

At the local level, these organizations are now a platform for political mobilization, making policy claims, delivering social services, and offering alternative visions of urban development and community life. Moreover, at a time when flows of undocumented immigrants represent a significant share of total migration to the United States, migrant civil society provides a mechanism for "political incorporation without citizenship."[26] Undocumented migrants residing in the United States are formally excluded from electoral politics. Yet, through their civil-society representatives, their concerns can be articulated and brought into public-policy debates and civic life.[27] Civil-society organizations, unlike undocumented immigrants, are typically seen as having standing and legitimacy to make claims on the state. Thus these organizations have come to occupy a central place in the contentious politics of immigration reform, affordable housing, workers' rights, access to education, the availability of healthcare, and other pressing social issues. It can be argued that immigrants' political activity through migrant civil society has now supplanted electoral politics and participation in political parties as the principal means of immigrant political incorporation and activism.[28]

The broad field of migrant civil society encompasses organizations of varying political orientations. Some might be characterized as assimilationist, focusing their efforts on the social, cultural, and linguistic integration of immigrant populations. Others take a more confrontational stance, advancing notions of social citizenship that call into question conventional definitions of national citizenship based in sovereign territories. Still others explicitly avoid framing their goals and activities in terms of citizenship rights, focusing instead on universal human rights. Similar debates have been occurring within academia. Helga Leitner and Christopher Strunk provide a reasoned synopsis of these differing intellectual currents, the terrain of which is worthy of summarizing given its resonance with the approaches taken by some prominent immigrant-rights advocates:

> Some scholars have been highly critical of deploying conceptions of citizenship to theorize and make meaningful the political activities and demands of immigrants and their allies. It is argued that even an expanded

conception of citizenship is too limiting because it reinforces citizenship as the foremost measure of belonging. [. . .] Although acknowledging these dangers associated with the concept of citizenship, we disagree that this necessitates abandoning the concept of citizenship altogether. To the contrary, we suggest that an expanded, agentic conception of citizenship, which dislodges citizenship as located and conferred by the nation-state, offers other insights and solutions.[29]

Leitner and Struck propose the concept of "insurgent citizenship" to describe "discourses and practices that challenge existing laws, policies, and institutions; promote alternative criteria for membership in a polity; and lay claims to and enact new forms of citizenship and rights. Insurgent citizenship moves the focus toward individual practices and organized collective actions."[30] This might include collective action to improve conditions in low-wage industries; struggles to expand access to education, health care, and social services; and efforts to challenge landlords who maintain substandard properties in immigrant port-of-entry neighborhoods, as well as "everyday acts of resistance" that restore a measure of autonomy and dignity to urban life. By opening up new spaces for immigrant political agency, insurgent citizenship challenges the prevailing liberal-democratic concept of citizenship that is rooted in bounded national territories. It represents a call to collective action to confront injustice and inequality, both by working through established societal institutions (including policy-making bodies and courts) and by contesting punitive policies through protest, civil disobedience, and other forms of resistance.

The remainder of this section examines innovative efforts initiated by migrant civil society to intervene in three arenas: workplace issues, social services and antipoverty programs, and municipal policies. These initiatives are emblematic of "new-generation" programs and urban policies to redress many of the hardships immigrant populations endure. Some entail relatively modest changes to policy and service delivery, while others hold greater potential for systemic change. Each, though, is a concrete manifestation of an upsurge in social activism that has gathered strength through the increasing acceptance of notions of insurgent citizenship, as well as migrant civil society's growing willingness to confront head-on the sources of systemic disadvantage. Yet these strategies have serious limitations, as well. As migrant civil society mobilizes to address issues, including entrenched urban poverty and growing inequality, it confronts major societal problems whose resolution ultimately lies beyond the sector's strained capacities.

Workplace Issues

Undocumented migrants comprise a substantial share of the workforce in agricultural production, manufacturing, construction, and the hospitality sector,[31] and they increasingly have become the "workers of choice" for employers seeking to hire employees at below-market rates of pay.[32] As a result, many immigrants enter urban economies through precarious jobs in low-wage industries and the informal economy, where they routinely endure violations of labor and employment laws, including the nonpayment of wages, violations of minimum wage and overtime laws, exposure to hazardous working conditions, and employer retaliation against workers who attempt to exercise their workplace rights.[33]

In response to these conditions, immigrant rights groups have established worker centers as an intervention into exploitative niches of local economies.[34] Worker centers are labor market intermediaries that assist workers in redressing wage theft, conduct workers' rights education, provide workforce development services, and organize workers so that they can exert greater leverage in the job market and contest substandard conditions. Increasingly, worker centers are entering into partnerships with government agencies that enforce labor standards, and they have been valuable partners in efforts to improve conditions in low-wage industries.[35] Worker centers also collaborate with other allies in the labor movement to organize workers, press for stronger enforcement of labor standards, and advocate for policies—including comprehensive immigration reform—that will improve employment conditions.[36]

Though the worker center movement has grown rapidly since 2000, its reach into exploitative niches of local economies is far from complete. The majority of immigrant workers in low-wage industries are employed without the benefit of representation, either by worker centers and other workers' rights organizations or by unions. Absent a significant expansion in government's capacity to monitor and enforce labor standards, it is unlikely that the incidence of exploitative conditions will be substantially reduced.

Social Services and Antipoverty Programs

Immigrant-serving nonprofit organizations administer a wide range of social services and antipoverty programs for their constituents. These include child care and early childhood education, health screening and counseling, housing counseling, job-search assistance, assistance accessing public benefits, financial literacy courses, programming for senior citizens, and emergency food and housing services. However, a series of public policy decisions has eroded the social services resources available to many immigrants. The 1996 Personal Responsibility and Work Opportunity Reconciliation Act, which reformed the U.S. welfare system, eliminated most federal programs for immigrants and devolved responsibility for setting eligibility criteria to states. Many immigrants and their families lost access to cash-transfer programs, food stamps, and health insurance, a move that was motivated by perceived fiscal savings and policy makers' desire to shift responsibility for support onto immigrants' sponsors who, under the Illegal Immigration Reform and Immigrant Responsibility Act of 1996, must pledge to assist immigrants until they become naturalized citizens.[37]

Restrictions on immigrant eligibility for assistance coincided with the large-scale devolution of social programs and the rise of nonprofit organizations as an unevenly developed "shadow state" that assumes increasing responsibilities for meeting the needs of low-income households.[38] Variations in sector capacities, owing to disparities in funding allocations by the state, as well as capabilities within the sector itself (e.g., leadership, financial support, or other resources), can result in unmet needs, particularly in areas, such as suburbs and new gateway cities, where migrant civil society is underdeveloped. There is a danger that greater reliance on nonprofit organizations might entrench inequities in access to services, given the spatial mismatch of organizations' service-delivery areas.[39] Furthermore, in locales where anti-immigrant sentiments are intense, political tensions may arise over resource allocations for immigrant services. Because devolved service delivery relies on public funding, in some parts of the country there may be little political will to support antipoverty programming for immigrants, and as a result the nonprofit sector will struggle to meet the demand for services.

Municipal Policies

Cities that are experiencing dramatic increases in immigration confront significant cultural, political, social, and economic changes associated with large-scale demographic shifts. The following programs are examples of the types of immigrant-incorporation initiatives municipalities have pursued, often at the urging of or in collaboration with migrant civil society.

LEGAL DEFENSE TO UNAUTHORIZED IMMIGRANTS. The New York Immigrant Family Unity Project (NYIFUP) is the first local program in the nation to provide legal defense to low-income immigrants facing deportation. The

NYIFUP is founded on the premise that a lack of legal safeguards denies immigrants due process under the law, while a lack of legal representation "leads to detentions that continue for months or years longer than necessary and deportations of New Yorkers who have viable legal claims to remain in the communities they call home." A coalition of immigrants' rights organizations estimates substantial savings to governments (primarily through reductions in healthcare and foster care costs) and employers (through decreased costs of employee turnover) from such a program, while also injecting a measure of fairness into proceedings to determine legal residency in the United States.[40]

MUNICIPAL IDENTIFICATION CARDS.   In 2007, New Haven, Connecticut, authorized the issuance of the Elm City Resident Card, the first municipal identification card in the nation. The municipal ID is intended to enable undocumented immigrant residents of the city, as well as other residents who might lack appropriate identification, to open bank accounts and make use of municipal services, such as public libraries.[41] Similar policies have been enacted in San Francisco, Oakland, New York City, and elsewhere.

COMMUNITY POLICING AND IMMIGRANT OUTREACH PROGRAMS.   Recognizing that immigrants may be disproportionately the victims of crimes, a number of cities have created programs to strengthen relationships between local police departments and immigrant communities. These programs help to allay concerns that undocumented immigrants may have, should they report crimes to authorities; expand language access for the police to enable officers to communicate to non-English speakers; and otherwise remove barriers between law enforcement authorities and the communities they serve.[42] El Paso, Texas, has created a Victims Services Unit to conduct legal-rights education and outreach to immigrant communities, and the local police department does not require victims to reveal their immigration status. Durham, North Carolina, has created a Victims Assistance Office and a Spanish-language neighborhood watch program, and the local police department has increased the number of Spanish-speaking personnel on staff. Seattle, Washington, has created a number of councils that advise the police department on public-safety issues affecting various immigrant groups, religious minorities, racial groups, and others who might face particular public-safety challenges. The advisory councils identify public-safety issues, help build trust between communities and law enforcement authorities, and ensure that police officers are culturally competent.

SENIOR SERVICES. Fremont, California, has created the Community Ambassadors Program for Seniors, a partnership between the Human Services Department and ten local cultural and faith-based organizations. The program provides support to seniors in their native languages and according to their own cultural norms. Ambassadors serve as a liaison between the city's social services and seniors' religious and cultural communities.

COMMUNITY DEVELOPMENT. The Community Development, Planning and Policy Department in Fort Wayne, Indiana, has a Hispanic and immigrant liaison who provides assistance for accessing city services and is involved in community development planning projects. The position is part of a wider effort in the city to promote immigrant naturalization as well as civic participation among the local Burmese and Latino communities.

FINANCIAL SERVICES. San Francisco launched the "Bank on San Francisco" initiative in 2006 to expand access to mainstream financial services to "unbanked" individuals. Participating banks and credit unions allow individuals with no or poor banking history to start low-fee accounts and gain access to financial counseling, college savings accounts, and responsible payday loans. The Mexican Matricula and Guatemalan Consular ID cards are accepted as primary identification. Similar programs have been created in Dallas, Fresno, Memphis, Shreveport, and dozens of other cities.

Migrant civil society intervenes in urban life at the intersection of major societal trends toward increasing immigration, polarizing politics, and the devolution of responsibilities for human needs to lower tiers of government and onto communities, organizations, and households. In some respects, migrant civil society can be regarded as the last line of defense for immigrant populations that otherwise would have few avenues through which to advocate for their interests. Problems of substandard jobs, inadequate housing, and other social ills are borne disproportionately by immigrants, and in particular by undocumented immigrants and recent arrivals. Migrant civil society has been an indispensable resource for countless immigrants as they adjust to life in the United States.

But is it appropriate for a segment of civil society to bear so much of the responsibility for addressing these social problems? Often underfunded and with their capacities overstretched, migrant civil-society organizations at best provide a patchwork approach to social assistance, leaving large populations underserved, particularly those in areas of the country where the political backlash against immigrants has been strongest. It is, therefore, unreasonable to think that devolving so much of the responsibility for immigrant incorporation to civil-society organizations will produce satisfactory outcomes in terms of social cohesion and expanded economic opportunities; governments can and must play a substantially greater role. At the municipal level, this includes eliminating anti-immigrant policies where they exist and developing comprehensive agendas for immigrant incorporation.

Notes

1. Betancur, John J., and Maricela Garcia, "The 2006–2007 Immigration Mobilizations and Community Capacity: The Experience of Chicago," *Latino Studies* 9, no. 1 (2011): 10–37; Cordero-Guzman, Hector, Nina Martin, Victoria Quiroz-Becerra, and Nik Theodore, "Voting with Their Feet: Nonprofit Organizations and Immigrant Mobilization," *American Behavioral Scientist* 52 (2008): 598–617; Das Gupta, Monesha, *Unruly Immigrants: Rights, Activism, and Transnational South Asian Politics in the United States* (Durham, N.C.: Duke University Press, 2006); Nicholls, Walter J., "From Political Opportunities to Niche-Openings: The Dilemmas of Mobilizing for Immigrant Rights in Inhospitable Environments," *Theory and Society* 43, no. 1 (2014): 23–49; Palleres, Amalia, and Nilda Flores-Gonzalez, eds., *¡Marcha! Latino Chicago and the Immigrant Rights Movement* (Champaign: University of Illinois Press, 2010).

2. Passel, Jeffery S., D'Vera Cohn, and Ana Gonzalez-Barrera, *Population Decline of Unauthorized Immigrants May Have Reversed* (Washington, D.C.: Pew Research Center, 2013).

3. Singer, Audrey, *The Rise of New Immigrant Gateways* (Washington, D.C.: Brookings Institution, 2004).

4. Passel, Cohn, and Gonzalez-Barrea, *Population Decline of Unauthorized Immigrants May Have Reversed*.

5. Singer, *Rise of New Immigrant Gateways*.

6. Pastor, Manuel, "Spatial Assimilation and Its Discontents: The Changing Geography of Immigration in Metropolitan America," in *The Oxford Handbook of Economics and Planning*, eds. Kieran Donaghy and Gerrit-Jan Knaap, 340–70 (Oxford: Oxford University Press, 2011).

7. Ellis, Mark, Richard Wright, and Matthew Townley, "The Great Recession and the Allure of New Immigrant Destinations in the United States," *International Migration Review* 4, no. 1 (2014): 3–33.

8. Wright, Richard, Mark Ellis, and Virginia Parks, "Immigrant Niches and the Intrametropolitan Spatial Division of Labour," *Journal of Ethnic and Migration Studies* 36, no. 7 (2010): 1033–59.

9. Bernhardt, Annette, Michael Spiller, and Nik Theodore, "Employers Gone Rogue: Explaining Industry Variation in Violations of Workplace Laws," *Industrial and Labor Relations Review* 66, no. 4 (2013): 808–32.

10. Massey, Douglas S., and Kerstin Gentsch, "Undocumented Migration to the United States and the Wages of Mexican Immigrants," *International Migration Review* 48, no. 2 (2014): 482–99. It appears that the positive effects of mobility on workers' wages have become muted over time. Massey and Gentsch have shown that by criminalizing the hiring of unauthorized immigrants, IRCA has been associated with a lowering of wages for undocumented immigrants as employers attempt to compensate for the risks they face in violating IRCA's employment provisions by reducing pay rates.

11. Pastor, "Spatial Assimilation and Its Discontents," 345.

12. Joassart-Marcelli, Pascale, "Ethnic Concentration and Nonprofit Organizations: The Political and Urban Geography of Immigrant Services in Boston, Massachusetts," *International Migration Review* 47, no. 3 (2013): 730–72.

13. Jones-Correa, Michael, "Bringing Outsiders In: Questions of Immigrant Incorporation," in *The Politics of Democratic Inclusion*, eds. Christina Wolbrecht and Rodney E. Hero, 75–101 (Philadelphia: Temple University Press, 2005).

14. Lacayo, Elena, *One Year Later: A Look at SB 1070 and Copycat Legislation* (Washington, D.C.: National Council of La Raza, 2011).

15. Varsanyi, Monica, "Immigration Policy Activism in U.S. States and Cities: Interdisciplinary Perspectives," in *Taking Local Control: Immigration Policy Activism in U.S. Cities and States*, ed. Monica W. Varsanyi, 1–27 (Stanford, Calif.: Stanford University Press, 2010).

16. National Conference of State Legislatures, *2011 Immigration-Related Laws and Resolutions in the States* (Washington, D.C.: National Conference of State Legislatures, 2012); National Conference of State Legislatures, *2012 Immigration-Related Laws and Resolutions in the States* (Washington, D.C.: National Conference of State Legislatures, 2013).

17. Hincapié, Marielena, "Aquí Estamos y No Nos Vamos: Unintended Consequences of Current Immigration Law," in *Global Connections and Local Receptions: New Latino Immigration to the Southeastern United States*, eds. Fran Ansley and Jon Shefner, 89–128 (Knoxville: University of Tennessee Press, 2009); Varsanyi, "Immigration Policy Activism in U.S. States and Cities"; Walker, Kyle E., and Helga Leitner, "The Variegated Landscape of Local Immigration Policies in the United States," *Urban Geography* 32, no. 2 (2011): 156–78.

18. Ramakrishnan, Karthick S., and Tom (Tak) Wong, "Partnership, Not Spanish: Explaining Municipal Ordinances Affecting Undocumented Immigrants," in Varsanyi, *Taking Local Control*, 89.

19. Krikorian, Mark, *Downsizing Illegal Immigration: A Strategy of Attrition Through Enforcement* (Washington, D.C.: Center for Immigration Studies, 2005), 1. See also Kris Kobach, "Attrition through Enforcement: A Rational Approach to Illegal Immigration," *Tulsa Journal of Comparative and International Law* 15 (2008): 153–61; Vaughan, Jessica M., *Attrition through Enforcement: A Cost-Effective*

Strategy to Shrink the Illegal Population (Washington, D.C.: Center for Immigration Studies, 2006).

20. Filindra, Alexandra, *The Myth of "Self-Deportation": How Behavioral Economics Reveals the Fallacies behind "Attrition through Enforcement"* (Washington, D.C.: Immigration Policy Center, 2012); see Mark Ellis et al., "The Migration Response to the Legal Arizona Workers Act," *Political Geography* 42 (2014): 46–56, for countervailing evidence.

21. Waslin, Michele, *Discrediting "Self-Deportation" as Immigration Policy: Why an Attrition through Enforcement Strategy Makes Life Difficult for Everyone* (Washington, D.C.: Immigration Policy Center, 2012); Theodore, Nik, *Insecure Communities: Latino Perceptions of Police Involvement in Immigration Enforcement* (Chicago: Great Cities Institute, University of Illinois at Chicago, 2013); Menjívar, Cecilia, "The 'Poli-Migra': Multilayered Legislation, Enforcement Practices, and Can We Learn about and from Today's Approaches," *American Behavioral Scientist*, 58, no. 13 (2014): 1805–19.

22. Cordero-Guzman, Hector, "Community-Based Organizations and Migration in New York City," *Journal of Ethnic and Migration Studies* 31, no. 5 (2005): 889–909.

23. Fox, Jonathan, and Gaspar Rivera-Salgado, eds., *Indigenous Mexican Migrants in the United States* (La Jolla: Center for U.S.-Mexican Studies and Center for Comparative Immigration Studies, University of California, San Diego, 2004); Fox, Jonathan, and Gaspar Rivera-Salgado, "Building Migrant Civil Society: Indigenous Mexicans in the US," *Iberoamericana* 17, no. 5 (2005): 101–15; Bada, Xóchitl, Jonathan Fox, and Andrew Selee, eds., *Invisible No More: Mexican Migrant Civic Participation in the United States* (Washington, D.C.: Mexico Institute, 2006).

24. Theodore, Nik, and Nina Martin, "Migrant Civil Society: New Voices in the Struggle over Community Development," *Journal of Urban Affairs* 29, no. 3 (2007): 269–87.

25. Bada, Xóchitl, *Mexican Hometown Associations in Chicagoacán: From Local to Transnational Civic Engagement* (New Brunswick, N.J.: Rutgers University Press, 2014); Martin, Nina, "'There Is Abuse Everywhere': Migrant Nonprofit Organizations and the Problem of Precarious Work," *Urban Affairs Review* 48, no. 3 (2012): 389–416; Joassart-Marcelli, "Ethnic Concentration and Nonprofit Organizations"; Smith, Michael Peter, and Matt Bakker, *Citizenship across Borders: The Political Transnationalism of El Migrante* (Ithaca, N.Y.: Cornell University Press, 2008).

26. Theodore and Martin, "Migrant Civil Society."

27. Chung, Angie, "'Politics without the Politics': The Evolving Political Cultures of Ethnic Non-Profits in Koreatown, Los Angeles," *Journal of Ethnic and Migration Studies* 31, no. 5 (2005): 911–29; Gupta, *Unruly Immigrants*; Wong, Janelle, *Democracy's Promise: Immigrants and American Civic Institutions* (Ann Arbor: University of Michigan Press, 2006).

28. Wong, *Democracy's Promise.*

29. Leitner, Helga, and Christopher Strunk, "Spaces of Immigrant Advocacy and Liberal Democratic Citizenship," *Annals of the Association of American Geographers* 104, no. 2 (2014): 348–56, 350.

30. Ibid.

31. Passel, Jeffrey S., and D'Vera Cohn, *A Portrait of Unauthorized Immigrants in the United States* (Washington, D.C.: Pew Hispanic Center, 2009).

32. Peck, Jamie, and Nik Theodore, "Contingent Chicago: Restructuring the Spaces of Temporary Labor," *International Journal of Urban and Regional Research* 25, no. 3 (2001): 471–96; Doussard, Marc, *Degraded Work: The Struggle at the Bottom of the Labor Market* (Minneapolis: University of Minnesota Press, 2013).

33. See Annette Bernhardt et al., *Broken Laws, Unprotected Workers: Violations of Employment and Labor Laws in America's Cities* (UIC Center for Urban Economic Development, National Employment Law Project, and UCLA Institute for Research on Labor and Employment, 2009), http://www.nelp.org/, accessed May 25, 2015.

34. Fine, Janice, *Worker Centers: Organizing Communities at the Edge of the Dream* (Ithaca, N.Y.: Cornell University Press, 2006); Martin, Nina, Sandra Morales, and Nik Theodore, "Migrant Worker Centers: Contending with Downgrading in the Low-Wage Labor Market," *GeoJournal* 68, no. 2–3 (2007): 155–65; United Workers Congress, *The Rise of Worker Centers and the Fight for a Fair Economy* (Oakland, Calif.: United Workers Congress, 2014).

35. Fine, Janice, and Jennifer Gordon, "Strengthening Labor Standards Enforcement through Partnerships with Workers' Organizations," *Politics and Society* 38, no. 4 (2010): 552–85.

36. Milkman, Ruth, *L.A. Story: Immigrant Workers and the Future of the U.S. Labor Movement* (New York: Russell Sage Foundation, 2006); Milkman, Ruth, and Ed Ott, eds., *New Labor in New York: Precarious Workers and the Future of the Labor Movement* (Ithaca, N.Y.: Cornell University Press, 2014).

37. Fix, Michael E., Randy Capps, and Neeraj Kaushal, "Immigrants and Welfare: Overview," in *Immigrants and Welfare: The Impact of Welfare Reform on America's Newcomers*, ed. Michael E. Fix, 1–36 (New York: Russell Sage Foundation, 2011).

38. Wolch, Jennifer R., *The Shadow State: Government and Voluntary Sector in Transition* (New York: Foundation Center, 1990).

39. Joassart-Marcelli, "Ethnic Concentration and Nonprofit Organizations."

40. Center for Popular Democracy et al., *New York Immigrant Family Unity Project: Good for Families, Good for Employers, and Good for All New Yorkers* (New York: Center for Popular Democracy, 2014), 5, 9–15.

41. Holtz, Jeff, "This Summer's Surprise Hit: An Elm City ID," *New York Times*, September 16, 2007, www.nytimes.com, accessed November 17, 2014.

42. Gambetta, Ricardo, and Zivile Gedrimaite, *Municipal Innovations in Immigrant Integration: 20 Cities, 20 Good Practices* (Washington, D.C.: National League of Cities, 2010).

Other References

Clarke, Susan E. "Splintering Citizenship and the Prospects for Democratic Inclusion." In *The Politics of Democratic Inclusion*, eds. Christina Wolbrecht and Rodney E. Hero (Philadelphia: Temple University Press, 2005), 210–37.

Martin, Nina. "The Crisis of Social Reproduction among Migrant Workers: Interrogating the Role of Migrant Civil Society." *Antipode* 42 (2010): 127–51.

Immigrant Civil Society and Incorporation in the Chicago Suburbs

DISCUSSANTS: NILDA FLORES-GONZÁLEZ,
ANDY CLARNO, AND VANESSA GURIDY-CERRITOS,
UNIVERSITY OF ILLINOIS AT CHICAGO

Nik Theodore argues that immigrant civil society plays an increasingly important role as a service provider and a political force for immigrants.[1] Consisting of social service organizations, voluntary associations, grassroots organizations, and advocacy groups, immigrant civil society addresses some of the most immediate needs and concerns of immigrant communities while also pushing city officials, school administrators, and institutions to adopt more inclusive policies. Most research on immigrant civil society has focused on cities like Chicago or New York that have historically served as gateways for new immigrants and therefore have resources and institutions to help migrants incorporate. But since there has been a large influx of immigrants—mostly from Mexico—into parts of the Midwest and South that have not historically served as immigrant gateways, it is important to understand the role of immigrant civil society in these "new destinations."[2]

In the Chicago Metropolitan Area (CMA), for instance, immigrants increasingly bypass the city itself and instead move directly to suburban locations. According to the 2010 U.S. Census, 52 percent of Latinos in Illinois live in the suburbs, 38 percent live in the city of Chicago, and 10 percent live outside of the CMA. Drawing on recent research about immigrant incorporation in six "new destinations" in the CMA, we offer insights on the impact of immigrant civil society institutions on immigration-related policy in emerging gateways.

From 2010 to 2012, University of Illinois at Chicago (UIC) faculty and students associated with the Chicago Area Study (CAS) carried out a multi-method research project to explain why some suburban locations have adopted supportive or neutral policies toward immigrants while others have adopted more restrictive policies. Our research focused on six locations in one suburban county: a wealthy suburb, a small immigrant enclave, two industrial cities, a rural town, and a growing exurban community. The first year of the project consisted of a survey of residents about their attitudes toward immigrants and immigration-related policy. During the second year, we focused on the political factors that shape local immigration policies. Teams of researchers conducted interviews with key individual and institutional actors, including elected officials, school administrators, and law enforcement officers as well as members of the public and representatives of voluntary associations, business organizations, churches, and labor unions.

Each of the six cities in our study was fraught with political contestation over the growing immigrant population. Groups and individuals with different views sought to influence the policies adopted by city councils, school boards, housing authorities, police, and other local institutions. As a result, the communities cannot be classified as "purely" integrative, restrictive, or neutral. Most are fairly inclusive, yet their approach is perhaps best described as "benign neglect." Many institutions in these cities express integrative or welcoming intentions but in practice do little to help immigrants. Some of these cities simply do not have the human or material resources necessary to assist immigrants. Other institutions subscribe to a "color-blind" approach, offering services to "all" residents rather than providing services specifically for immigrants. And a few local institutions adopt explicitly restrictive policies such as housing ordinances and policing procedures that target immigrants. Yet, often these policies are not fully enforced; while some actors attempt to administer the policies, others ignore them and render them ineffective.

Because these policies are shaped by political struggles, there are no simple predictors of whether localities will adopt inclusive or exclusionary policies. Analyzing demographic factors such as race, social class, the political attitudes of existing residents, or even the rate of immigrant population growth does not yield predictable patterns or outcomes. For instance, the two cities in our study that had adopted the most integrative policies were the same cities in which residents held the most negative attitudes toward immigrants. In the town that experienced the most rapid growth in its immigrant population—more than 1,200 percent since 1980—residents expressed largely negative views of immigrants, but the city council and school board adopted inclusionary policies. Residents in another town that experienced precipitous growth held more positive views of immigrants, yet the policies adopted by the city were largely restrictive. What is clear is that community political dynamics are complex and that demographics and political attitudes do not determine local policies.

In each of the communities in our study, immigrant civil society organizations were actively engaged in policy struggles involving the city council, the school board, and other key institutions for immigrant integration. Our research demonstrates the importance of these institutions in shaping local immigration policy. These findings support decades of research on local government. Since the 1950s, scholars have repeatedly pointed to the importance of informal networks, local institutions, and civic organizations in shaping policy decisions at the local level.[3] Scholars of migrant civil society have argued that these institutions are especially important for providing a voice to people who are excluded from formal electoral politics.[4] Because these institutions lie outside the grasp of traditional power structures, they have relative autonomy to pursue their interests.

Ultimately, we found that the ability of social institutions to build connections with the local political power structure had more of an impact on policy making than merely the density or number of social institutions in a community. For instance, the city with the most restrictive policies had multiple immigrant organizations fighting for affordable housing, labor rights, immigrant businesses, and other resources. But their impact was limited due to organizational and strategic differences, interpersonal rivalries, and an inability to penetrate the informal networks through which policy making took place. This community's power structure was characterized by an old guard that closely protected access to power and decision making. In contrast, the city with the most inclusive policies had only one immigrant-oriented organization. But because that organization was deeply connected to the political structure and held regular meetings with city officials, police commanders, and school administrators, it was able to effectively advocate for immigrants. Even in this city, however, there were not enough Spanish-speaking teachers in the schools, the parents had to fight for educational opportunities for their children, and the police carried out regular crackdowns on immigrant youth.

To be effective, these social institutions must engage with the immigrant community. Serving as a broker is initially important in opening doors for immigrants, but ultimately these social institutions need to build capacity and leadership among immigrants. This can be a difficult task; when professional Latinos become brokers between immigrants and the local power structure, they often have an incentive to maintain conditions as they are. The largest Latino organization in the area—a network of multiple organizations that bills itself as committed to improving the quality of life for Latinos—serves as little more than a professional referral network. Though members have strong connections to formal power structures throughout the county, and often occupy positions of relative authority in public institutions, these connections are seldom pressed to provide more than a contribution to their scholarship fund. In contrast, a local advocacy organization that is particularly effective at developing leadership skills, has limited—if any—relationships with the formal power structure in the area. As a result, interventions by this organization are often restricted to demand protests.

A third organization illustrates the importance of combining community engagement and political networking. The organization has good relationships with the power structure, but its own employees are strongly discouraged from political advocacy. Instead, the organization has found creative ways to support leadership training among its clients. Training local women as health promoters, for example, allowed the organization to facilitate leadership development in such a way that participants take on divisive political struggles independently. In addition, the organization provided local parents with outside resources that helped them clarify their demands on the local school district. Though the organization itself did not control the content of the meetings, it provided an outside facilitator as well as meeting space. It later organized a community forum giving these parents a platform through which to address members of the local power structure, who attended precisely because of the organization's care to preserve its non-advocacy stand. This organization's success is due in large part to its ability to combine good relationships with the local power structure with the development of capacity and leadership among immigrant residents.

This delicate balance is not easy to achieve. Another organization affiliated with a local church provides significant capacity building to new immigrants. But the organization itself has so many goals (as a service provider, advocacy agent, and spiritual guide) that its efforts are inefficient and often ineffective. During a particularly contentious struggle between the immigrant community and the city council, one priest's attempt to mediate between the two sides resulted in him being shunned by both sides. Rather than being able to serve as an effective mediator, the priest—along with the church and its affiliates—was seen both as a traitor to the immigrant community *and* as anti-American.

As broader processes of social, political, and economic restructuring make local governments increasingly reliant on non-state actors to determine and carry out public policies, there may be increasing opportunities for civil society to gain access to local power structures. As a result, immigrant civil-society organizations find themselves in a unique position to further the incorporation of immigrants. Those able to create lines of communication with city officials can function as a bridge between their constituents and the local government.[5] Yet, the most successful organizations are those that maintain good relationships with the local power structure but at the same time provide the immigrant community with tools that enable them to develop their own capacity to become the political force that ultimately tilts the scale toward inclusive policies.

Notes

The larger project was funded by the National Science Foundation; the Russell Sage Foundation; and UIC Great Cities Institute, Institute for Research on Race and Public Policy, Office of Social Science Research, and Institute for Policy and Civic Engagement.

1. Theodore, Nik, "Migrant Civil Society and the Metropolitics of Belonging," chapter in this book.

2. Massey, Douglas, ed., *New Faces in New Places: The Changing Geography of American Immigration* (New York: Russell Sage Foundation, 2008); Singer, A., S. W. Hardwick, and C. B. Bretell, eds., *Twenty-First Century Gateways: Immigrant Incorporation in Suburban America* (Washington, D.C.: Brookings Institution Press, 2009); Zuniga, Victor, and Ruben Hernandez-Leon, *New Destinations: Mexican Immigration in the United States* (New York: Russell Sage Foundation, 2005).

3. Hunter, Floyd, *Community Power Structure: A Study of Decision Makers* (Chapel Hill: University of North Carolina Press, 1953); Dahl, Robert, *Who Governs?* (New Haven, Conn.: Yale University Press, 1969); Banfield, Edward C., and James Q. Wilson, *City Politics* (Cambridge, Mass.: Harvard University Press and MIT Press, 1963); Elkin, Stephen, *City and Regime in the American Republic* (Chicago: University of Chicago Press, 1987); Stone, Clarence N., *Regime Politics: Governing Atlanta 1946–1988* (Lawrence: University Press of Kansas, 1989); Mossberger, Karen, and Gerry Stoker, "The Evolution of Urban Regime Theory: The Challenge of Conceptualization," *Urban Affairs Review* 36, no. 6 (2001): 810–35; Logan, John R., and Harvey L. Molotch, *Urban Fortunes: The Political Economy of Place* (Berkeley: University of California Press, 1987).

4. Bada, Xóchitl, et al., "Politicizing the Civic and Socializing the Political: Latino Civic and Political Engagement in Chicago and the Metropolitan Area," in *Latinos in Chicago: Reflections of an American Landscape*, White Paper Series, ed. John P. Koval,

171–210 (Notre Dame, Ind.: Institute for Latino Studies, University of Notre Dame, June 2010); Cordero-Guzman, H., N. Martin, V. Quiroz-Becerra, and N. Theodore, "Voting with Their Feet: Non-Profit Organizations and Immigrant Mobilization," *American Behavioral Scientist* 52, no. 4 (2008): 598–617; Marwell, N., "Privatizing the Welfare State: Non-Profit Community Based Organizations as Political Actors," *American Sociological Review* 69, no. 2 (2004): 265–91; Ramakrishan, S. Karthick, and Irene Bloemraad, "Introduction: Civic and Political Inequalities," in *Civic Hopes and Political Realities: Immigrants, Community Organizations, and Political Engagement,* ed. S. Karthick Ramakrishan and Irene Bloemraad, 1–42 (New York: Russell Sage Foundation, 2008); Theodore, N., and N. Martin, "Migrant Civil Society: New Voices in the Struggle over Community Development," *Journal of Urban Affairs* 29, no. 3 (2008): 269–87.

    5. Fine, Janice, *Worker Centers: Organizing Communities at the Edge of the Dream* (Ithaca, N.Y.: Cornell University Press, 2006); Valenzuela Jr., Abel, *Day Laborers in Southern California: Preliminary Findings from the Day Labor Survey* (Los Angeles: Center for the Study of Urban Poverty, Institute for Social Science Research, University of California at Los Angeles, 1999).

PART THREE

SYNTHESIS AND RECOMMENDATIONS

Not Your Parents' Neighborhood

Tradition, Innovation, and the Changing Face of Community Development

STEPHANIE TRUCHAN

UNIVERSITY OF ILLINOIS AT CHICAGO

Chicago has long been regarded as a city of neighborhoods. Its seventy-seven community areas are home to over two hundred neighborhoods, each with their own character and history, defined by real estate development, demographics, faith, and culture. These neighborhoods formed the foundation for Chicago and continue to shape the city's built and social environments. But neighborhoods are not unique to Chicago. They can be found in large cities and small towns, in every country across the globe. The 2014 Urban Forum provided a medium through which socially conscious academics, professionals, and students could discuss the importance and value of the neighborhood to urban society.

Susana Vasquez, executive director of LISC Chicago, set the tone for the morning's discussions by asking this question: "Who thinks neighborhoods stopped being an urban strategy, and where do those people think it went?" As a woman who has spent her career building communities, Vasquez acknowledged that she does see the world through "neighborhood-colored glasses," but the question is still a valid one. As members of an increasingly urban society, we often look to city officials to solve block-level problems, sometimes neglecting the fact that solutions can exist right in our own backyards. School closings, crime and violence, and unemployment, as Vasquez pointed out, are all urban issues, but they require neighborhood strategy. A community's anchor institutions and the people who support them have the power to be a first line of defense when it comes to neighborhood resilience.

In her keynote address, Aon's vice president of global affairs and Cook County commissioner Bridget Gainer said that community development is not for the faint of heart. Indeed it isn't; community development is not just a buzzword. It is an action that requires a plan, but the foundation of this plan is not always easy to come by. Neighborhoods are living creatures, constantly changing, and the tools we use to build and maintain them must also evolve. The tried-and-true solutions for problems in one neighborhood may not work in another. Similarly, the "traditional" way of doing things might now be outdated in some instances. As Gainer said, "Our job isn't to recreate neighborhoods in the way they looked in the past. It's to support communities by doing the right thing, by challenging each other, and by focusing on how we can think differently in the future." The forum's morning discussion focused on these tools more broadly and provided overarching inspiration on how we can apply them in our own neighborhoods to catalyze positive change.

BUILDING LIVABLE NEIGHBORHOODS:
CREATIVE DESTRUCTION OR CULTURAL EXPULSION?

As Janet Smith points out in her overview white paper, defining both the physical neighborhood and the more abstract idea of neighborhoods has been a struggle for even the most highly regarded scholars. Smith says that "our frameworks for experiencing neighborhoods and interpreting what happens in them are shaped by many of the same social norms, historical moments, and cultural preferences, which in turn determine their significance to policy makers and academics at different points in time." In short, neighborhoods are constantly changing, and as such, their definitions must evolve as society evolves. But even as physical boundaries and public discourse change, civic institutions remain constant, and their presence—or lack of—can make or break a neighborhood.

"The notion of creative destruction and cultural expulsion really speaks to the conflict that can often happen within neighborhoods," said WBEZ's Niala Boodhoo. "Often times we look at forces, and people, and change in neighborhoods—as we all know—that doesn't always happen in a cooperative way." To further explore this idea, the following people joined Boodhoo for a conversation about building livable neighborhoods: Brian Bannon, commissioner of the Chicago Public Library; Philip Blackwell, retired senior minister with the First United Methodist Church at Chicago Temple; Robin Steans, executive director of Advance Illinois and the Steans Family Foundation; and Robert Winn, associate vice president for community-based practice at the University of Illinois Hospital and Health Sciences Systems.

Generally speaking, what role do libraries, religious institutions, nonprofit organizations, and health care centers play at the neighborhood level, and how does this support the creation of livable neighborhoods?

Brian Bannon noted that the Chicago Public Library operates branches in every neighborhood across the city. These branches are located in high-resource neighborhoods that have good schools and extracurricular programs, but they are also located in neighborhoods that lack even a grocery or convenience store. Oftentimes when people talk about libraries, the discussion goes directly to books. But a library's role is greater than that. Libraries serve as a platform for education, for community building and strengthening, and for connecting people to the emerging ideas of the day in order to build strong, democratic, and competitive communities.

Philip Blackwell shifted the focus to the role of religious institutions in neighborhoods. He pointed out that the Loop, where his church is located, is a neighborhood but not a community. Churches can provide a sacred space and time, a safe place, and a sense of belonging within a neighborhood and eventually foster a sense of community. The First United Methodist Church at Chicago Temple is attempting to do this in the Loop.

"One of the roles that religious traditions are able to play in the city has to do with shaping the vocabulary of how we talk about these issues," he said. Blackwell acknowledged that identifying the difference between neighborhoods and communities—the word *neighborhood*, whose root of *neighbor* refers historically to the "nigh Boer," or nearby farmer, whereas *community* comes from the Latin for "common task or vision"—can help religious institutions enrich current conversation. Corporate, political, and economic language are considered standard and traditional, but their vocabularies can be deadening. The challenge religious institutions face lies in incorporating themes such as the common good, compassion, and enhancing human life to change the public discourse.

According to Robin Steans, the role of nonprofit organizations is to support individuals and families so they can live healthy, productive lives. In order to do this, these organizations have to care about safety, health, education, employment, and other factors that bear on individuals and families. Neighborhoods become a logical place to work because they are home to factors and the existing infrastructure that supports community-building and community-strengthening efforts.

Robert Winn likened the tripartite mission of academic health institutions—patient care, research, and education—to the tripartite mission of communities. Communities have the opportunity to be healthy, well-educated, and wealthy (not simply in the monetary sense), but the discussion lately has focused so closely on health that many have forgotten the importance of wellness. Winn points out that the medical field is often so tied to the "bedside" that it has neglected the community. A health institution that is totally integrated has the ability to identify the kind of resources needed within a community and then focus those resources on providing health *care* as opposed to the rote delivery of procedures and prescriptions.

What are these same civic institutions doing—both traditionally and nontraditionally—to fill gaps in services, resources, and overall education in neighborhoods?

Chicago's library system is large and complex, and Chicago's neighborhoods are incredibly diverse. One challenge the system faces is balancing equity to make sure neighborhoods have what they need. To meet this challenge, the Chicago Public Library refers to data but also utilizes recommendations from community members and library employees to set a program of core services that can be found in every branch throughout the city.

Bannon acknowledged that books are usually the first things that come to mind when we talk about libraries. But libraries can also act as community centers that provide myriad services to neighborhood residents. Branches of the Chicago Public Library system provide resources, materials, citizenship and new-American services, and trained research librarians; and all eighty locations offer a free homework help program—the largest in the city—that is supported through private philanthropy and the Chicago Public Library Foundation. The Chicago Public Library system is also the city's largest provider of free and open access to computers. During the 2013 Urban Forum, Karen Mossberger pointed out that nationally, and in the city of Chicago, approximately 30 percent of the population does not have regular and effective access to the internet at home.[1] Bannon reemphasized this statistic and added that of the 30 percent of the population who do not have regular and reliable access, 19 percent of Chicago households do not have *any* access to the internet. They are unable to access the internet at home. Chicago Public Library branches provide residents in each community with internet access, which is helping to close the digital divide, and the system is taking its efforts one step further by launching a pilot project that would lend wireless hotspots in underserved communities.

Libraries, as Bannon stressed, play nontraditional neighborhood roles, as well. By partnering with other community organizations, Chicago's libraries are able to identify community needs and either provide referrals or create services to support these needs. For example, some of Chicago's libraries have brought in social workers to help operate shelters in the evening hours and to provide employment and educational services to the homeless. Other branches have worked with the Greater Chicago Food Depository to provide snacks or serve dinner to kids after school.

Libraries are not the only civic institutions that are concerned with language. Earlier in the morning's conversations, Blackwell said that religious institutions have the power to shape language and change the public discourse, but language is not always about the spoken word. Through the actions of congregation members, religious institutions can help shape their communities. And churches, like neighborhoods, also face evolution-related problems. It is often the case that a neighborhood church was there before the neighborhood changed. To stay relevant and to provide an anchor or tethering point, the institution must change with the neighborhood.

Blackwell brought up the example of Old St. Patrick's Roman Catholic Church (known locally as Old St. Pat's), which has stood in Chicago's West Loop neighborhood for almost 170 years. "Old St. Pat's used to have a neighborhood," Blackwell said, "before [the neighborhood] got bulldozed to make room for the Kennedy Expressway." The church could have easily followed the fate of the physical neighborhood, but instead it reinvented itself, empowered its congregation, and created a *community* based on both the strength of its belief system and its public service. Old St. Pat's has anchored a section of the city, despite the fact that the whole city around it has changed.

The First United Methodist Church at Chicago Temple was founded in 1831, six years before the City of Chicago, making it one of the oldest and most established congregations. A study of neighborhood churches in Chicago conducted by the University of Pennsylvania found that First United Methodist Church at Chicago Temple adds about $8 million in value to its neighborhood annually. Other large churches in the city come up with similar numbers. This value is not what the institution financially contributes to the neighborhood, but rather the value of the services (e.g., soup kitchens, child care facilities, support groups for alcohol and drug users, homeless shelters, pro bono legal advice) it provides to neighborhood residents, usually at no cost. These institutions can play a role in adding significant value to a neighborhood independent of parochial and religious intent.

Nonprofits that focus on education, like Advance Illinois, have the power to support schools to catalyze community change. Schools have historically been neighborhood anchors where teachers and community leaders can reach adults and children alike. Steans pointed out that one of the problems some schools face is attracting high-quality educators and administrators who are dedicated not only to their school but also to the neighborhood in which it is located. Most new teachers are very young, and they turn to parents and mentors for career advice. These teachers are sometimes counseled away from certain neighborhoods without fully understanding the potential available there. Advance Illinois has partnered with other organizations to place educators in underserved schools. The organization takes teachers on neighborhood tours and provides them with the opportunity to meet parents and students.

Similar to other civic institutions, schools also play more nontraditional roles and face nontraditional problems. Often, school quality is judged by test scores, student budget, and teacher ratings. But schools need to be equipped with more resources than just money and manpower. In some neighborhoods, students face safety issues traveling to and from school. Other neighborhoods might lack counseling services, mental health services, or health care facilities. Schools have the potential to meet these needs, but the challenge is determining how to meet these needs even when the system is not set up to deal with them. By bringing awareness to these issues and training principals and teachers in how to remedy them, schools can nontraditionally fill the community resource gap.

Not all neighborhood schools need to provide extensive health care services to students and families. Indeed, some neighborhoods are well-served by clinics, hospitals, and pharmacies. In these neighborhoods, health care facilities serve as community anchors by providing comprehensive services ranging from treatment to wellness education.

Winn believes that this is an exciting time for health care. For decades, health care professionals believed that patients evolved around their neighborhood health care facilities. But the perspective is shifting, and professionals are now talking about ways for facilities and services to evolve around the needs of the communities they serve. While still focused on the delivery of treatment, practitioners are also becoming more vocal advocates for larger health care opportunities, like combating health deserts and food deserts. The image of health care, according to Winn, is no longer that of a brick building that forces patients to come to it. To truly make a difference in today's society, health care providers must now go to their patients.

What are some of the external forces your organization deals with?

Institutions often struggle from compartmentalization and isolation. Libraries work within their own space and provide their own services, just as churches, schools, nonprofits, and clinics do. Putting these historically dis-jointed (but potentially symbiotic) services together would undoubtedly do more good than operating separately. So what prevents this from happening?

Macro forces like policy changes and economic shifts play major roles. All institutions are hopeful that they can somehow influence these policies or adapt to these shifts, but unfortunately not all institutions are successful in this. In the most underserved communities, lows (resources, finances, etc.) are lower and highs are not as high, placing these communities in constant catch-up mode. But there are other micro and more localized forces shap-ing the connective tissue within neighborhoods. According to Steans, some neighborhoods are very transient, which works against the common goal. Other neighborhoods have safety issues that give people pause about travel-ing to and working in those communities.

Blackwell mentioned the Newberry Center, which served a local school through Head Start programs and exemplifies how localized micro forces are influenced by larger macro forces. City decisions and economic changes caused the displacement of the neighborhood's population. Because the cen-ter could not follow its patrons, it went out of business.

Perhaps one of the largest of the macro forces impacting the health care field is the Affordable Care Act (ACA). The ACA has been a hot-button is-sue since it was proposed in 2009. Experts, health care professionals, and regular Americans alike are still struggling to understand the law, but Winn believes this act brings opportunities and hope, especially to communities that are underserved. According to Winn, providing more health insurance is a good thing, but most of the patients who have purchased affordable insurance coverage through the federal marketplace are not traditional pa-tients. Among underserved populations, ACA insurance does not look like the premium insurance that most health care providers are used to seeing.

Premium insurance plans—sometimes referred to as "Cadillac" plans—have historically been employer-sponsored, meaning patients must be em-ployed in order to receive coverage. These plans often feature low deductibles; deductibles are the amount of money a patient must pay out-of-pocket for health care before an insurer will start covering costs. Once an out-of-pocket maximum is met, the insurer pays 100 percent of covered services. Low-deductible insurance usually comes with a higher premium—the amount of money a patient pays each month (or quarter, or year) for insurance cover-age. These plans reimburse physician services at or above market rates.

In contrast, plans offered through the federal health insurance marketplace can be purchased by anyone, whether they are employed or unemployed. These plans cover a broad range of services, but many feature high deductibles in exchange for a lower premium. This means that although a patient has health insurance, he or she may not be able to take advantage of an insurer's payment agreement until he or she foots the bill for all medical expenses up to a certain amount. For low-income individuals, these expenses can become a significant burden and can result in delayed or missed payments to physicians.

Fortunately, many doctors in Chicago are embracing the ACA—including plans that carry higher deductibles—which has helped to reduce health inequities. The ACA has helped health care providers shift the emphasis back to primary care and has driven the concept that providers need to return to and become active in communities. Doctors face a very real pressure to stay away from primary care when the reimbursement is not good. The system has been so focused on high-cost, high-care specialties that it cannot save money to put toward primary care. The medical field has also spent so much money on technologies, further decreasing the amount left over for extra resources. The challenge now lies in determining how to partner with other organizations to spread primary care and wellness concepts. As the country moves out of the implementation period, Winn is hopeful that providers will be placed in the communities where they are needed most. By moving away from "institutionalized" medicine—hospitals with the goal of filling more beds—and moving toward a more ambulatory approach that integrates social services with traditional medicine, health care providers can create a more nimble system that bridges equity gaps and provides more comprehensive care.

Bannon recalled how the ACA has influenced operations at the library. When the health care exchanges were first opened, hundreds of people lined up at libraries to log on to public computers and enroll in an insurance plan. But many of the people looking to purchase insurance through this marketplace did not even know how to use a computer mouse, let alone sign on to the internet and navigate a complex website. Chicago is one of the leading global cities and has one of the fastest-growing tech sectors in the country, but at the neighborhood level, the city is still trying to conquer the digital divide. When we think of the way we apply for jobs or start businesses, or even apply for health care or housing benefits: we need to be able to not only access technology but know how to utilize it. Through the library, the city provides internet help sessions that give residents the digital skills they need to navigate the web's basic uses. By ensuring competitiveness and success at the neighborhood level, the city can strengthen its own position in the country and the world.

A city of immigrants, Chicago has strong roots in migrant civil society. As we look at these rich and varied resources, what role do immigrants play?

Immigrants arrive on our shores with food, language, religious beliefs, and familial traditions, and it can be interesting to watch second and third generations assimilate to U.S. culture. But in Chicago, as Blackwell pointed out, the sense of migration is not just confined to families moving into the city from other countries. There is a sense that the whole population is migrating from one place to another, even within the city.

Bannon said that the library is an interesting place to do some on-ramping, but it is also important to this institution to not become set in its ways. Each neighborhood has a unique culture, and the library's services and resources often reflect this. Bannon pointed out that it is important for libraries to be flexible so they can best address the needs of their patrons in an equitable way.

Blackwell echoed Bannon's sentiment, saying that sometimes religious institutions can become an impediment to this change and assimilation because they are conservative by definition and frequently reflect the values and beliefs of the generation that founded the church. The challenge lies in changing the institution to fit the evolving culture of the second and third generations while still staying true to a core set of beliefs.

There is a huge opportunity for Chicago to welcome these migrants, whether they are coming from another country, another city in the United States, or are simply moving from one Chicago neighborhood to another. Being a welcoming city that can thoughtfully understand the experiences of its residents and provide them with the tools they need to succeed will in turn ensure Chicago's success.

The conversation frequently turns to neighborhoods that have serious challenges. What does it mean that a neighborhood is under-resourced?

In a healthy neighborhood, there are supportive resources and institutions, places to play and learn, and a sense of culture and vibrancy. Neighborhoods lacking the basic building blocks or infrastructure inherently have a harder time growing stronger and more powerful. In a city like Chicago, resources do not need to be allocated equally. As Steans has said earlier in this forum, Chicago's low-resource neighborhoods experience lower lows and highs that are not as high as other communities. To create equity, resources need to be allocated on a differential, since a small, incremental change may not make the necessary impact in a low-resource community. Nonprofit organizations and community development practitioners are working to provide neighborhoods with these resources, but the problem will not be solved without thoughtful public investment.

But we cannot create strong, healthy neighborhoods if we are working in isolation and if neighborhoods are working in isolation. Strong neighborhoods have infrastructure, but they also possess a sense of movement and free flow of people coming into the neighborhood from other areas. Steans said that in addition to being under-resourced, many neighborhoods are also operating in isolation. The hyper-segregation that has plagued Chicago for decades has meant that policy makers, city officials, and others can go months, years, or even an entire lifetime without interacting in a meaningful way with people who live in very different conditions, and vice versa. A free-flowing dynamic causes people to think differently and act differently than when they are isolated in segregated neighborhoods.

"All roads lead to the Loop, but not equally," Blackwell said. Transit is both a resource and a tool to combat isolation. The entire city is served by public transportation via CTA buses and the "L"(elevated) train system, and many of the surrounding suburbs are served by the Metra and South Shore commuter rail lines. However, the distribution of this service poses an issue. The CTA's Red Line swoops in from the city's northernmost border, stopping frequently between Howard and the Loop Stations to pick up younger professionals from north side neighborhoods. But on the city's South Side, the CTA only operates stations as far south as 95th Street. The neighborhoods south of 95th Street are generally considered lower-resource neighborhoods, and a transit line would connect these residents to jobs and services on Chicago's south side and in the Loop. The CTA has recognized this and is extending the Red Line south from 95th Street to 130th Street, but there are still other neighborhoods facing similar problems.

A lot of times decision makers look at resources that are underutilized—for example, a library with a low circulation rate or a transit line with low ridership—and say "this is not being used to its full potential, so let's stop investing in it." Steans points out that it is important before acting to ask the question "But what would happen to the community if you did take away this resource?" Moving away from the hard data on traditional measures and looking at a broader, neighborhood perspective effect—since sometimes these same resources are used *nontraditionally*—can help officials better understand who they are serving and how these groups are being served.

Do you see anything remarkable in Chicago's neighborhoods?

Domestic violence, which is an issue in many neighborhoods, sometimes looks different in lower-income neighborhoods that have a number of residents accepting public aid. In these neighborhoods, police and social service professionals often see fewer reports of domestic violence and less use of domestic violence services, despite its presence. Steans pointed out that many women (and men) in these neighborhoods are wary about reporting that there is a partner in their life or their home because they feel this may jeopardize their public aid. There is now a system in place citywide that allows victims of domestic violence to report these issues without having their relationship status reported to public-aid officials. This is an example of a small change at the neighborhood level that ended up positively impacting families across the city. For other issues, though, practitioners need to think bigger. In the health care field, these issues have led to larger-scale solutions that are also exhibiting positive impacts.

In the Back of the Yards, Cicero, Englewood, Humboldt Park, New City, North Center, and South Shore, Mile Square Health Center clinics are working to change the way we think about federally qualified health centers (FQHC). A new clinic opened in January 2014 in the Illinois Medical District on the city's near-west side. At Mile Square in the Illinois Medical District, the departments of medicine, surgery, radiology, pediatrics, and many other specialties that historically have not worked in tandem with primary and urgent care, are now housed under one roof.

These clinics serve lower-resource neighborhoods that previously did not have access to primary and urgent-care facilities. The clinics are also striving to shift the conversation from "underserved" versus "everybody else" to simply "patients." Winn said that when he takes care of a patient, he provides the same level of care regardless of where that patient comes from. This is a standard to which all doctors are held.

While clinics aim to create physical wellness through health education, other initiatives aim to create cultural wellness through thoughtful actions and community collaboration. Blackwell recalled Fred Rogers, the beloved namesake behind the popular children's show *Mister Rogers' Neighborhood*. Through his "neighborhood," Mr. Rogers was able to create a space where children felt they were understood and appreciated. While it's admittedly odd to compare a television personality with a Catholic priest, in Chicago, Father Michael Pfleger is working to create these safe spaces for children. Blackwell believes Father Pfleger's work is commendable and worth noting.

Working on Chicago's South and West Sides, Father Pfleger is credited with creating a youth basketball program that places rival gang members on the same team, where they can work together toward a common goal of winning. The basketball program has garnered attention from the city's mayor and the Chicago Bulls, but the additional benefit of the basketball program is that it has given Father Pfleger's parish (St. Sabina) an extraordinary opportunity to do something visionary. Contrary to common wisdom, the program demonstrates that there is a way youths can belong and feel accepted in these neighborhoods without resorting to gang life.

Bannon closed the panel by recalling Federal Communications Commission commissioner Mignon Clyburn's tour of the Harold Washington Library in the heart of the Chicago Loop. Bannon said that Commissioner Clyburn was especially impressed with the number of people utilizing the library's computer lab (on that day, patrons were using all 150 computers, with others waiting in line). At some computers, users were receiving free training from library employees. Across the hall in the library's advanced manufacturing lab, individuals were receiving higher-skills training in emerging technologies that may very well be the future of the city. The digital media center on the library's lower level was also filled with teenagers participating in after-school workshops.

"This is the library I didn't grow up in," Bannon said, "and on this particular day, I was reminded that we have come such a long way. While our mission hasn't changed, the way we perform that mission has changed in the context of where we are today." Bannon's statement reaches far beyond the walls of the library. As all of the panelists have emphasized, the way we build strong and successful neighborhoods and communities evolves in response to changing ideas, cultures, and policies. By keeping this in mind moving forward, we can build equity and enact positive neighborhood change.

ENVISIONING SMART NEIGHBORHOODS:
OLD SCHOOL, NEW SCHOOL, OR NO SCHOOL?

The panel discussions bookended a unique keynote presentation that offered a personal, ground-level view of life in one of Chicago's lower-resource neighborhoods. On July 28, 2014, the *Chicago Tribune* had printed a guest commentary by fifth graders from the Bradwell School of Excellence in South Shore. The short piece provides a strong counter-narrative to the reports of crime and violence that tend to make headlines. The students say these negative reports—which fuel negative perceptions—are perpetuated by people who do not really know the community. The focus on random acts of crime and violence overshadows the random acts of kindness that occur in South Shore and across the city every single day, and it overshadows the struggle that residents face to change these perceptions.

Linsey Rose, the teacher who had helped the students draft their narratives, brought three of her former students to deliver their own personal stories to the UIC Urban Forum's audience as the keynote address. While each of the students focused on different topics unique to their lives, a common thread appeared in all three. Each student stressed the importance of family, both in the traditional and nontraditional sense. From their anecdotes, it is obvious that family extends much farther than just blood relatives in South Shore. "Family" includes brothers and sisters, the woman who lives next door who babysits once in a while, the owner of the corner store who gives the kids treats after school, and the group of kids in the park who are best friends and really care about one another. The students' commentaries prove that South Shore is more than a neighborhood. It is a *community* filled with love and committed residents who work hard to give back and change the narrative.

The keynote set the tone for the panel discussion that followed. On the panel were Herman Brewer, bureau chief for the Cook County Bureau of Economic Development; Bernita Johnson-Gabriel, executive director of Quad Communities Development Corporation (QCDC); Terry Mazany, president and CEO of the Chicago Community Trust; Isiah Thomas, founder and CEO of Isiah International LLC; and WBEZ's Richard Steele. The idea of schools as community anchors and catalysts for change is not a new one. But, as the first panelists observed, institutions are now finding themselves performing nontraditional roles. "Old school, new school, or no school" refers to the disparate historical and modern ways we think about schools and how they interact with their neighborhoods.

What experience do you or your organization have with neighborhood schools and education?

Isiah Thomas began by saying that the students from the Bradwell School had an excellent point that neighborhoods are about the people who live there—in a sense, family. Growing up below the poverty line on Chicago's West Side, Thomas said resources were scarce, but his community was dedicated to making sure the neighborhood kids received an education. As the education gaps began to close, sports and recreation became another way to learn while playing.

The quality-of-life issues in different communities resemble pieces of a puzzle. Bernita Johnson-Gabriel values that in her job she gets to look at these puzzle pieces and how they fit together in North Kenwood, Oakland, Douglas, and Grand Boulevard. At one time, these neighborhoods were saturated with public housing. They are now being revitalized as mixed-income communities, and these quality-of-life building blocks are becoming an even larger part of the conversation, especially when community development practitioners talk about schools.

Herman Brewer noted that the suburban concerns around education are broader and more dire than just what is occurring in historically targeted areas of Cook County. The media and civic leaders tend to focus on issues occurring in Chicago Public Schools (CPS), but there are mini pockets of disparity in suburban communities, as well. The most drama surrounds school funding, particularly from property tax allocation, which impacts what practitioners can plan and implement in suburban Cook County.

Terry Mazany said the Chicago Community Trust (CCT) plays a significant role, looking broadly at both urban and suburban issues in the six-county metropolitan region. Mazany stressed that it is important to act as a region on the global stage, since that is where the Chicago region is economically competitive. The region's success leads to prosperity at the local level. CCT's grant making covers a broad range of issues, from human needs to health care and health access to affordable housing, but Mazany believes that education lies at the root of this funding.

When equity decisions are made, who decides who gets what?

For civic leaders, "a rising tide lifts all boats" has become an idealistic phrase that cannot be accomplished. In today's bifurcated economy, the keys to success and opportunity are not felt from the ground up. Mazany recalled one of Philip Blackwell's earlier comments that civic leaders are responsible for opening a larger moral vocabulary about issues of equity, fairness, and justice. Equity decisions are a matter of leadership, which is expressed at all levels within communities. These decisions must be made for the benefit of the "common good," which is an essential part of any neighborhood.

In May 2014, CCT hosted "On the Table," a community-wide, ongoing workshop set up as a conversation about Chicago's future. The resounding consensus of the eleven thousand participants was that education is the most important issue we face, because education is the key to opportunity. But education in isolation will not achieve its full potential. To be a success, education must be combined with community engagement and collaboration.

What are some equity issues in Chicago and the suburbs?

At the base of community engagement are the people who live in a neighborhood. Philosophy is often pitted against data; Thomas was quick to point out that love, compassion, and caring are neighborhood qualities that are not measured by the census. We use numbers when we make decisions about equity, but Thomas said we should really be looking more closely at these more philosophical community qualities as well. Thomas has witnessed firsthand how sports can bring out collaboration and compassion among neighbors. He has worked closely with Father Pfleger's rival-gang basketball program and has seen the positive impacts that on-court play has on life off the court.

Thomas stated that sports and recreation programs are usually the first cuts made when a municipality is economically disinvesting in a neighborhood. He has witnessed the creation of territorial barriers caused by the removal of sports programs and said that when kids cannot meet each other through recreation, their only remaining option is to meet others at school. But in economically disinvested communities, schools also suffer. Thomas said that he grew up in a very poor community surrounded by neighbors intent on instilling the value of education in children. His community understood that you can educate in poverty if the community is engaged and committed. Because his was, many of his classmates moved up in class and out of the community, going on to lead successful lives.

One of the challenges that schools face, though, is a ranking system that presents the looming threat of closure. Level 1 schools are high-performing schools that exceed basic standards. Level 2 schools are performing moderately, and level 3 schools are under-performing and often on probation. Johnson-Gabriel has witnessed the effects of this system firsthand in Chicago. CPS closed six schools in her community, three of which had been on probation for years. This gives a sense of what communities are dealing with, particularly in neighborhoods with fewer resources. Many people think that schools are the center of the neighborhood, but in reality, this is not the case.

In QCDC's focus area, Johnson-Gabriel said there is only one community school. A community school opens early and closes late, providing before- and after-school care and services to parents and students. These schools also house resources and services for members of the larger community. These much-needed institutions are still scarce, leaving opportunity gaps in many communities. The majority of the schools in QCDC's area are neighborhood schools, which are defined by attendance boundaries. Johnson-Gabriel said that, according to performance data, the majority of neighborhood schools within QCDC's community are level 2 schools, but these are either charter, magnet, or specialty schools that employ selective enrollment. Johnson-Gabriel said that she attended a neighborhood high school in North Carolina where students of all levels and abilities—from honors students to students in special-education programs—learned and played in the same building. This contributed to a sense of community, she recalled. In Chicago, the emphasis on "specialty" and selective enrollment highlights the disparities in socioeconomic status and ability among school-age children. In this way, the school system itself is contributing to anger, unease, stress, and isolation in neighborhoods. This poses a challenge in trying to rebuild a community because it exacerbates the problem of inequity.

What are some of the challenges in leveling the playing field between specialty schools and neighborhood schools?

Overdesign and overspecialization have come with a good deal of pushback. By focusing so closely on creating niche education, we have lost sight of the fundamental role that schools play in neighborhoods as community centers and gathering places. In addition to creating undue stress and self-esteem issues in children, overspecialization puts stress on and causes challenges for parents. Brewer rightfully said that trying to get a child into the "right" school is one of the most emotional decisions a parent will make, regardless of economic stratum. There is a calculus that parents must overcome in order to place their children into "good" schools. This calculus often comes in the form of "shopping around" for school districts, which, according to Brewer, has led to mini pockets of disparity in Chicago's suburbs. In northern Illinois, this decision has become even more acute due to the close tie between property taxes and school quality.

"We have people living in homes that are valued at $50,000, who may have a tax bill of $7,000 or $8,000, or $9,000. If you dig deeper, you'll find that home is probably in a community that has a low-performing K–8 school district," said Brewer. These K–8 school districts have a dramatic impact on the property tax bills in their communities because many large businesses and corporations look at schools in the context of neighborhood quality when choosing to locate in an area. In low-performing school districts, it is often solely the burden of residential property to fund this school, a classic example of the rich (or in this case, the high-performing, high-resource school) getting richer and the poor getting poorer.

The way to combat this, Mazany said, is through the value of plans. Plans contain the vision that leadership has for a community. Plans are moral documents that describe the movement of resources and address problems.

At the neighborhood level, CCT has helped implement quality of life plans that galvanize and create coherence in how these particular neighborhoods move forward. These plans are designed around the macro forces that drive population and resources to and from neighborhoods. Chicago has become keenly interested in reestablishing a set of plans that can help make more equitable allocation decisions to create a more even playing field between neighborhood schools and specialty schools.

What should we focus on as we move forward?

In order to be truly effective, the plans Mazany spoke about cannot continue to dance around the issues of poverty and segregation. Steele pointed out that children of African American and Hispanic ethnicities make up about 90 percent of CPS's student body. In Chicago, and in many cities across the country, schools are more segregated than ever, but segregation is only part of the issue. Economics and poverty are also driving a wedge between low-performing and high-performing schools. People with the wherewithal to navigate the system can put their kids into better schools, but people without these resources have no option but to send their kids to neighborhood public schools. Part of fixing the system, according to Mazany, is also recognizing that race is not just about African Americans and Hispanics. We need to recognize that there is a sense of white privilege in the United States. One of the biggest questions we need to ask is "how do we get back to equitable opportunities for *all* young people?"

But socioeconomic data are not the only numbers behind this system. Educational statistics in the form of test scores are increasingly driving resource allocation decisions. There is frustration among educators about the overemphasis on testing because a broad set of high-stakes decisions are being made around the narrow spectrum of student performance. While these data have the ability to be inclusive, it is often the case that the numbers end up excluding those who fall below the baseline. Under-performing schools are placed on probation instead of receiving more resources to help bring up the test scores and enhance the learning environment. Teachers whose students do not pass receive reprimands that send the dispiriting message that they have not done enough to educate their students. Students who do not pass are held back, but instead of receiving true remediation, they are often forced to return to the same situation they tried to test out of.

Thomas stressed that to move forward and fix the system, we need to focus on *real* education. Real education is not limited to the classroom. Education is about what is being taught in the schools and in the home. It involves treating the mind and the body through arts, sports, recreation, and it involves learning and incorporating compassion, care, and understanding into the decision-making process. It is also about setting high expectations and encouraging students to meet them, but this conversation must involve more than just educators and administrators. Education is about recognizing that everyone has a contribution and involving parents in these community-specific conversations.

Moving forward also involves changing the narrative. As the children from the Bradwell School said in their keynote, Chicago sees their neighborhood as a wasteland of gang violence, abandoned buildings, and few amenities, but crime and violence are not occurring every day. What *is* occurring every day in South Shore and in neighborhoods across Chicago and across the country is education. We all know that education is a community effort, but perhaps it is time to expand the boundaries of these "communities" and include *everyone* in the conversation.

As children we were admonished not to judge a book by its cover, and it is time we as leaders and decision makers take this into account when talking about community development in Chicago and beyond. Political clout, private morals and values, and unbiased data all heavily influence where and how money is allocated. We reward institutions that are succeeding in their missions while leaving struggling institutions to flounder and often fail. Often times, these rewards are based on a narrow and nit-picky meritocracy. A library branch with a high check-out rate in an affluent community might receive more resources and funding than a library in a lower-income community that has a low check-out rate but is a haven for individuals who need internet access. The second library is filling a gap and meeting a need—and likely well-respected by its patrons—but its service to its community does not resemble the traditional service we are used to seeing. The same is true for schools, churches, clinics, and social service organizations.

Community development sometimes gets placed on the back burner in favor of debate on what we have deemed more pressing issues—economics, homeland security, international relations, employment, and so on. What we sometimes neglect to consider, though, is that our society would not be half as successful as it is without strong communities. Neighborhood blocks and the people and resources found on them are the foundation for our cities; our cities are the foundation for our states; and our states form the foundation of our country. Susana Vasquez perfectly captured the importance of community development: "As long as where you live informs how well you live, we have an urgent need to support effective neighborhood strategies and the practitioners who lead them."

Note

1. Mossberger, Karen, Chen-Yu Kao, and Kuang-Ting Tai, "Toward Connected, Innovative, and Resilient Metro Regions," in *Technology and the Resilience of Metropolitan Regions*, ed. Michael A. Pagano, 3–21 (Urbana: University of Illinois Press, 2015).

What's Next?

The UIC Urban Forum contributors identified some of today's most pressing neighborhood-centric issues, and panelists and audience members alike spent the day thoughtfully discussing strategies for building strong, livable urban regions. While everyone's contributions differed, a few reoccurring themes wove a common thread between the day's discussions.

Bridge the equity gap.

- Acknowledge that equity is not only about race; poverty does not discriminate. Focusing solely on black-white equality has the chance to solve only part of the whole problem.
- Data tell a story, though only from one side. Talking about equity in terms of larger, more philosophical qualities (i.e., love, compassion, collaboration, empathy) can help paint a fuller, more accurate picture of life within a neighborhood.
- Plan strategically for a common community vision. Quality-of-life plans designed around macro forces can build resiliency and help stabilize neighborhoods.
- Allocate resources on a differential to ensure that all neighborhoods have the services and funding they need in order to be strong and livable.

Think outside the box in terms of how institutions function.

- Judge the success of a civic institution (i.e., a library or a clinic) by how well it meets the needs of its specific community, not by how well it fits within its traditional role or definition.

- Bring together institutions that historically have not worked together, for example, churches and health care facilities. Collaboration and the pooling of resources has the potential to fill a needs gap and reach a greater population than working in isolation.
- Flexibility can help keep civic institutions relevant and successful. The roles of civic institutions need to change in order to keep pace with constantly changing neighborhood dynamics.
- Expanding nontraditional services can help existing institutions fill needs gaps in low-resource neighborhoods. For example, an existing library with a set budget may be able to reallocate funding to support a homeless shelter or job training center. A community school may have the capital to operate a small health care clinic or soup kitchen.

Invest strategically in education to positively retool the current system.

- Education is not limited to the classroom. Lessons learned at home and through arts, sports, recreation, and extracurriculars carry over into schools and create a more robust and inclusive dialogue about how to move forward.
- Recognize that specialization, overdesign, and selective enrollment exacerbate the problem of inequity in schools; combat this by investing in and revitalizing neighborhood and community school systems.
- Provide parents with the tools they need to choose the right school for their child. Parents do not always realize or understand all of their options, with the result that the child winds up in an environment not suited to his or her intellectual level.
- Education policy is tied closely to tax policy. Reviewing property tax allocation within the context of school districts can help ensure that all schools—and in turn, all students—have the resources needed to build success.

Find a balance between growth and change on one hand and community conservation on the other.

- Economic restructuring can be played out in the form of gentrification or in the form of disinvestment. The challenge in reversing the negative effects of economic restructuring lies in changing the ways we think and talk about neighborhoods.
- Thoughtfully understand the experiences of residents, whether they have lived in the neighborhood for years, have just moved from out of town, or have recently moved from another country with a different

culture. Assist newcomers with integration while being respectful of traditions, beliefs, and values.

- Balance finance capitalism with community capitalism. In other words, allow geographically distant, large-scale developers to invest in neighborhoods, but avoid letting this occur at the expense of small businesses and neighborhood groups seeking to funnel their smaller profits directly back into the community.

- Ultimately, bear in mind that communities are about the people who live there. Neighborhood residents form a type of family, and all families face different issues. By focusing solely on negative traits, outsiders perpetuate a cycle of negative perceptions and undermine residents' efforts to change the narrative.

Contributors

ANDY CLARNO is assistant professor of sociology and African American studies at the University of Illinois at Chicago. His research focuses on the race
and class dynamics of political-economic restructuring in South Africa and
Palestine/Israel.

TERESA L. CÓRDOVA is director, Great Cities Institute, and professor of urban
planning and policy at the University of Illinois at Chicago. As an applied
theorist and political economist, she is interested in a scholarship of engagement, and her work integrates research, pedagogy, and service. Her analysis
of global and local dynamics, including impacts of globalization on Latino
communities, informs her publications in community development and Latino studies. Córdova is a former elected or appointed member, or chair, of
national, regional, and local boards, commissions and steering committees
of county government, community development corporations, grassroots
organizations, editorial boards, research centers, planning organizations,
policy groups, and campus committees. She has been instrumental in affecting economic development policy and projects, the provision of infrastructure, local governance, and neighborhood change. She is president of
the board of the Praxis Project, a national nonprofit organization. Her PhD
is from the University of California, Berkeley.

NILDA FLORES-GONZÁLEZ is an associate professor with a joint appointment in
sociology and Latin American and Latino studies at the University of Illinois at
Chicago. Her work focuses on race and ethnicity, children and youth, identity,

Latino sociology, and education. Her current research explores the effects of racialization on the ways in which Latino youth understand citizenship and belonging and struggle with their paradoxical status as marginalized citizens and as racial minorities. She is codirector of two ongoing research projects: the Immigrant Mobilization Project, and New Destinations in an Old Gateway: The Interplay between Public and Private Actors in Shaping Local Immigration Policy. Flores-González is the incoming coeditor of the leading sociology journal, *Social Problems*, author of *School Kids, Street Kids: Identity Development in Latino Students* (2002), coeditor of *Marcha: Latino Chicago in the Immigrant Rights Movement* (University of Illinois Press, 2010), and coeditor of *Immigrant Women Workers in the Neoliberal Era* (University of Illinois Press, 2013).

VANESSA GURIDY-CERRITOS is a doctoral candidate in the Department of Political Science at the University of Illinois at Chicago. Her dissertation examines how social and cultural capital and local context impact political participation among Latinos in Chicago and surrounding suburbs.

PEDRO ANTONIO NOGUERA is the Peter L. Agnew Professor of Education and the executive director of the Metropolitan Center for Urban Education at New York University. He is the author of nine books and over 150 articles and monographs. Noguera serves on the boards of numerous national and local organizations, including the Economic Policy Institute, the Young Women's Leadership Institute, the After School Corporation, and the Nation Magazine. He is also a member of the National Academy of Education. In 2014 Noguera received an award from the McSilver Institute at NYU for his research and advocacy efforts aimed at fighting poverty.

ALICE O'CONNOR is professor and director of graduate studies in the Department of History at the University of California, Santa Barbara. She teaches and writes about poverty and wealth, social and urban policy, the politics of knowledge, and the history of organized philanthropy in the United States. Among her publications are *Poverty Knowledge: Social Science, Social Policy, and the Poor in Twentieth-Century U.S. History*; *Social Science for What? Philanthropy and the Social Question in a World Turned Rightside Up*; and the coedited volume *Urban Inequality: Evidence from Four Cities* (with Chris Tilly and Lawrence Bobo). Her current research focuses on wealth and inequality in the post–World War II United States, and the origins of the second Gilded Age.

MARY PATTILLO is the Harold Washington Professor of Sociology and African American Studies, and a faculty affiliate at the Institute for Policy Research at Northwestern University. Her research focuses on race and ethnicity, inequality, urban sociology, and policy. She is the author of numerous journal articles, coeditor of *Imprisoning America: The Social Effects of Mass Incarceration*, and author of the award-winning *Black Picket Fences: Privilege and Peril among the Black Middle Class* and *Black on the Block: The Politics of Race and Class in the City*. She is a member of the MacArthur Research Network on Housing, Children, and Families, which is conducting a four-city, multi-method study of the effects of housing on children's development.

JANET L. SMITH is an associate professor of urban planning and codirector of the Nathalie P. Voorhees Center for Neighborhood and Community Improvement, a research center that focuses on working to improve the conditions and lives of people in the Chicago metropolitan area. Her teaching, research, and community service focuses on local housing planning and policy implementation. Research includes public-housing transformation; housing and health outcomes; expanding housing opportunities for people with disabilities; and implementing community-driven strategies to preserve affordable housing. Her forthcoming book written with John Betancur is *Reclaiming Neighborhoods*. Smith earned a bachelor of fine arts (1985) and master of urban planning degree (1990) from the University of Illinois at Urbana-Champaign, and a doctorate in urban studies from Cleveland State University (1998).

NIK THEODORE is a professor of urban planning and policy as well as a senior associate of the Great Cities Institute at the University of Illinois at Chicago. He has held posts as visiting professor at the University of Johannesburg, University of Manchester, and York University. His research focuses on low-wage labor markets, migration, and urban inequality. His forthcoming book with Jamie Peck is titled *Fast Policy: Experimental Statecraft at the Thresholds of Neoliberalism*.

ELIZABETH S. TODD-BRELAND is an assistant professor of history at the University of Illinois at Chicago. She is a 2014–15 fellow at the Institute for Research on Race and Public Policy. Her research and teaching focuses on twentieth-century U.S. urban and social history, African American history, and the history of education. Todd-Breland is completing a book that analyzes transformations in black politics, shifts in education organizing, and the racial politics of education reform in post–civil rights Chicago. She has also coordinated professional development workshops and courses for K–12 teachers on critical pedagogy, African American history, urban education, and college readiness.

STEPHANIE TRUCHAN graduated from the University of Illinois at Chicago with a master of urban planning and policy in May 2015. She worked as a graduate assistant for the College of Urban Planning and Public Affairs, was a member of the Urban Forum planning committee, and interned with the Chicago Metropolitan Agency for Planning. Her research interests include land use law, economic development, and communications/public-engagement strategies. Truchan received a bachelor of arts degree in English from Valparaiso University, where she wrote regularly for the *Torch* and on rotation with the *Times of Northwest Indiana*.

RACHEL WEBER is associate professor in the Urban Planning and Policy Department at the University of Illinois at Chicago, where she conducts research in economic development, real estate, and public finance. She is coeditor of the *Oxford Handbook of Urban Planning* (2012) and author of the *Why We Overbuild* (forthcoming). Weber was appointed by Chicago mayor Rahm Emanuel to the Tax Increment Financing Reform Task Force and was a member of the Urban Policy Advisory Committee for then-presidential candidate Barack Obama. She received her undergraduate degree from Brown University and her master's degree and doctorate in city and regional planning from Cornell University.

THE URBAN AGENDA

Metropolitan Resilience in a Time of Economic Turmoil
  Edited by Michael A. Pagano

Technology and the Resilience of Metropolitan Regions
  Edited by Michael A. Pagano

The Return of the Neighborhood as an Urban Strategy
  Edited by Michael A. Pagano

The University of Illinois Press
is a founding member of the
Association of American University Presses.

Composed in 10.5/13 Minion Pro
with Franklin Gothic display
by Jim Proefrock
at the University of Illinois Press
Manufactured by Cushing-Malloy, Inc.

University of Illinois Press
1325 South Oak Street
Champaign, IL 61820-6903
www.press.uillinois.edu